The United Nations
and
Human Rights

By
JAMES FREDERICK GREEN

THE BROOKINGS INSTITUTION
WASHINGTON, D.C.

SOUTHERN METHODIST UNIVERSITY
Libraries

BRIDWELL LiBRARY

Library of Congress Catalog Card Number 56-7899

Printed in the United States of America
George Banta Company, Inc.
Menasha, Wisconsin

Preface

IN THE SUMMER OF 1951, the Brookings Institution began a series of studies on the United Nations. The series was initiated by the late Dr. Leo Pasvolsky who, until his untimely death on May 5, 1953, was Director of the International Studies Group at the Institution. The general plan for the research was formulated in the winter of 1949-50 when many proposals for changes in the United Nations system were being widely discussed in the United States. Much of the public discussion indicated the need for a systematic analysis of the issues arising from the experience with the United Nations system and for a careful evaluation of the immediate and ultimate implications of the various courses of action being proposed. To assist in meeting this need, became therefore the central purpose of the Brookings studies.

While this research has been under way, new developments have further affected the attitude of many Americans toward the United Nations. Paramount among these have been the difficulties encountered in dealing with aggression in Korea and in trying to achieve a settlement of the situation there, within the broader context of the whole Far Eastern situation. Some American pressures for changes in the United Nations system have been increasing, and now that the General Assembly and the Security Council have agreed in principle that a General Conference should be called for the purpose of reviewing the Charter, it is hoped that the Brookings studies will be of special value in contributing to better public understanding of the problems that will be involved.

The studies are being published in seven volumes, of which two have already appeared. Although these volumes form a related series, each of them constitutes a separate study of a major feature of the United Nations system. The order given below is not the actual order of publication, but it represents the logical arrangement of the series.

One volume is entitled *A History of the United Nations Charter.* It will present, from the American point of view, the evolution and negotiation of the Charter as part of the developing United Nations system during the period from 1940 to 1945. A major purpose of the volume will be to show the principal ideas and proposals considered by the United States Government in reaching its final position on the specific provisions of the Charter.

Three volumes will analyze and appraise the principal activities and organizational problems of the United Nations and its related agencies since January 1946 when the Organization came into being.

One of these, entitled *The Organization and Procedures of the United Nations,* will cover the general organizational development of the United Nations. It will be concerned both with particular organizational problems in each of the principal organs—the General Assembly, the Security Council, the Economic and Social Council, the Trusteeship Council, the International Court of Justice, and the Secretariat—and with some of the general problems encountered, such as the interpretation of the Charter, the definition of domestic jurisdiction, and the admission of new Members.

The second of these, which has already been published, is entitled *The United Nations and the Maintenance of International Peace and Security.* It deals with methods and processes for maintaining peace and security through the United Nations. It covers the procedures that have been developed under the Charter for the peaceful settlement or adjustment of disputes and situations, the use of collective measures in threats to or breaches of the peace, and the regulation of armaments, and seeks to evaluate these methods and processes in light of the conditions in which the United Nations has had to function.

The third, entitled *The United Nations and Promotion of the General Welfare,* will cover the major activities undertaken by the United Nations in response to the insistent pressures that, during the postwar period, have brought to the fore issues in the field of general welfare. The work of the Organization and its related agencies in dealing with problems of international co-operation in economic and social affairs, in the promotion of human rights, and in the advancement of dependent peoples will be analyzed, and the efforts made to harmonize conflicting national views in solving these problems will be appraised.

Another volume in the series will deal with *Regional Security and the United Nations.* It will analyze and appraise the history and activities of the principal regional security, collective defense, and similar arrangements that have developed within the framework of the United Nations Charter. The volume will describe how and why the arrangements came into existence and the manner in which they have functioned, and will analyze some of the problems raised by their establishment and operation, both within the scope of the individual groupings and in relation to the broader United Nations system.

A sixth volume, which has already been published, is entitled *Proposals for Changes in the United Nations.* It presents a description and analysis of the principal proposals advanced by governments and by private groups and individuals for changes in the United Nations system. The analysis includes a review of the major arguments advanced both for and against particular proposals, the impact of the proposals on the United Nations, and their implications for United States policy.

The final volume, entitled *The United States and the Future of the United Nations,* will attempt an over-all appraisal of the United Nations system from the American point of view. This volume, which will be based primarily on the studies in the other six volumes, will present general conclusions and recommendations regarding such changes as may appear to be desirable in the United Nations Charter or in the organization and functioning of the system.

The present publication consists of the four chapters, dealing with human rights, that will comprise Part Three of the volume on *The United Nations and Promotion of the General Welfare.* Because of the current public interest in the subject of these chapters, they are being published in advance of the rest of the volume, which will include them when it appears later this year.

The study on which the present publication is based was essentially completed a year ago, but at several points in the analysis, brief references are made to developments during 1955 in the field of human rights that occurred after the study was completed. Although the study draws some conclusions from the analysis it makes, a further appraisal of the activities of the United Nations in the field of human rights will be contained in Part Five of the volume on *The United Nations and Promotion of the General Welfare.* Furthermore, the general conclusions and recommendations that will be printed in the final volume on *The United States and the Future of the United Nations* will take into account the conclusions reached in this and the other studies in the series, but they will be formulated from the point of view of the United Nations system as a whole and of United States policy with respect to it.

The four chapters in this publication have been written by James Frederick Green, Deputy Director, Office of International Economic and Social Affairs, Department of State. He has written these chapters in a personal capacity, however, and his comments and conclusions do not necessarily reflect the official views of the Department of State. The author acknowledges with gratitude the assistance of A. Evelyn Breck, who with the aid of Medora Richardson edited the final manuscript.

The author and the Institution also acknowledge with gratitude the many thoughtful comments and constructive suggestions made by a number of present and former officials in both government and international organizations who responded to inquiries or read drafts of the manuscript. Their courtesy and willingness in making their expert knowledge and experience available have aided in clarifying many difficult points and issues. Although custom precludes the citing of these persons by name, the Institution greatly appreciates the individual assistance of each of them.

After Dr. Pasvolsky's death, Robert W. Hartley was given the responsibility for bringing to completion the Brookings studies on the United Nations, and the manuscript for the present publication has been prepared under his direction. We have had the benefit of continuing consultation with Ernest A. Gross, James N. Hyde, Joseph E. Johnson, C. Easton Rothwell, and Willard L. Thorp, who comprise an informal group, organized during the summer of 1953, to advise on the direction of the project, and to whom the Institution is heavily indebted for many helpful suggestions.

Finally, on behalf of the Institution, I wish to express grateful appreciation to the A. W. Mellon Educational and Charitable Trust of Pittsburgh for the generous grants that have made possible this series of studies on the United Nations system. The conclusions and recommendations of these studies have been reached, however, wholly independently of the Mellon Trust, which is not to be understood as approving or disapproving the views expressed in this and the other volumes in the series.

ROBERT D. CALKINS
President

January 31, 1956

Contents

	PAGE
PREFACE	iii

CHAPTER I

EXPANDING INTERNATIONAL CONCERN WITH HUMAN RIGHTS	3
Three Aspects of Liberty	5
The League of Nations and Human Rights	8
Emphasis on Human Rights in Second World War	13
Formulation of the United Nations Charter	15
Interpretation of the Charter	18

CHAPTER II

THE ATTEMPT TO DEFINE HUMAN RIGHTS	24
Universal Declaration of Human Rights	26
Completion of the Declaration	28
Scope of the Declaration	29
Content of the Declaration	31
Significance of the Declaration	34
The Draft Covenants on Human Rights	37
Differing Approaches to the Problem	38
Question of One or Two Covenants	39
Civil and Political Rights	42
Economic, Social, and Cultural Rights	44
Limitations on the Covenants	46
Self-Determination	48
Measures of Implementation	50
Federal-State Article	53
Territorial Clause	55
Reservations	57
The New United States Position	59
Future of the Covenants	65

CHAPTER III

SPECIAL ACTIVITIES TO FOSTER HUMAN RIGHTS	68
Promotion of Human Rights	69
Yearbook on Human Rights	70
Proposals for an Action Program	73
Freedom of Information	76
Drafting of Conventions	77
Drafting of a Code of Ethics	81
Promoting a Freer Flow of Information	83

PAGE

Prevention of Discrimination 88
    Work of the Subcommission 88
    Expansion of the Work Program 90
Protection of Minorities 92
Prevention and Punishment of Genocide 95
    The General Assembly Resolution 96
    The Genocide Convention 97
Equal Rights for Women 102
    Work of the Commission on the Status of Women 103
    Promotion of Political Rights 106
    Nationality of Married Women 110
    Status of Women in Private Law 112
The Right of Self-Determination 114

CHAPTER IV

EFFORTS TO DEAL WITH VIOLATIONS OF HUMAN RIGHTS 119
Communications Concerning Human Rights 120
Slavery, Forced Labor, and Trade Union Rights 125
    Slavery 126
    Forced Labor 130
    Trade Union Rights 135
Racial Discrimination in South Africa 139
    Status of Indians in South Africa 139
    Race Relations in South Africa 143
    Effect of United Nations Action 146
Violation of Human Rights in Bulgaria, Hungary, and Rumania 147
Prisoners of War of the Second World War 153
Violations of Rights of Individuals 158
    Soviet Spouses of Foreign Nationals 159
    Greek Prisoners 162
    Spanish Prisoners 165
    Oatis Case 168

APPENDIXES

A. Universal Declaration of Human Rights 175
B. Draft Covenant on Civil and Political Rights 179
C. Draft Covenant on Economic, Social and Cultural Rights 190

THE UNITED NATIONS AND HUMAN RIGHTS

CHAPTER I

Expanding International Concern with Human Rights

THE MANY different activities of the United Nations in the field of human rights over the past ten years have constituted a pioneer effort in the history of international relations.[1] With certain exceptions, this has been the first attempt to make the rights of the individual a matter of international concern and a subject of international action or agreement. In the past, the issue has been, for the most part, the rights of the individual under the state. For the last ten years, however, the issue has concerned the extent to which an international organization could and should assume responsibility for promoting and encouraging respect for the rights of the individual.

The issue is complicated by the fact that there is no agreed definition of the term "human rights" and often no agreed understanding of the several facets of that term. In earlier usage, the word "right" had a legal connotation: the individual had an "inalienable" right to life, for example, and he could not be deprived of that right by the state without due process of law. Today, the word "right" has also the connotation of a goal: for example, the individual has the right to a free education, which the state is expected to provide. Furthermore, promotion of respect for human rights is at once a legal problem, requiring the definition and codification of rights in the form of laws and treaties; a political problem, requiring enforcement action by the state; and a social problem, requiring the development of public opinion. All of these elements have been involved in international activity, as well as in national and local activity, with regard to human rights.

[1] There are few general surveys of the development of international concern in human rights and of the activities of the United Nations in this whole field. The most useful recent works are U.N. Secretariat, Department of Public Information, *These Rights and Freedoms* (1950); and Marian Neal, "The United Nations and Human Rights," *International Conciliation*, No. 489 (March 1953). Other more specialized works are cited later.

This issue is further complicated by the efforts of many Members of the United Nations to relate group rights to individual rights—that is, to insist on the right of peoples and nations to self-determination as a parallel to personal freedom. This increasing emphasis on the right to self-determination is part of the preoccupation of a majority of Members with problems of non-self-governing and trust territories.[2] It is also part of their preoccupation with problems of discrimination on the ground of race or color. Although the insistence of the Near Eastern, Asian, and Latin-American Members on relating self-determination to the rights of individuals is understandable, it has been regarded by other Members as illogical and even unacceptable.

The effort to deal with human rights has been profoundly influenced by the political atmosphere in the United Nations. For the first two years, there seemed to be hope for agreement in this field. The early resolutions on human rights, freedom of information, genocide, and related subjects, which were couched in very general terms, were adopted in the General Assembly by unanimous or nearly unanimous votes. As the substantive issues were explored more thoroughly, as the split between the Soviet bloc and the free world became more evident, and as the differences between the underdeveloped countries and the more advanced countries became more serious, there appeared to be less and less agreement on the detailed application of basic principles. Indeed, the whole subject of human rights has become a focal point of disagreement, surcharged with emotion, between the Communist countries and the democratic countries, between developed countries and underdeveloped countries, between white peoples and colored peoples, and between colonial powers and anti-colonial powers. The record of recent years has thus been one of mounting controversy and of resulting frustration and failure.

The altered position of the United States, the most important Member of the Organization, has also been of crucial significance in the field of human rights. At the outset, there appeared to be support, particularly among many of the nongovernmental organizations, for the effort to draft the Universal Declaration of Human Rights and the covenants, although many had doubts and misgivings about the latter. More recently, however, a combination of

[2] See Part Four of the volume in this Brookings series, *The United Nations and Promotion of the General Welfare.*

domestic political forces has aroused large-scale American opposition to the conclusion of treaties in the field of human rights. As a result, the United States has shifted its policy from support of the drafting of international conventions, involving controversial national commitments, to the encouraging of exchange of information, studies, inquiries, and technical assistance.

During the past ten years, the United Nations has experimented with a wide variety of measures for promoting human rights, and it has considered and rejected others. These measures have included the following: definition of human rights in international instruments; collection and exchange of information; appointment of subcommissions or *rapporteurs* to study particular problems; establishment of commissions to conduct investigations or to exercise good offices; examination of complaints by nongovernmental organizations against governments; provision of technical assistance; and debates and adoption of recommendations by various United Nations organs. The recommendations of the General Assembly and other organs have been directed usually at all Members, but occasionally at a single Member.

Each of these methods has its advantages and its disadvantages. Methods that have satisfied one group in the United Nations have tended to antagonize another and to precipitate controversy over the nature of the powers and functions of United Nations organs and the extent to which the United Nations can act without violating the domestic jurisdiction clause in Article 2(7) of the Charter. The sum total of these actions in all the different fields has been to make human rights one of the major activities of the United Nations and to focus public attention on a new and controversial area of international activity.

Three Aspects of Liberty

The three aspects of liberty—civil and political rights, economic and social rights, and the right of self-determination—although closely related, have received different emphases at different times in history. The current international preoccupation with human rights, however, represents a new and dramatic chapter in man's unending struggle for freedom—freedom to speak and worship as he chooses, to earn a living and improve his status, and to live under a government of his choice.

The concern of governments with the first aspect of freedom—civil and political rights of the individual—had been well established in the Western world by the end of the First World War. The English Magna Carta and Bill of Rights of 1689, the American Declaration of Independence, the French Declaration of the Rights of Man—these and hundreds of lesser-known bills of rights, constitutional provisions, and legislative acts had secured the basic rights of the citizen throughout Western Europe, North America, the British Dominions, and to varying degrees in Latin America and other parts of the world. Such basic rights included freedom of speech and of the press, freedom of worship and of assembly, freedom from arbitrary arrest and detention, the right to a fair trial, and freedom from cruel and unusual punishment. They were, in the language of the eighteenth century, the "inalienable" rights of the individual under natural law. They belonged inherently in the individual, and he could neither divest himself of them nor be divested of them by the state.

International law and relations between states were not generally concerned with such rights, which traditionally involved the relation of the citizen to the national state. The individual was not regarded as a subject of international law, and consequently his rights were not regarded as a matter of international concern, for international law regulated the relations of states, and international tribunals arbitrated or adjudicated cases between them.[3] There were, of course, a few notable exceptions to the principle that human rights were of no concern internationally. For example, under international law states were expected to respect the rights of foreigners in their territory. And the suppression of slavery and the slave trade was a matter of international concern as early as 1815 and the subject of a number of treaties throughout the nineteenth century. These agreements, however, made the states parties to them responsible for suppressing slavery and the slave trade. The suppression of

---

[3] See, for example, L. Oppenheim, *International Law, A Treatise*, Vol. I (1948), pp. 19-22; Charles Cheney Hyde, *International Law, Chiefly as Interpreted and Applied by the United States*, Vol. I (1945), pp. 33-40; and Charles G. Fenwick, *International Law* (1934), pp. 86-87. For a contrary view, maintaining that individuals have always been subjects of international law with a "restricted capacity" for rights, see Willard B. Cowles, "The Impact of International Law on the Individual," *Proceedings of the American Society of International Law* (1952), pp. 71-85. For a discussion of the individual as a subject of contemporary international law, see Philip C. Jessup, *A Modern Law of Nations: An Introduction* (1948), pp. 15-42.

religious freedom in the Ottoman Empire, including massacres of Christian minorities, the persecution of Jews in Russia, and the suppression of civil and religious rights in the Spanish Empire occasionally provoked official condemnations and even intervention by foreign governments. But they remained exceptions to the acknowledged principle that the rights of the individual were a matter wholly of the domestic concern of states.

The concept of economic and social rights developed later and much more slowly. By the end of the First World War, the idea that workers needed special safeguards was beginning to take hold in many industrial countries. Labor unions were establishing the right to collective bargaining; wages were being increased and hours were being reduced. Many of the worst abuses of the industrial revolution, which had aroused religious and political leaders, had been remedied in the more advanced countries. But the idea that the citizen required and deserved certain basic protection from the state—in the form of the right to collective bargaining, to social security, and to minimum standards of housing and medical care— divided social classes and political parties in most countries. At one extreme, the doctrines of Marx had captured the imagination of millions throughout the world and had gained control in Russia. In other countries, where the tradition of democracy and individual liberty prevailed, the idea that the citizen had certain basic economic and social rights, admittedly more difficult to define than political rights and not readily susceptible of judicial interpretation, had been recognized in constitutions and legislation. As in the case of civil rights, however, the problem of economic and social rights was regarded as one primarily of national, and not international, concern. Again it was the relation of the citizen to the state that was at issue, and international action in the problem was virtually nonexistent.

The third concept, that of the right of self-determination, was a matter of major importance by the time of the Paris Peace Conference in 1919. The nineteenth century had left a heritage of nationalism—involving the growth of new states in Europe, the growth of explosive forces among nationalities that were later to shatter the German, Austro-Hungarian, and Ottoman empires in the First World War, and the desire of many minority groups in Europe for protection of their separate cultures. This third force, linked to the drive for civil and political rights and to the desire for economic and social security, involved the concept of a group or territorial right, not of an individual right.

By its very nature, however, the concept of the right of peoples and nations to self-government was more a matter of international concern than problems of civil and political rights or problems of economic and social rights. In special circumstances, states occasionally intervened for the protection of minority groups or of the rights of peoples to self-government, although such intervention may have been motivated by other considerations as well. The collective action of the European powers against the Ottoman Empire to free Greece in 1821-32 and the Balkan states in 1878, and the intervention of the United States in the misrule of Cuba by Spain— these are the most familiar examples of the development of the modern concern for the right of self-determination of nations and peoples.

The First World War resulted in part from the explosive forces of nationalism, and it released new forces of nationalism the consequences of which are still being felt. It crystallized the concept of self-determination, for which President Wilson became champion. Even before the United States entered the war, he voiced the concept in these eloquent terms: "No peace can last, or ought to last, which does not recognize and accept the principle that governments derive all their just powers from the consent of the governed, and that no right anywhere exists to hand peoples about from sovereignty to sovereignty as if they were property."[4] These principles were developed in more detail by President Wilson in the "Fourteen Points" of his address of January 8, 1918 and in later addresses, and they became a basis for the peace settlement.

The League of Nations and Human Rights

The Covenant of the League of Nations reflected the very limited international concern with human rights. The phrase, "human rights and fundamental freedoms," which is of such significance in the Charter of the United Nations, did not appear in the Covenant. The drafters of the Covenant were preoccupied with the maintenance of security, the pacific settlement of disputes, the establishment of a mandates system for former German and Ottoman territories,

---

[4] Address to the Senate, January 22, 1917, *Congressional Record*, Vol. 54, Pt. 2, 64 Cong. 2 sess., p. 1742.

and the protection of minorities in Central Europe. Neither the Council nor the Assembly of the League subsequently dealt with questions of human rights as such or considered charges of violations of human rights. The wholesale and systematic suppression of human liberty in Communist Russia, Fascist Italy, and Nazi Germany went officially unnoticed by the League, although the implications of these acts of tyranny were recognized by many of its Member states.

The fact that the whole subject of human rights—whether civil and political or economic, social, and cultural—was not mentioned in the Covenant and was not dealt with by the League, reflects the traditional idea that the rights of the citizen are a matter for the state concerned and not for the international community. The Covenant contained, in Article 15(8), a paragraph on domestic jurisdiction, but it related only to pacific settlement of disputes.[5] The powers and functions of the League in the economic and social fields were sufficiently limited so that the question of domestic jurisdiction did not attain any major significance.[6] It would appear from the records of the Paris Peace Conference and of the League of Nations that Member governments continued to feel that international law covered relations between states and not the relation of the citizen to the state.[7]

[5] Article 15 (8) was as follows: "If the dispute between the parties is claimed by one of them, and is found by the Council, to arise out of a matter which by international law is solely within the domestic jurisdiction of that party, the Council shall so report, and shall make no recommendation as to its settlement."

[6] In 1926, the British Government introduced a resolution at the Assembly of the League, backed by a memorandum, asking that the Assembly "request the Council to appoint a committee to consider and report what questions are and what are not within the sphere of action of the League within the meaning of the Preamble and Articles 3 and 4 of the Covenant, especially with reference to questions which are now being dealt with by organs of the League or are proposed to be so dealt with." The supporting memorandum described communications, traffic in narcotic drugs, and disease as "primarily national matters," and argued that to enable the League to intervene there must be either a treaty, or (under Article 24 of the Covenant) an international bureau, and a bureau must of necessity be the creature of a treaty or an agreement. The committee discussing the matter concluded, however, that it would be preferable not to try to define the jurisdiction of the League, and the British Government did not press the matter further. Howard B. Calderwood, "Borderlines of National and International Jurisdiction," *Proceedings of the Thirty-Eighth Annual Meeting of the American Society of International Law* (Apr. 28-29, 1944), pp. 44-46.

[7] In this connection it should be noted that the fourth of the reservations to the Covenant of the League proposed by the Senate Committee on Foreign Relations and refused by President Wilson was: "The United States reserves to

The League Covenant and the constitution of the International Labour Organisation provided machinery for co-operation in the economic and social fields. This machinery, which marked a significant departure in international relations, worked satisfactorily for the most part and laid the ground work for the more elaborate agencies and broader functions of the United Nations system. The concept of economic and social rights did not appear in the Covenant, however, and did not often arise in the work of the League. The principal exception was perhaps the Geneva Declaration of the Rights of the Child, which was endorsed by the Assembly of the League in 1925. However, international action to eliminate the worst social evils— slavery, forced labor, the traffic in narcotics, and the traffic in women and children—was greatly strengthened under the League.[8] In particular, the development of conventions and recommendations by the International Labour Organisation emphasized a new international concern in labor questions—wages, hours, working conditions, and social security—that traditionally had been regarded as a matter for national action alone.[9] These activities of the League did not, for the most part, create the idea that any new economic

---

itself exclusively the right to decide what questions are within its domestic jurisdiction and declares that all domestic and political questions relating wholly or in part to its internal affairs, including immigration, labor, coastwise traffic, the tariff, commerce, the suppression of traffic in women and children and in opium and other dangerous drugs, and all other domestic questions, are solely within the jurisdiction of the United States and are not under this treaty to be submitted in any way either to arbitration or to the consideration of the Council or of the Assembly of the League of Nations, or any agency thereof, or to the decision or recommendation of any other power." *Congressional Record*, Vol. 59, Pt. 5, 66 Cong. 2 sess. p. 4599.

[8] The following comment by the former Deputy Secretary-General on the work of the committees of the League on the traffic in women and on child welfare is of interest: "These Committees formed a minor element in the structure of the League and their work had no great influence on the general course of international affairs. Some of their undertakings, particularly those connected with child welfare, were international only in the general sense that social advance in any country is beneficial to the rest, while evil social conditions in any country may hamper the advance of others. Foreign ministers and diplomatists were apt to regard them with distrust: Sir Austen Chamberlin not infrequently suggested that they should guard against interfering in the internal affairs of Member States. Nevertheless, the general historian will find in their records much that is of interest . . . such acts may continue to produce their effects long after many a frontier dispute has been forgotten." F. P. Walters, *A History of the League of Nations*, Vol. I (1952), pp. 186-87.

[9] See Parts One and Two of the volume in this Brookings series, *The United Nations and Promotion of the General Welfare*.

and social "rights" existed; but they did reflect the growing acceptance of the concept that the affairs of labor were matters of international as well as national concern.

In two fields of human rights, however, the League of Nations
made a particularly significant advance over the past—in dealing
with mandated territories and minorities problems. The activities
of the League in both these fields represented in part international
concern with the rights of individuals living in territories formerly
governed by the defeated enemy powers, and in part, the growing
international concern with the right of self-determination of peoples
and nations, which President Wilson had proclaimed during the
war.

The mandates system, established by Article 22 of the Covenant,
constituted an entirely new—indeed, an almost revolutionary—development in international affairs. That article proclaimed that to
the German and Ottoman colonies and territories "there should be
applied the principle that the well-being and development of such
peoples form a sacred trust of civilization." The Council of the
League, which, with the assistance of the Permanent Mandates
Commission, supervised the administration of the mandated territories, gave special attention to safeguarding the rights of the inhabitants in these territories. Moreover, provision was made for the
receipt and examination by the Council, through the commission,
of petitions from individuals and organizations regarding the territories, with special safeguards to eliminate those that were trivial,
anonymous, or abusive. Petitions emanating from within the territory had to be forwarded by the mandatory power, which was entitled to add its comments. Petitions from outside the territory were
communicated to the chairman of the Permanent Mandates Commission, and those that he decided required attention were forwarded to the mandatory power for comment. The Permanent
Mandates Commission then discussed the petitions and comments
and decided which of them should be transmitted to the Council
for further consideration. There was no provision for hearing the
petitioners. But the right of an individual or of a group to petition
an international organization, in limited form, was thus recognized.
This represented a notable departure from the traditional idea that
relations between national states are the sole concern of international
law.

The Covenant contained no provisions concerning the minorities of Europe, but a series of treaties and declarations concluded during and after the Paris Peace Conference went even further than the mandates system in attempting to secure the rights of special groups of individuals. Special minorities treaties were concluded between the Principal Allied and Associated Powers and Czechoslovakia, Greece, Poland, Rumania, and Yugoslavia. Provisions on the rights of minorities were included in the peace treaties with Austria, Bulgaria, Hungary, and Turkey. Declarations were made before the Council of the League by Albania, Estonia, Finland (for the Aaland Islands), Iraq, Latvia, and Lithuania on or after their admission to the League. Special provisions were included in the convention regarding Memel concluded by France, Italy, Japan, Lithuania, and the United Kingdom, and in the convention concerning Upper Silesia concluded by Germany and Poland.

These instruments guaranteed, *mutatis mutandis,* protection of life and liberty and freedom of religious worship for all inhabitants of each country. They provided that the nationality of the country might be acquired by domicile in the country or by possessing rights of citizenship when the treaty came into force and by birth in the territory. In particular, they guaranteed the following rights to nationals who belonged to minorities: equality before the law and equality of civil and political rights, especially for admission to public employment; free use of the mother tongue in private intercourse, commerce, religion, the press or publications, and at public meetings and before the courts; a right equal to that of other nationals to maintain at their own expense charitable, religious, social, or educational institutions; in districts where a considerable proportion of the population belonged to the minority, instruction in the state elementary schools in the language of the minority and assurance to the minority of a fair share of the sums provided by the state, municipal, or other budgets for educational, religious, or charitable purposes.

The minorities system went even further in providing for petitions from the inhabitants of these areas.[10] The inhabitants could petition directly to the Council of the League; but the petition was communicated, for any observations, to the government concerned. The government was given three weeks in which to inform the Secretary-General whether it intended to forward any observations. If it did

[10] See P. de Azcárate, *League of Nations and National Minorities, an Experiment* (1945), pp. 102-09.

not, then the petition was immediately communicated to all members of the Council for their information. If the government desired to reply, it was given two months in which to present its comments, which were communicated with the petition to the Council. The Council established very strict screening procedures to eliminate, in particular, petitions that requested severance of political relations between the minority and the state of which it formed a part; that emanated from an anonymous or unauthenticated source; or that contained violent language.

The League of Nations and the International Labour Organisation thus touched some aspects of the field of human rights. Concern was shown especially in the fields of slavery, forced labor, mandated territories, and minorities. In general, however, the traditional concept that the civil, political, economic, and social rights of the individual were strictly a concern of the national state was respected. The major work of the League and the International Labour Organisation was to provide an efficient system for developing and co-ordinating new international machinery for economic and social co-operation rather than to define rights and to devise measures for promoting them. It required a world depression, the Second World War, and the rise of totalitarianism to expand the concern of the international community for the rights of the individual.

Emphasis on Human Rights
in Second World War

The Second World War marked a turning point in the development of international concern for human rights. The excesses of the Fascists in Italy and the Nazis in Germany, and the horrifying massacres by the Hitler regime of millions of Jews and Poles, shocked public opinion throughout the world. President Roosevelt's Four Freedoms—set forth in his message to the Congress in January 1941—inspired and encouraged the forces resisting the Axis powers. These freedoms—freedom of speech and expression, freedom of worship, freedom from want, and freedom from fear—provided, in a sense, some of the "war aims" that had been lacking in the conflict and defined the interests of the United States, which had not yet entered the war.

Two of the four—freedom from want and freedom from fear—were reaffirmed in the Atlantic Charter of August 1941, as a statement of Anglo-American goals. The Atlantic Charter also recognized the principle of self-determination, for the United States and the United Kingdom agreed to "respect the right of all peoples to choose the form of government under which they will live." All of them were given general endorsement in the Declaration by United Nations of January 1, 1942, when twenty-six nations subscribed to the following in the preamble:

Being convinced that complete victory over their enemies is essential to decent life, liberty, independence and religious freedom, and to preserve human rights and justice in their own lands as well as in other lands, and that they are now engaged in a common struggle against savage and brutal forces seeking to subjugate the world. . . .

The wartime speeches of American leaders—President Roosevelt, Secretary of State Hull, and Under Secretary of State Welles—as well as of British leaders—Prime Minister Churchill, Foreign Secretary Eden, and the Labour Party members of the Cabinet—gave special emphasis to the need for exorcising the Fascist and Nazi tyranny and safeguarding human rights in the peace settlement. The American spokesmen also stressed the need for international measures to promote economic and social co-operation and the need for advancing non-self-governing peoples toward self-government or independence.

It was at the height of the war that President Roosevelt set forth, for the United States, what is perhaps its first official statement of economic and social rights. This statement, contained in a message to the Congress on January 11, 1944, so clearly presages the later debates in the United Nations that it warrants quotation in full, even though it did not evoke a widespread response, either from the public or the Congress.

We have come to a clear realization of the fact that true individual freedom cannot exist without economic security and independence. . . .

In our day these economic truths have become accepted as self-evident. We have accepted, so to speak, a second Bill of Rights under which a new basis of security and prosperity can be estabished for all regardless of station, race, or creed.

Among these are:

The right to a useful and remunerative job in the industries, or shops or farms, or mines of the Nation;

The right to earn enough to provide adequate food and clothing and recreation;

The right of every farmer to raise and sell his products at a return which will give him and his family a decent living;

The right of every businessman, large and small, to trade in an atmosphere of freedom from unfair competition and domination by monopolies at home or abroad;

The right of every family to a decent home;

The right to adequate medical care and the opportunity to achieve and enjoy good health;

The right to adequate protection from the economic fears of old age, sickness, accident, and unemployment;

The right to a good education.[11]

The general concept of international recognition of individual rights was accepted by the American republics, at the Inter-American Conference on Problems of War and Peace, held at Chapultepec, Mexico, in March 1945. The conference requested the Inter-American Juridical Committee to prepare a Declaration of the International Rights and Duties of Man, which later would be adopted "as a convention." The *considerandum* of this resolution contained two paragraphs that reflected the new international concern with human rights and one that reflected the Latin-American concern with the principle of nonintervention:

WHEREAS:

The Declaration of the United Nations has proclaimed the need for establishing international protection of the essential rights of man;

In order to make such protection effective it is necessary to define these rights, as well as the correlative duties, in a declaration to be adopted as a convention by the States;

International protection of the essential rights of man would eliminate the misuse of diplomatic protection of citizens abroad, the exercise of which has more than once led to the violation of the principles of nonintervention and of equality between nations and aliens, with respect to the essential rights of man. . . .[12]

The proposed declaration was completed, as will be noted later, at the Bogotá Conference in the spring of 1948.[13]

Formulation of the United Nations Charter

The Dumbarton Oaks Proposals contained only a brief reference to the promotion of human rights as one of the activities to be performed by the proposed General Assembly, and, under its authority, the Economic and Social Council. The single sentence on this sub-

[11] *Congressional Record,* Vol. 90, Pt. 1, 78 Cong. 2 sess., p. 57.

[12] Inter-American Conference on Problems of War and Peace, Mexico City, February-March 1945, *Final Act,* p. 79.

[13] See below, Chap. II.

ject in the Proposals, which carefully stressed the political and security purposes of the new Organization, was as follows: "With a view to the creation of conditions of stability and well-being which are necessary for peaceful and friendly relations among nations, the Organization should facilitate solutions of international economic, social, and other humanitarian problems and promote respect for human rights and fundamental freedoms."[14]

At the San Francisco Conference, many delegations of the participating states, as well as nongovernmental organizations, urged the inclusion of more detailed provisions concerning human rights.[15] The four sponsoring powers of the Conference introduced amendments to incorporate specific reference to the promotion of human rights and fundamental freedoms. After consultations with the representatives of forty-two American nongovernmental organizations, the United States delegation agreed to propose a specific reference to the creation of a commission on human rights under the Economic and Social Council.[16]

The desire of the Latin-American states for a declaration of human rights, which had led to the decision of the Chapultepec Conference, also had its effect at San Francisco. Chile suggested that Chapter I of the Charter include a provision that every state must guarantee: complete protection of individual freedom; the right to live and work; freedom of religion, profession, science, and art; and freedom of the press and information. Cuba proposed that Chapter II of the Charter provide that the Members conform their acts to the principles contained in a "Declaration of Rights and Duties of Nations" and "Declaration of the International Duties and Rights of the Individual," which the General Assembly should adopt "within the shortest possible time after it is constituted."[17] Panama went even further by suggesting that a "Declaration of Essential

[14] Chap. IX, Sec. A (1) of the Dumbarton Oaks Proposals, U. S. Department of State, *Dumbarton Oaks Documents on International Organization,* Publication 2192 (1944), p. 19.

[15] For the origin of these new provisions on human rights see the volume in this Brookings series, *A History of the United Nations Charter.* For a brief discussion, with emphasis on proposals of nongovernmental organizations and individuals, see also Jacob Robinson, *Human Rights and Fundamental Freedoms in the United Nations: A Commentary* (May 1946).

[16] It is of interest to note that the inclusion of these provisions in the Charter was one of the first occasions in history in which unofficial groups at the scene of an international conference had influenced the drafting of a treaty.

[17] U.N. Information Organizations and U. S. Library of Congress, *Documents of the United Nations Conference on International Organization,* Vol. 6 (1945), p. 560.

Human Rights" be appended as an integral part of the Charter. The draft declaration, in a preamble and eighteen articles, provided for such matters as: freedom of religion, opinion, speech, assembly, and association; freedom from wrongful interference with person, home, reputation, privacy, activities, and property; freedom from arbitrary detention and retroactive laws; the right to a fair trial and the right to own property; the right to education; and the right to work, to reasonable conditions of work, and to social security. Each article provided, correspondingly, that the state had an obligation to assure the right or freedom.[18]

A number of delegations supported these proposals in the Conference committee, but did not press for a vote. It was generally felt that time did not permit adequate consideration of the question, and that the Organization would have to take it up later.

As a result of this new interest in human rights, the following seven specific references were incorporated in the Charter of the United Nations:

The Preamble refers to human rights in its second paragraph: "We the peoples of the United Nations determined . . . to reaffirm faith in fundamental human rights, in the dignity and worth of the human person, in the equal rights of men and women and of nations large and small. . . ."

Article 1 states as one of the purposes of the United Nations: "To achieve international cooperation . . . in promoting and encouraging respect for human rights and for fundamental freedoms for all without distinction as to race, sex, language, or religion. . . ."[19]

Article 13 states that the General Assembly shall initiate studies and make recommendations for the purpose of "assisting in the real-

---

[18] *Ibid.*, pp. 545-49.

[19] The idea that the United Nations should *protect* human rights as well as promote and encourage respect for those rights was specifically rejected at the San Francisco Conference. When Committee I/1 was considering the purposes of the Organization to be set forth in Article 1 of the Charter, the delegate of Panama proposed an amendment by which the third paragraph would read: "To achieve international cooperation in the . . . promotion and protection of human rights and fundamental freedoms. . . ." Several others supported his view that the phrase "promotion and encouragement of respect for" was too weak. The United States and United Kingdom delegates, as well as the *rapporteur* (Farid Zeineddine of Syria), objected, on the ground that the amendment "would raise the question as to whether or not the Organization should actively impose human rights and freedoms within individual countries, and that it would lead many peoples of the world to expect more of the Organization than it could successfully accomplish." The amendment proposed by Panama was subsequently rejected. *Ibid.*, pp. 324-25.

ization of human rights and fundamental freedoms for all without distinction as to race, sex, language, or religion."

Article 55 provides that "the United Nations shall promote . . . universal respect for, and observance of, human rights and fundamental freedoms for all without distinction as to race, sex, language, or religion." Under Article 56, "All Members pledge themselves to take joint and separate action in cooperation with the Organization for the achievement of the purposes set forth in Article 55."

The Economic and Social Council was empowered in Article 62 to "make recommendations for the purpose of promoting respect for, and observance of, human rights and fundamental freedoms for all."

The Commission on Human Rights was specifically provided for in Article 68, which reads: "The Economic and Social Council shall set up commissions in economic and social fields and for the promotion of human rights, and such other commissions as may be required for the performance of its functions."

Finally, one of the basic objectives of the trusteeship system, as set forth in Article 76, is "to encourage respect for human rights and for fundamental freedoms for all without distinction as to race, sex, language, or religion, and to encourage recognition of the interdependence of the peoples of the world."

There were however, two significant omissions in these references to human rights. In the first place, the phrase "human rights and fundamental freedoms" was not defined, with the result that statements made in the United Nations and documents issued by it use this phrase to connote both rights and aspirations and both individual and group rights. In the second place, the key words used were "promoting," "encouraging," "assisting in the realization of" and not "protecting," "safeguarding," and "guaranteeing." The result of these two omissions has been the absence of any agreement on exactly what constitutes the field of human rights and on precisely what are the powers and functions of the Organization in that field.

Interpretation of the Charter

There is a real question of what, if any, legal obligation the provisions of the Charter place on individual Members of the United Nations to promote human rights in their own territories. This question has been often considered in the General Assembly and other organs, in court decisions in the United States and elsewhere, and in the interpretation of jurists.[20] The International Court of Justice has not been asked to pass on the question; and the General Assembly has taken no definitive position on it, although, as will be noted later,[21] the Assembly has found that the actions of the Union of South Africa concerning racial discrimination have not been "in keeping with its obligations and responsibilities under the Charter."[22]

The legal effect of the Charter in the field of human rights has probably received greater attention in the United States than in other countries, because of the constitutional provision that treaties are part of the "supreme Law of the Land" and because of the relation of this provision to the jurisdiction of the states. In the most significant case thus far, *Sei Fujii* v. *The State of California*, the California Supreme Court took the position, in effect, that the Charter is a non-self-executing treaty and that the general obligation to promote human rights in co-operation with the Organization would not supersede existing domestic legislation.[23]

[20] For the argument that the Charter imposed express legal obligations on Members of the United Nations to promote human rights, see H. Lauterpacht, *International Law and Human Rights* (1950), pp. 145-65. For the opposing point of view, see Hans Kelsen, *The Law of the United Nations: A Critical Analysis of Its Fundamental Problems* (1950), pp. 99-101; Pieter N. Drost, *Human Rights as Legal Rights* (1951), pp. 28-31; René Brunet, *La garantie internationale des droits de l'homme, d'après la Charte de San-Francisco* (1947), p. 164; and Manley O. Hudson, "Integrity of International Instruments," *American Journal of International Law*, Vol. 42 (1948), pp. 105-08.

[21] See below, Chap. III.

[22] Res. 719 (VIII), Nov. 11, 1953.

[23] This case concerned the Alien Land Law, which forbids aliens from acquiring land in California. The District Court of Appeal, after quoting at length from the Charter and the Universal Declaration of Human Rights, held as follows in April 1950: "Clearly such a discrimination against a people of one race is contrary both to the letter and to the spirit of the Charter which, as a treaty, is paramount to every law of every state in conflict with it. The Alien Land Law must therefore yield to the treaty as the superior authority. The restrictions of the statute based on eligibility to citizenship, but which ultimately and actually are referable to race or color, must be and are therefore declared untenable and unenforceable." *Pacific Reporter*, 2nd Series, Vol. 217 (1950), p. 488. This decision has been frequently quoted as demonstrating the need for curtailing the treaty-making powers of the President. The decision was reversed in April 1952, however, by the Supreme Court of California, which made the following interpretation of the Charter: "The provisions in the Charter pledging cooperation in promoting observance of fundamental freedoms lack the mandatory quality and definiteness which would indicate an intent to create justiciable rights in private persons immediately upon ratification. Instead, they are framed as a promise of future action by the member nations. . . . The Charter repre-

This was the position taken by the Legal Adviser of the Department of State in 1947, and it has not been altered since that time. In a memorandum to the Attorney General, in connection with the cases of *McGhee* v. *Sipes* and *Shelley* v. *Kraemer* before the Supreme Court, the Department made the following statement with respect to Articles 55 and 56 of the Charter:

The Articles of the Charter referred to in your letter are not interpreted by the Department of State as imposing a legal obligation to guarantee observance of specific human rights and fundamental freedoms without distinction as to race, sex, language or religion. The Articles do appear to place member States under the obligation to co-operate with the United Nations in the carrying out of its function, which is stated here and elsewhere in the Charter as being the promotion of universal respect for and observance of human rights and fundamental freedoms.[24]

In opposition to Articles 55 and 56 concerning the promotion of respect for human rights stands Article 2(7) of the Charter, which provides: "Nothing . . . in the . . . Charter shall authorize the United Nations to intervene in matters which are essentially within the domestic jurisdiction of any state or shall require the Members to

---

sents a moral commitment of foremost importance, and we must not permit the spirit of our pledge to be compromised or disparaged in either our domestic or foreign affairs. We are satisfied, however, that the Charter provisions relied on by plaintiff were not intended to supersede existing domestic legislation, and we cannot hold that they operate to invalidate the alien land law." *Ibid.,* Vol. 242 (1952), pp. 621-22. In *Oyama* v. *California,* another case relating to the Alien Land Law, the United States Supreme Court based its decision on the Fourteenth Amendment and made no reference to the United Nations Charter. However, Justice Black, with Justice Douglas in agreement, made the following statement in a concurring opinion: "There are additional reasons now why that law stands as an obstacle to the free accomplishment of our policy in the international field. One of these reasons is that we have recently pledged ourselves to cooperate with the United Nations to 'promote . . . universal respect for, and observance of, human rights and fundamental freedoms for all without distinction as to race, sex, language, or religion.' How can this nation be faithful to this international pledge if state laws which bar land ownership and occupancy by aliens on account of race are permitted to be enforced?" Justice Murphy, in a concurring opinion, made the same interpretation: "Moreover, this nation has recently pledged itself, through the United Nations Charter, to promote respect for, and observance of, human rights and fundamental freedoms for all without distinction as to race, sex, language and religion. The Alien Land Law stands as a barrier to the fulfillment of that national pledge. Its inconsistency with the Charter, which has been duly ratified and adopted by the United States, is but one more reason why the statute must be condemned." 332 U.S. 633.
[24] Quoted in Lauterpacht, *op. cit.,* p. 149. Although arguments in the case and *amicus curiae* briefs referred to the Charter, the Court did not mention it but rested its decision on constitutional grounds. 334 U.S. 1.

submit such matters to settlement under the present Charter." To what extent, if any, this clause on domestic jurisdiction limits the powers and functions of the General Assembly and other organs has become a matter of great controversy especially throughout the whole field of human rights. This controversy has revolved around two questions: What is meant by the word "intervene"? What is meant by the phrase "matters . . . essentially within the domestic jurisdiction of any state"?[25]

The traditional interpretation of intervention has been dictatorial interference in the affairs of another state—a peremptory demand for positive action or abstention from action involving a threat or recourse to compulsion of some form. Intervention usually connoted the use, or threat of ultimate use, of force, and involved measures short of war.[26] It is clear from the records of the San Francisco Conference and the subsequent statements of the United States delegation that the word "intervene" was used in a much broader and less technical sense than this. The fact that the records of the Conference state that, with regard to economic and social matters, the Organization was not empowered to intervene in the domestic affairs of Members, makes clear that the traditional concept of intervention was not meant. On the other hand, mere discussion by the General Assembly, under Article 10 of the Charter, of an alleged violation of human rights within a state has been regarded by all but a few Members of the United Nations as not constituting inter-

[25] For recent analyses of these two questions, both of which cite official statements and unofficial commentaries, see U.N. General Assembly, Eighth Session, *Report of the United Nations Commission on the Racial Situation in the Union of South Africa*, Doc. A/2502, pp. 10-34; and Aleksander Witold Rudzinski, "Domestic Jurisdiction in United Nations Practice," *India Quarterly*, Vol. IX (October-December 1953), pp. 313-54.

[26] "Intervention is dictatorial interference by a State in the affairs of another State for the purpose of maintaining or altering the actual conditions of things." Oppenheim, *op. cit.*, p. 272. "The term intervention is here used simply to refer to the interference by a State in the domestic or foreign affairs of another in opposition to its will and serving by design or implication to impair its political independence." Hyde, *op. cit.*, p. 246. "This word is often used quite generally to denote almost any act of interference by one state in the affairs of another; but in a more special sense it is confined to acts of interference either in the domestic or the foreign affairs of another state which violate that state's independence. A mere tender of advice by one state to another state about some matter within the competence of the latter would not be an intervention in this sense; though it might be popularly so described; the interference must take an imperative form; it must either be forcible or backed by the threat of force." J. L. Brierly, *The Law of Nations: An Introduction to the Law of Peace* (1949), p. 247.

vention. The kind of intervention proscribed by Article 2(7) probably lies somewhere in between these two extremes.[27] Thus the establishment of a commission to study forced labor throughout the world would not appear to constitute intervention; but the establishment of a commission to study race relations in South Africa, over the objections of that state, might be considered to do so. The adoption of recommendations directed at all Members would similarly not contravene Article 2(7); but the adoption of a recommendation condemning a single state might be considered to be intervention. It is obviously difficult to draw any precise line; and, indeed, the line may move in one direction or another at any given time according to existing political circumstances.

The second question—what constitutes "matters . . . essentially within the domestic jurisdiction" of any state—is equally difficult to define. At first glance it would seem that rights of the individual —e.g. the right to a fair trial, the right to vote and hold office, or the right to belong to a trade union—are "matters . . . essentially within the domestic jurisdiction" of a state. On the other hand, the wholesale suppression of such rights by Hitler and the massacre of millions of persons for religious or ethnic reasons were regarded at the time as a threat to the peace and stability of Europe. Today, wholesale and systematic violation of human rights by governments of the Soviet bloc and by the Chinese Communist regime are considered a proper matter for discussion and for some kind of action by the General Assembly. The primary question again is: Where to draw the line? This raises several questions: When is a violation of human rights a matter essentially within the jurisdiction of a state? When does it become a violation of a general obligation of a Member, under Articles 55 and 56 of the Charter, to promote respect for and observance of human rights? When does it become, under Article 14 of the Charter, a situation "likely to impair the general welfare or friendly relations among nations"?

[27] "The practice of the United Nations makes it clear, as indeed does the phraseology of Article 2(7), that the word 'intervention' as used in the paragraph is not to be given a narrow technical interpretation. While discussion does not amount to intervention, the creation of a commission of inquiry, the making of a recommendation of a procedural or substantive nature, or the taking of a binding decision constitutes intervention under the terms of this paragraph. To limit intervention to coercive measures would have the result of largely limiting the application of the paragraph to the field of the exception which obviously could not have been intended." Leland M. Goodrich and Edvard Hambro, *Charter of the United Nations: Commentary and Documents* (1949), p. 120.

These questions—resulting from the presence in the Charter of Articles 10, 14, 55, and 56, on the one hand, and of Article 2(7), on the other—arise continually in the efforts of the United Nations to promote respect for human rights. Only in the attempt of the United Nations to define human rights has the problem been of relatively minor importance.[28] The Universal Declaration of Human Rights has been generally recognized as setting forth goals and standards to guide governments, and not as an extension of the obligations contained in the Charter. The formulation of the draft covenants on human rights has constituted an attempt to make the individual a subject of international law and to define his rights precisely; but this would directly affect only those states that become parties to the covenants, when completed, and not all Members of the United Nations. The efforts of the United Nations to promote human rights in other ways raise questions about domestic jurisdiction to a greater extent, especially as the various organs debate, study, and make recommendations about specific rights.[29] It is in the efforts of the United Nations to remedy violations of human rights—as in the questions of the peace treaties with Bulgaria, Hungary, and Rumania, and of race relations in South Africa—that the problem of competence becomes acute.[30] It is here that the definitions of the words "intervene" and "matters . . . essentially within the domestic jurisdiction of any state" become of major significance.

Most of these activities, experimental in character, have thus involved to varying degrees an interpretation of the powers and functions of the United Nations under the Charter. Some of them have provoked serious political controversy and perhaps jeopardized the unity and stability of the Organization. All of them reflect, however, the new and growing concern of the international community with the rights of the individual.

[28] See below, Chap. II.
[29] See below, Chap. III.
[30] See below, Chap. IV.

CHAPTER II

The Attempt to Define Human Rights

THE IDEA of drafting an "International Bill of Rights," which by the time of the San Francisco Conference had captured the imagination of many individuals and organizations and had been accepted by many governments, came to the fore again at the first session of the General Assembly, in early 1946. At that time, Cuba and Panama reintroduced proposals for the preparation of a bill of rights. The Assembly did not take action on these proposals until the second part of its first session, in December 1946, when it engaged in a brief debate, largely procedural in character. On the initiative of the United States delegation, the Assembly decided not to consider the "Declaration on Fundamental Human Rights and Freedoms" proposed by Panama but rather to transmit it to the Economic and Social Council for consideration by the Commission on Human Rights "in its preparation of an international bill of rights."[1] Thus the United Nations embarked on a pioneer venture that was to become increasingly difficult and controversial in each successive year—the attempt to define human rights through international instruments.

Meanwhile, the Economic and Social Council, at its first session in February 1946, had established the Commission on Human Rights, to consist initially of a nucleus of only nine members, and decided that its work should be directed toward submitting proposals, recommendations, and reports regarding:

  (a) an international bill of rights;
  (b) international declarations or conventions on civil liberties, the stat
of women, freedom of information and similar matters;
  (c) the protection of minorities;
  (d) the prevention of discrimination on the grounds of race, language or religion.[2]

The "nuclear" commission decided that it should not itself proc

[1] Res. 43(I), Dec. 11, 1946.
[2] Res. 5(I), Feb. 16, 1946.

with any detailed consideration of an international bill of rights but recommended that the full Commission on Human Rights should draft such a document as soon as possible. On the basis of the recommendations of the "nuclear" commission, the Council, at its second session in June 1946, decided that the full commission should consist of eighteen members. The full commission was given the same terms of reference, with the addition of a fifth item, as follows:

(e) any other matter concerning human rights not covered by items (a), (b), (c), and (d).[3]

The Commission on Human Rights held its first session in January-February 1947. It elected Mrs. Franklin D. Roosevelt (United States) as chairman and Dr. Charles Malik (Lebanon) as *rapporteur*.[4] Also, at its first session the commission gave priority to the first item in its terms of reference—consideration of an international bill of rights. The commission asked the chairman, the vice-chairman, and the *rapporteur*, with the assistance of the Secretariat, to formulate a preliminary draft of the international bill of rights. The chairman later appointed, with the approval of the Economic and Social Council, a drafting committee consisting of Australia, Chile, China, France, Lebanon, the Soviet Union, the United Kingdom, and the United States, and the Council adopted an eight-point schedule for preparing the document in time for submission to the General Assembly in 1948.

As a result of the work of its drafting committee, the commission, at its second session in December 1947, had before it three sets of proposals: a draft declaration, which the United States favored, setting forth general principles; a draft convention, which the United Kingdom proposed, to become binding on governments that ratified it; and measures for implementing human rights.

The United States, reluctant to embark on the preparation of a treaty that would ultimately require approval by the Senate, preferred an instrument that would contain goals and aspirations rather than legally binding commitments. In its view, moreover, a declaration might win unanimous or near unanimous support in the General Assembly and thus reflect the consensus of the international

[3] Res. 9(II), June 21, 1946.
[4] Mrs. Roosevelt served as chairman of the commission throughout the first five years, a record for any United Nations organ, and was succeeded by Dr. Malik in 1951 and 1952 and by the late Dr. Mahmoud Azmi (Egypt) in 1953 and 1954.

community, whereas a treaty would almost certainly be accepted only by a smaller part of that community. The United Kingdom, on the other hand, was skeptical about the value of declarations of goals, stated in general and perhaps ambiguous terms. As in the days of the League of Nations, the United Kingdom preferred a treaty, containing detailed and precise obligations, that would bind only those Members accepting it.

The commission created three working groups to consider these three proposals, which it ultimately submitted to the Economic and Social Council and to all Member governments for comment. The draft declaration covered civil, political, economic, social, and cultural rights, but the draft convention was limited to civil and political rights. The report of the third working group, containing suggestions for possible measures of implementation, either as part of the convention or separately, was not acted on by the commission. The commission decided that the term "International Bill of Rights" would embrace all three documents.

By the end of 1947, therefore, the pattern of United Nations activity in this field was clearly delineated. Two major documents were in preparation—a declaration of general principles and a convention or covenant of binding obligations. The measures of implementation, still in inchoate form, were generally envisaged as part of the covenant. The more general and somewhat ambiguous term "International Bill of Rights," which from historical association could be applied to either a declaration or a covenant, gradually disappeared.

Universal Declaration of Human Rights

The drafting of the Universal Declaration of Human Rights represented a painstaking effort, first by the Commission on Human Rights and then by the General Assembly, to take account of the differing religious traditions, political philosophies, legal systems, and economic, social, and cultural patterns represented among the then fifty-eight Members.[5] The commission first considered a doc-

[5] For a commentary, see Nehemiah Robinson, *Universal Declaration of Human Rights: Its Origins, Significance and Interpretation* (1950). For an analysis of the divergent approaches to human rights among the major cultures, prepared by the United Nations Educational, Scientific, and Cultural Organization as a contribution to the work of the Commission on Human Rights, see U.N. Educational, Scientific and Cultural Organization, *Human Rights, Comments and Interpretations: A Symposium* (1949).

ument of 408 pages prepared by the Secretariat, containing an annotated draft of forty-eight suggested articles, together with the draft declarations and proposals of Chile, Cuba, India, Panama, and the United States, and excerpts from the constitutions and legislation of many countries. The commission devoted most of its session in May-June 1948 to revising the draft declaration in the light of comments received from governments. It also drew on proposals received from the Geneva Conference on Freedom of Information, the Commission on the Status of Women, and the Subcommission on the Prevention of Discrimination and the Protection of Minorities. Several of the specialized agencies and many of the nongovernmental organizations participated actively in the debates of the commission.

The Commission on Human Rights also had the benefit of the American Declaration of the Rights and Duties of Man, adopted by the Ninth International Conference of American States, held at Bogotá in March-May 1948. This declaration was based on the text that had been prepared by the Inter-American Juridical Committee at the request of the Chapultepec Conference in 1945.[6] Although the earlier resolution did not make clear whether the document was to be a declaration of principles or a legally binding convention, the Bogotá Conference agreed upon the former.

The American Declaration contains an unusually eloquent preamble, twenty-eight articles on the rights of the individual, and ten articles on his duties. Most of the first twenty-eight articles begin with the phrase, "Every person has the right to." They cover a wide range of civil, political, economic, social, and cultural rights, and conclude with an article of general limitations: "The rights of man are limited by the rights of others, by the security of all, and by the just demands of the general welfare and the advancement of democracy." The last ten articles set forth the duty of every person, *inter alia,* to support, educate, and protect his minor children; to acquire at least an elementary education; to vote, to obey the law, to render whatever civil and military service his country may require; and to pay taxes and to work.[7]

The American Declaration of the Rights and Duties of Man constituted the first intergovernmental statement of human rights in history. It symbolized the deep concern of the postwar period

[6] See above, Chap. I.
[7] For text, see Ninth International Conference of American States, Bogotá, Colombia, March 30-May 2, 1948, *Final Act,* pp. 38-45.

with defining these rights, as well as the special Latin-American emphasis on the duties of the individual. As the American Declaration and the Universal Declaration of Human Rights were being drafted simultaneously, the former contained some elements of both substance and style that characterized the text proclaimed by the United Nations later in the year.

Completion of the Declaration

The text of the draft Universal Declaration of Human Rights, as completed by the Commission on Human Rights in June 1948, contained a preamble and twenty-eight articles.[8] The previous drafts were made briefer, clearer, and more precise. Limitations on rights in individual articles were replaced by a single, comprehensive article on limitations. Earlier references to the way in which certain rights should be carried out were eliminated. The draft declaration was approved in the commission by a vote of 12 to 0, with only Byelorussia, the Ukraine, the Soviet Union, and Yugoslavia abstaining. The representative of Iran did not participate in the session, and the alternate representative of the Philippines stated that if he had the right to vote, he would vote in favor. The draft declaration was then forwarded by the Economic and Social Council, after a brief debate, to the General Assembly for consideration.[9]

The third session of the General Assembly, held in Paris in the fall of 1948, completed this first general instrument on human rights. The spirit that animated most representatives in the Assembly in trying to set new goals for mankind was expressed in these frequently quoted words of United States Secretary of State Marshall at the opening of the session:

Systematic and deliberate denials of basic human rights lie at the root of most of our troubles and threaten the work of the United Nations. It is

[8] For a comparison of the text of each article as drafted by the Secretariat, the drafting committee, the commission at its second and third sessions, and the General Assembly, see U.N. Secretariat, Department of Public Information, *These Rights and Freedoms* (1950), pp. 17-86.

[9] On this occasion, as on later ones relating to the draft covenants, the Council acted as a "post office" between the General Assembly and the Commission on Human Rights, and refrained from tampering with the resolution that passed across its table. This passive role resulted from at least two factors: the fact that much of the work of the commission on the Universal Declaration and the draft covenants related to civil and political rights; and a reluctance to engage in debate and drafting that would inevitably be duplicated in the General Assembly.

not only fundamentally wrong that millions of men and women live in daily terror of secret police, subject to seizure, imprisonment, or forced labor without just cause and without fair trial, but these wrongs have repercussions in the community of nations. Governments which systematically disregard the rights of their own people are not likely to respect the rights of other nations and other people and are likely to seek their objectives by coercion and force in the international field.[10]

The Third (Social, Humanitarian, and Cultural) Committee of the Assembly, to which the declaration was referred, held eighty-six meetings, in addition to twenty meetings of its drafting sub-committees, to consider and revise the text. The committee went over every word of the text prepared by the commission, and the forty Members not represented on the commission reopened many of the issues and presented countless amendments. The committee finished its task, however, in time for the plenary session to approve the final text on December 10, 1948—only two days before the end of the session. The final text was adopted without objection—48 to 0, with 8 abstentions (Byelorussia, Czechoslovakia, Poland, Saudi Arabia, the Ukraine, the Union of South Africa, the Soviet Union, and Yugoslavia) and 2 absences (Honduras and Yemen).[11] Although the eight delegations that abstained took strong exception to certain provisions in the Universal Declaration, as will be indicated below, they apparently did not wish to cast a negative vote on this occasion.

Scope of the Declaration

The Universal Declaration of Human Rights begins with a preamble the first three paragraphs of which so capture the mood and intent of the Assembly of 1948 that they deserve quotation in full:

Whereas recognition of the inherent dignity and of the equal and inalienable rights of all members of the human family is the foundation of freedom, justice and peace in the world,

Whereas disregard and contempt for human rights have resulted in barbarous acts which have outraged the conscience of mankind, and the advent of a world in which human beings shall enjoy freedom of speech and belief and freedom from fear and want has been proclaimed as the highest aspiration of the common people,

Whereas it is essential, if man is not to be compelled to have recourse,

[10] U. S. Department of State *Bulletin,* Vol. 19 (Oct. 3, 1948), p. 432.

[11] Honduras later made it known that if its representative had been present he would have voted in favor of the declaration. It may be noted that in United Nations usage, this vote of 48-0-8 is called "unanimous," even though all did not vote "yes." The more accurate phrase in English parliamentary procedure is *"nemine contradicente"* *("nem. con.").*

as a last resort, to rebellion against tyranny and oppression, that human rights should be protected by the rule of law.[12]

At first glance, the substantive articles of the Declaration give the impression that the document is a treaty, but the language of the opening paragraph makes clear that the Declaration is a statement of goals and standards. Here the emphasis is on the concept of progressive achievement of these goals:

The General Assembly

Proclaims this Universal Declaration of Human Rights as a common standard of achievement for all peoples and all nations, to the end that every individual and every organ of society, keeping this Declaration constantly in mind, shall strive by teaching and education to promote respect for these rights and freedoms and by progressive measures, national and international, to secure their universal and effective recognition and observance, both among the peoples of Member States themselves and among the peoples of territories under their jurisdiction.

The nature of the Declaration was a matter of considerable debate in the General Assembly. Some hoped, and others feared, that the Declaration might have some legally binding effect on the Members. In fact, the Union of South Africa abstained from voting because it felt that the Declaration, although not a convention, would impose certain obligations on the Members once it had been accepted by the Assembly. South Africa maintained there was a danger that the Declaration would be interpreted as an authoritative definition of "human rights and fundamental freedoms," which had been left undefined in the Charter. The scope of the Declaration was such, moreover, that many questions that had hitherto been considered as falling wholly within the domestic jurisdiction of Member states would in the future be considered a proper subject of international discussion and even of condemnation.

This was not the interpretation of the principal draftsmen of the Declaration. As the chairman of the Commission on Human Rights (Mrs. Roosevelt) stated as the Assembly neared its final vote:

In giving our approval to the declaration today, it is of primary importance that we keep clearly in mind the basic character of the document. It is not a treaty; it is not an international agreement. It is not and does not purport to be a statement of law or of legal obligation. It is a declaration of basic principles of human rights and freedoms, to be stamped with the approval of the General Assembly by formal vote of its members, and

[12] For text of the Universal Declaration of Human Rights, see App. A.

to serve as a common standard of achievement for all peoples of all nations.[13]

Article 1 of the Declaration, which the Assembly adopted unanimously, expresses the basic philosophy of the whole document: "All human beings are born free and equal in dignity and rights. They are endowed with reason and conscience and should act towards one another in a spirit of brotherhood." During the debates, there was some criticism, which has been repeated on occasion in recent years, that this first article does not state whether human beings are endowed with reason and conscience by God, by Nature, or by some other source. In view of the widely differing religious traditions represented in the Assembly, however, it would have been virtually impossible to reach unanimous agreement on such a text.

The second article proclaims that no distinction shall be made with respect to these rights and freedoms either because of the status of the individual or because of the status of the country or territory to which he belongs. The first sentence of this article merely expands the four categories of discrimination mentioned in the Charter to include: "race, colour, sex, language, religion, political or other opinion, national or social origin, property, birth or other status." The second sentence, introduced by Yugoslavia, marked one of the earliest of the now familiar efforts to make certain that human rights are safeguarded in every territory, "whether it be independent, trust, non-self-governing or under any other limitation of sovereignty."

Content of the Declaration

The civil and political rights proclaimed in the Universal Declaration are those that have been most widely recognized in constitutions and laws throughout the world. The civil rights included: the right to life, liberty, and security of person; prohibition of slavery and the slave trade; freedom from torture or cruel, inhuman, or degrading treatment or punishment; the right to recognition as a person before the law; equal protection of the law; right to an effective judicial remedy; freedom from arbitrary arrest, detention, or exile; the right to a fair and public hearing by an independent

[13] U.S. Department of State *Bulletin*, Vol. 19 (Dec. 19, 1948), p. 751. This significant paragraph is not fully reflected in the summary record as given in U.N. General Assembly, Third Session, First Part, *Official Records*, 180th Meeting (Dec. 9, 1948), pp. 860-63.

and impartial tribunal; the right to be presumed innocent until proved guilty, and freedom from *ex post facto laws;* freedom from arbitrary interference with one's privacy, family, home, or correspondence and from attacks on one's honor or reputation; freedom of movement; the right of asylum; the right to a nationality; equal rights of men and women concerning marriage and the family; freedom of thought, conscience, and religion; freedom of opinion and expression; and freedom of peaceful assembly and association.

These civil rights gave rise to two principal problems, in addition to the innumerable amendments designed either to take account of one or another legal tradition or to adapt the style to the five official languages. The Soviet bloc tried constantly to impose its concept of state guarantees of individual rights and its limitations of certain of these rights. The Soviet Union, for example, proposed that Article 3 should provide that the state should guarantee the right of life and should abolish the death penalty. It urged that Article 18 be modified to provide that freedom to perform religious services should be in accordance with the laws of the country concerned and the requirements of public morality. It also insisted, with regard to Article 19, that freedom of speech and the press should not be used for purposes of propagating fascism and aggression, and for provoking hatred as between nations. The Soviet Union also proposed that freedom of assembly, in Article 20, be qualified by a prohibition on societies and organizations of a fascist or antidemocratic nature. All of these amendments, and many others, were rejected.

Freedom of religion, as set forth in Article 18, created difficulties for the Moslem states. The first clause—"Everyone has the right to freedom of thought, conscience and religion"—was accepted by representatives of all religious faiths. The second clause—"this right includes freedom to change his religion or belief"—was strongly opposed by some of the Moslem delegates. They pointed out that the Koran forbids a Moslem to change his faith and criticized the Christian missionaries for their efforts to win converts in Mohammedan countries. Saudi Arabia felt obliged to abstain on the final vote because of this clause. Other Moslem representatives were content merely to register their objections, however, while Pakistan defended the article on the ground that the Moslem faith is itself a missionary religion.

Political rights are defined by the Declaration in the three parts of Article 21: the right to take part in the government of one's country; the right of equal access to public service; and a provision that "the will of the people shall be the basis of the authority of government." This third clause created the greatest difficulty, in view of the widely divergent political systems represented. After long argument, however, it was unanimously agreed that "this will [of the people] shall be expressed in periodic and genuine elections which shall be by universal and equal suffrage and shall be held by secret vote or by equivalent free voting procedures."

Eight articles are devoted to economic, social, and cultural rights, many of them described in considerable detail. A number of these are similar in substance and spirit to those proclaimed by President Roosevelt in January 1944 and by the American Declaration of the Rights and Duties of Man. These include: the right to own property; the right to social security; the right to work and protection from unemployment, to equal pay for equal work, to just and favorable remuneration, and to form and join trade unions; the right to rest and leisure; the right to an adequate standard of living, with special care and assistance for motherhood and childhood and the same social protection for all children, whether born in or out of wedlock; the right to education; the right freely to participate in the cultural life of the community and to the protection of scientific, literary, or artistic works; and the right to a social and international order in which the freedoms set forth in the Declaration can be fully realized.

The idea that the individual has duties as well as rights, which was incorporated in the draft declaration submitted by Panama at the San Francisco Conference and in the American Declaration of the Rights and Duties of Man, is also included in the Universal Declaration. Article 29 prescribes these duties in a very comprehensive manner as well as the general limitations on the exercise of the rights and freedoms:

1. Everyone has duties to the community in which alone the free and full development of his personality is possible.
2. In the exercise of his rights and freedoms, everyone shall be subject only to such limitations as are determined by law solely for the purpose of securing due recognition and respect for the rights and freedoms of others and of meeting the just requirements of morality, public order and the general welfare in a democratic society.

An additional safeguard is included in Article 30, which was designed to make clear that freedom implies respect for the rights of others: "Nothing in this Declaration may be interpreted as implying for any State, group or person any right to engage in any activity or to perform any act aimed at the destruction of any of the rights and freedoms set forth herein."

Two additional proposals were omitted, after long deliberation, from the final text of the Declaration. The early drafts of the Declaration contained an article on the right, either individually or in association with others, to petition the state or the United Nations. The Commission on Human Rights did not include this provision in its final text, because it had not yet discussed measures of implementation. After a long debate, in which a number of delegations urged the inclusion of such a provision in the Declaration, the General Assembly ultimately agreed merely to ask the commission to examine the problem further when studying the covenant and measures of implementation. The preamble of the resolution approved by the Assembly stated, however, that "the right of petition is an essential human right, as is recognized in the Constitutions of a great number of countries."[14]

The early drafts of the Declaration had also included an article on the rights of ethnic, linguistic, and religious minorities, but this too was deleted by the commission from its final text. During the debates in the General Assembly, the delegations of Denmark, the Soviet Union, and Yugoslavia submitted proposals for articles on this subject. The Assembly decided, however, merely to request the Commission on Human Rights and the Subcommission on the Prevention of Discrimination and the Protection of Minorities to make a thorough study of the problem of minorities "in order that the United Nations may be able to take effective measures for the protection of racial, national, religious or linguistic minorities."[15]

Significance of the Declaration

After the General Assembly had adopted the Universal Declaration of Human Rights on December 10, 1948, the President of the Assembly (Evatt of Australia) declared:

It is the first occasion on which the organized community of nations has made a declaration of human rights and fundamental freedoms, and it has

[14] Res. 217B(III), Dec. 10, 1948.
[15] Res. 217C(III), Dec. 10, 1948.

the authority of the body of opinion of the United Nations as a whole, and millions of men, women and children all over the world, many miles from Paris and New York, will turn for help, guidance and inspiration to this document.[16]

It is undoubtedly true that the adoption of the Universal Declaration without a dissenting vote marked a notable event in history, but it is too early yet to determine the place of this international document among the great national statements of the rights of man. Nevertheless, the Universal Declaration already has had an impressive impact not only on the resolutions of United Nations organs but also on the constitutions, laws, and judicial decisions of many countries, for it is becoming, as it was intended to be, a yardstick for measuring the progress of governments and peoples toward the full respect for human freedom.

The Universal Declaration is frequently cited in resolutions of the General Assembly and other organs of the United Nations; and proposals concerning future work of the Commission on Human Rights and its Subcommission on Prevention of Discrimination and Protection of Minorities envisage reports, studies, debates, and other activities based on the specific rights set forth in that document. Of particular significance is the fact that the General Assembly has frequently cited the Universal Declaration in its resolutions on the status of Indians in South Africa. Several of these references have been in the preamble of the resolution; but two of them have been in the operative paragraphs where the objectives of the Universal Declaration have, in effect, been equated with the obligations of the Charter—just as the Union of South Africa had feared when it abstained in the final vote on the Universal Declaration. In 1952, the Assembly established a Good Offices Commission "in order that a satisfactory solution of the question in accordance with the Purposes and Principles of the Charter and the Universal Declaration of Human Rights may be achieved."[17] In 1953, the Assembly expressed regret that the South African Government was "proceeding with further legislation contrary to the Charter and the Universal Declaration of Human Rights."[18]

[16] Quoted in U.N. Department of Social Affairs, *The Impact of the Universal Declaration of Human Rights*, Doc. ST/SOA/5/Rev. 1 (June 29, 1953), p. 7. Only a summary version is given in U.N. General Assembly, Third Session, First Part, *Official Records*, 183rd Meeting (Dec. 10, 1948), p. 934.

[17] Res. 615(VII), Dec. 5, 1952.

[18] Res. 719(VIII), Nov. 11, 1953.

Within seven years, the Universal Declaration of Human Rights has had its influence on the constitutions of Indonesia, Costa Rica, Syria, El Salvador, Haiti, Jordan, the Federal Republic of Germany, and Puerto Rico; the instruments relating to Eritrea, Libya, and Somaliland; the peace treaty with Japan; and the legislation of several other states.[19] The Universal Declaration has also been cited by the International Court of Justice and by courts in a number of countries. It has been the subject of intensive educational work on the part of the United Nations Educational, Scientific, and Cultural Organization.

The Universal Declaration has become the subject of an annual world-wide celebration—Human Rights Day on December 10, the anniversary of its proclamation by the Assembly. On the initiative of the United States, the General Assembly, at its session in 1950, invited all states and interested organizations to observe Human Rights Day and to report to the Secretary-General on their activities. One measure of popular interest is the fact that the special commemorative Human Rights Day stamp, issued by the United Nations Postal Administration on December 10, 1952, received 200,000 advance orders; and a number of countries have issued their own stamps or made special cancellations to honor this occasion. The Secretary-General's annual summary of the celebrations—involving meetings, government proclamations, radio programs, and similar activities—shows the continuing importance of the Universal Declaration as a statement of goals toward which to strive.

The fact that the General Assembly, after the most painstaking efforts by various United Nations organs over a period of three years, was able to reach agreement on the Universal Declaration has had, however, one adverse effect. The very success of this enterprise has led some governments, nongovernmental organizations, and individuals to place too much emphasis on the value of defining human

---

[19] For an informative summary of developments since 1948, see U.N. Department of Social Affairs, *The Impact of the Universal Declaration of Human Rights*. The most recent example was the Special Statute for Trieste, which was annexed to the memorandum of understanding concluded by Italy, the United Kingdom, the United States, and Yugoslavia on October 5, 1954. In the first article of the Special Statute, Italy and Yugoslavia agreed as follows: "In the administration of their respective areas the Italian and Yugoslav authorities shall act in accordance with the principles of the Universal Declaration of Human Rights adopted by the General Assembly of the United Nations on the 10th of December, 1948, so that all inhabitants of the two areas without discrimination may fully enjoy the fundamental rights and freedoms laid down in the aforesaid Declaration." U.S. Department of State *Bulletin*, Vol. 31 (Oct. 18, 1954), p. 558.

rights. During the third session of the Assembly in 1948, Argentina introduced a proposal for a Declaration on the Rights of the Aged. The Social Commission has considered a Declaration of the Rights of the Child, designed to amplify the declaration adopted in 1924 by the League of Nations. The United Nations Educational, Scientific, and Cultural Organization has given consideration to a Declaration on the Rights of Teachers. No final action has been taken on these proposals; but this tendency, if continued, might eventually detract from the dignity and significance of the Universal Declaration of *all* rights.

The Draft Covenants on Human Rights

The problem of translating the Universal Declaration of Human Rights into treaty form was, however, an entirely different problem, one which absorbed the attention and energies of the Commission on Human Rights after 1947. With the completion of the Declaration, it was generally agreed—in fact, it had long been assumed— that the conclusion of the proposed Covenant on Human Rights was the next task of the United Nations in this field.[20] The Commission on Human Rights had already prepared a very tentative text, based in part on the initial proposal of the United Kingdom. This effort to define human rights in treaty form, to which the commission had already devoted much of its first three sessions, was destined to occupy most of the next five sessions of the commission, during 1949 to 1954.[21] This effort has also taken much of the time

[20] That this was the prevailing view in 1948 is illustrated by the following statement by John Foster Dulles, who was then a member of the United States delegation: "I hope and believe this Assembly will endorse this Declaration. But we must not stop there. We must go on with the drafting of a Covenant which will seek to translate human rights into law. It does not minimize the importance of our own Declaration of Independence to recognize that the Constitution and its Bill of Rights were required to establish the body of law necessary to achieve practical results. So with the Declaration before the Assembly. It is an important proclamation of principle and should be approved. But that approval is only a step toward fulfilling the faith in fundamental human rights, in the dignity and worth of the human person, and the pledge to practice tolerance that is contained in the preamble of the United Nations Charter." Address at Paris House of the Carnegie Endowment for International Peace, Sept. 29, 1948, reprinted in *International Conciliation*, No. 445 (November 1948), pp. 584-85.

[21] The fourth session was held on April 15, 1949 for the sole purpose of electing the members of the Subcommission on Freedom of Information and of the Press. The subsequent sessions were as follows: fifth, May 9-June 20, 1949; sixth, March 27-May 19, 1950; seventh, April 16-May 19, 1951; eighth, April 14-June 14, 1952; ninth, April 7-May 30, 1953; tenth, February 23-April 16, 1954.

of the Third Committee of the General Assembly, which has dealt with matters of general principle rather than with specific texts.

Differing Approaches to the Problem

The longer these debates have continued, the more it has become apparent that the Members of the United Nations are in fundamental disagreement over the nature and scope of a treaty on human rights. On the one hand, the United States, the older members of the British Commonwealth, and Western Europe have urged that the proposed Covenant on Human Rights should be limited to a relatively few civil and political rights that are generally accepted around the world. They have maintained that such a treaty, to be effective, must give international recognition to rights that have already been given national recognition in most countries and are enforceable in their courts. They have regarded the proposed covenant as a "floor," containing the minimum rights that most governments already respect. Similarly, they have taken a cautious approach to the problem of implementation and have refused to go beyond a narrowly defined procedure by which one state party to the covenant may complain of a violation by another state also party to it. In this way, they argued, a large number of governments would be willing to assume a treaty obligation to respect and promote at least certain basic rights.

Most of the Latin-American, Near Eastern, and Asian representatives, on the other hand, have taken a much broader view of the nature of such a treaty. They have felt that treaties, like many of their own constitutions, should contain a broad statement of goals to be achieved—a "ceiling" toward which governments and peoples should strive. They have been less concerned with the legal niceties of drafting than with the inclusion of the widest possible range of rights. Some of them have intimated that their governments could not carry out all of the obligations proposed for the covenant, but the conclusion of such a treaty would enable public opinion to bring pressure to bear on governments. A number of them, although by no means all, have been willing to accept elaborate implementation procedures, including examination of petitions from individuals and organizations. This group, which usually controls a majority of votes, has succeeded in including in the draft covenants many provisions about which they feel deeply.

Still a third approach has been advocated by the Soviet bloc. The Soviet Union and its satellites have consistently supported the underdeveloped countries in their desire to extend the scope of the covenant to include economic, social, and cultural rights. They have insisted, however, on the inclusion of provisions that will express their totalitarian philosophy and have steadfastly opposed all measures of implementation. They have maintained that any kind of machinery for examining petitions, reviewing state-to-state complaints, or creating judicial procedures would constitute an infringement of domestic jurisdiction in violation of Article 2(7) of the Charter.

Question of One or Two Covenants

The conflicting views of Members of the United Nations over the nature and scope of the proposed covenant became apparent in many different issues. The most important of these was over the question whether to include economic, social, and cultural rights as well as civil and political rights in the covenant. This question first arose during the session in 1949 of the Commission on Human Rights, when Australia and the Soviet Union proposed that the covenant should include economic and social rights. The commission deferred a decision on this question at that session, and instead requested the Secretary-General to prepare a survey of the activities of other organs of the United Nations and the specialized agencies in the economic and social fields "for the purpose of enabling the Commission to determine what action it should take in these fields, in particular for the inclusion of these subjects either in the covenant on human rights or in later conventions."[22] At its session in 1950, the commission decided—by a vote of 13 to 2—not to include economic and social rights in the "first" covenant and to postpone consideration of "additional covenants" dealing with these rights until its 1951 session.

In 1950, the General Assembly, at the request of the Economic and Social Council, considered four policy issues: (1) the general adequacy of the first eighteen substantive articles on civil and political rights; (2) the application of the covenant to federal states

[22] U.N. Commission on Human Rights, *Report of the Fifth Session*, Doc. E/1371 (June 23, 1949), pp. 8-9. The vote was 12 to 0, with 3 abstentions.

and to non-self-governing territories; (3) the desirability of including articles on economic, social, and cultural rights; and (4) the adequacy of the articles relating to implementation.

The debate on the third issue was especially long and bitter, because it went to the very heart of the matter. Throughout the years of negotiations and debates, the United States and a number of other delegations insisted that only civil and political rights, generally recognized and enforceable in courts, were suitable for inclusion in a treaty. The United States delegation, in particular, was intent on concluding a covenant that would be acceptable to the Senate and therefore took the lead in urging that the covenant be limited to civil and political rights, in order that the United States and other Members might be able to ratify it. To this end, the United States delegation made clear in its public statements that the United States would find it difficult to accept a treaty containing economic, social, and cultural rights, because these went far beyond the rights contained in the United States Constitution and were not enforceable—apart from particular legislation—by the federal and state courts in the United States.

The United States, Brazil, and Turkey introduced a draft resolution requesting the Commission on Human Rights to proceed with "the consideration of additional instruments and measures dealing with economic, social, cultural and other human rights" not included in the covenant.[23] The majority was not convinced, however, and the Third Committee adopted a Yugoslav amendment by which economic, social, and cultural rights would be included in the covenant. The vote was 23 in favor, 17 against, with 10 abstentions.[24] The vote in the plenary session of the Assembly on the amended text was overwhelming: 35 in favor, 9 against, with 7 abstentions.[25]

The Commission on Human Rights, in response to the will of the Assembly, proceeded at its 1951 session to draft economic, social, and cultural rights. The commission made clear, however, that these rights differed from the civil and political provisions of the covenant in a number of ways, as follows:

[23] U.N. General Assembly, Fifth Session, Third Committee, Doc. A/C.3/L. 76 (Nov. 1, 1950).

[24] India, most of the Latin-American nations, and the Soviet bloc were in favor; the United Kingdom and United States were against; China and France abstained.

[25] The negative votes included Australia, Canada, the United Kingdom, and the United States.

The economic, social and cultural rights were recognized as objectives to be achieved "progressively." The civil and political rights were regarded as rights to be given effect almost immediately.

It was also recognized that the economic, social, and cultural rights were to be achieved by many means, private as well as public, and not solely through legislation. Although the Soviet bloc repeatedly urged that these rights should be stated in terms of state legislation only, the other members of the commission rejected this approach.

Different implementation machinery was considered for the two groups of rights. It was generally held that some form of reporting on progress made in promoting economic, social, and cultural rights would be preferable to the kind of state-to-state complaint machinery being formulated for civil and political rights.

At the end of its session, the commission debated an Indian proposal that the General Assembly be asked to reconsider its decision to include economic, social and cultural rights in the same covenant with civil and political rights. The proposal was defeated by a vote of 5 in favor, 12 against, with 1 abstention.[26] Several months later, the Economic and Social Council—on the initiative of India, France, the United Kingdom, the United States, and Uruguay—moved in the opposite direction and requested the Assembly to reconsider its 1950 decision. This time the vote was 11 in favor and 7 against, a number of Members having reversed their positions.[27]

Another debate on this issue took place in 1951-52 during the sixth session of the General Assembly. In the Third Committee, a draft resolution was submitted by Chile, Egypt, Pakistan, and Yugoslavia proposing that the Assembly reaffirm its 1950 decision. An amendment submitted by Belgium, India, Lebanon, and the United States proposed that the two covenants should be completed and opened for signature simultaneously, and, after a long debate, the amendment was adopted by the committee. In the plenary meeting of the Assembly, a Chilean amendment proposing a single covenant was defeated by 25 votes in favor, 29 against, with 4 abstentions. The text of the resolution by the committee in favor of two covenants

[26] Denmark, Greece, India, the United Kingdom, and the United States were in favor; Chile, China, Egypt, France, Guatemala, Lebanon, Pakistan, Sweden, the Ukraine, the Soviet Union, Uruguay, Yugoslavia were against; and Australia abstained.

[27] Belgium, Canada, China, France, India, Iran, Peru, Sweden, the United Kingdom, the United States, and Uruguay were in favor; Chile, Czechoslovakia, Mexico, Pakistan, the Philippines, Poland, and the Soviet Union were against.

was then adopted by 27 votes in favor, 20 against, with 3 abstentions. These very narrow majorities reveal how deeply the Members of the United Nations were divided on the basic approach to the problem of the covenants.

Two subsequent attempts were made by the Soviet Union during the sessions of the commission in 1952 and 1953 to have the decision of the Assembly reconsidered once again, but both attempts were defeated. The decision of the Assembly to deal with human rights in two separate covenants, thus twice reaffirmed by the commission, was the result of several different factors: first, the growing realization by a number of Members (especially China, France, India, Lebanon, and Uruguay, which reversed their positions in this period) that economic, social, and cultural rights are completely different in character from civil and political rights; second, the intensive efforts by the United States in foreign capitals and in United Nations lobbies and committee rooms, in favor of two covenants; and third, the willingness of some Members to acquiesce, reluctantly, in the separation of the two covenants in order to make it possible for the United States, the British Commonwealth, and others to ratify at least a covenant on civil and political rights.

Civil and Political Rights

The Draft Covenant on Civil and Political Rights, as completed by the commission at its tenth session (February-April 1954), contains six parts, which deal with the following subjects in the order given: the right of self-determination; the general obligation to respect and ensure the rights contained in the covenant, and certain limitations on these rights; the substantive rights; complaint procedure; reports concerning measures adopted to give effect to these rights; and final clauses.[28] The Draft Covenant on Economic, Social, and Cultural Rights is similar in structure, except that it contains no complaint procedure.[29]

The twenty-one rights contained in Part III of the Draft Covenant on Civil and Political Rights define and amplify, in more precise language, most of the corresponding rights set forth in the Universal Declaration. With some notable exceptions, most of them

[28] For text of the Draft Covenant on Civil and Political Rights, see App. B. For a detailed commentary, prepared for the use of the General Assembly at its tenth session, see U. N. Secretariat, *Draft International Covenants on Human Rights, Annotation,* Doc. A/2929 (July 1, 1955).

[29] For text of the Draft Covenant on Economic, Social, and Cultural Rights, see App. C.

are similar in substance, although not always in language, to those in the constitutions of the United States and many other countries. These rights may be summarized as follows: freedom from arbitrary deprival of life; freedom from torture and from cruel, inhuman, or degrading treatment and punishment; prohibition of slavery and the slave trade; right to liberty and security of person; humane treatment for prisoners; freedom from imprisonment for indebtedness; freedom of movement; freedom of an alien from arbitrary expulsion from a country; equal rights before the law; freedom from *ex post facto* laws; right to recognition as a person before the law; freedom from arbitrary or unlawful interference with privacy, home, or correspondence and from unlawful attacks on honor and reputation; freedom of thought, conscience, and religion, including the right to change one's religion or belief; right to hold opinions without interference, and freedom of expression; right of peaceful assembly; freedom of association; right to marry and to found a family; right and opportunity to take part in the conduct of public affairs, to vote and be elected, and of access to public service; equal status before the law; rights of ethnic, religious, or linguistic minorities; and prohibition of any advocacy of national, racial, or religious hostility that constitutes an incitement to hatred and violence.

One of the articles that departs most strikingly from the kind of right contained in the more familiar bills of rights in the Western democracies is Article 22, concerning the right to marry and to found a family. The article, based on Article 16 of the Universal Declaration, was recommended by the Commission on the Status of Women and adopted in 1953 by the Commission on Human Rights. The article begins with a statement of principle somewhat unusual in a treaty: "The family is the natural and fundamental group unit of society and is entitled to protection by society and the State." The next two clauses provide that the right of men and women of marriageable age to marry and to found a family shall be recognized, and that no marriage shall be entered into without the free and full consent of the intending spouses.[30] The final clause is the only one among the substantive rights of this covenant to provide for the attainment of the right through progressive legislation: "The legislation of the States Parties to this Covenant shall be directed towards

[30] The Commission on Human Rights found it difficult—in view of the widely differing traditions, laws, and customs throughout the world—to translate the words of the Universal Declaration, "Men and women of full age," into treaty language. After a long and slightly risible debate, the commission agreed on the phrase, "The right of men and women of marriageable age."

equality of rights and responsibilities for the spouses as to marriage, during marriage and at its dissolution. In the last-mentioned case the law shall lay down special measures for the protection of any children of the marriage."

A second provision that is not usually found in bills of individual rights—and indeed one that was omitted from the Universal Declaration—is Article 25 of the covenant, which pertains to the rights of minorities. The text of Article 25 is based on one submitted by the Subcommission on Discrimination and Minorities. More extreme texts were submitted by the Soviet Union and by Yugoslavia at the 1953 session of the commission; but the former was rejected and the latter was withdrawn. The text as adopted sets forth a generally recognized principle, but many states, because of local conditions or political circumstances, might be unable to accept it: "In those States in which ethnic, religious or linguistic minorities exist, persons belonging to such minorities shall not be denied the right, in community with the other members of their group, to enjoy their own culture, to profess and practise their own religion, or to use their own language."

Another atypical provision, and one that provoked much controversy, is Article 26: "Any advocacy of national, racial or religious hostility that constitutes an incitement to hatred and violence shall be prohibited by the law of the State." This text was based on a recommendation of the Subcommission on Discrimination and Minorities, which was limited to incitement to violence, and was strongly supported by delegations of the Soviet bloc. The commission in 1953 rejected a Polish proposal to replace the words "national, racial" by the words "national or racial exclusiveness, hatred and contempt." It accepted, however, a Chilean proposal to add the words "hatred and" before "violence." The United States, the United Kingdom, and other Member states opposed the addition of "hatred" as a subjective concept not easily justiciable. They also opposed the idea that the state should censor and punish propaganda, although they deplored this kind of activity.

Economic, Social, and Cultural Rights

The Draft Covenant on Economic, Social, and Cultural Rights, contains, in Part III, eleven articles. All but one of these articles begins with a similar phrase. It reflects the concept that the state recognizes everyone should have a certain right, but does not declare that everyone has the right in fact.[31] The phrasing of these articles thus takes account of the fact that these rights cannot be made immediately effective by legislative and judicial action and, indeed, that they are far beyond the means of most states. This is in distinct contrast to the Draft Covenant on Civil and Political Rights, which provides in most of its articles that everyone actually has a particular right.

The economic, social, and cultural rights follow the general pattern of the Universal Declaration, but they are far more detailed. This resulted in part from the overriding concern of the majority with this category of rights and their determination to spell them out at length. It also resulted from the active participation in the work of the commission by the International Labour Organisation, and particularly by the United Nations Educational, Scientific and Cultural Organization and the World Health Organization, each of which submitted detailed proposals in its own field.

These rights are as follows: to work; to just and favorable conditions of work, fair wages and equal remuneration for work of equal value, and to rest, leisure, and reasonable limitation of working hours, and periodic holidays with pay; to form and join trade unions; to social security; accordance of special protection to motherhood and children; adequate food, clothing, and housing; to an adequate standard of living and the continuous improvement of living conditions; to the enjoyment of the highest attainable standard of health; to education; the provision of free, compulsory primary education; to take part in cultural life, and the obligation of the state to respect the freedom indispensable for scientific research and creative activity.

This group of eleven articles is obviously comprehensive in scope and almost utopian in character. However, one important right—the right to own property—is conspicuous by its absence. The Commission on Human Rights, at its session in 1951, considered a United States proposal to include an article on the right to own property

[31] For example, a number of the articles begin: "The States Parties to the Covenant recognize the right of everyone to. . . ." The only exception is Article 8, which begins: "The States Parties to the Covenant undertake to ensure the free exercise of the right of everyone to form and join local, national and international trade unions. . . ." This, in effect, guarantees "the right to freedom of association with others, including the right to form and join trade unions," contained in Article 21 of the Draft Covenant on Civil and Political Rights.

that was a paraphrase of Article 17 of the Universal Declaration. After an inconclusive debate on the problems of expropriation of private property and of compensation, the commission decided "not to include at present, an article on the right of property."[32] At its session in 1952, France introduced a more elaborate proposal, which included a clause on expropriation and compensation; but this time the commission decided to adjourn the debate.

The most recent attempt to include in the covenant an article on the right to own property was made by the United States at the session of the commission in 1954. The text submitted by the United States was the exact language of Article 17 of the Universal Declaration, preceded by the customary introductory phrase of the later document. During the course of seven meetings, all members of the commission, even those in the Soviet bloc, expressed willingness, in principle, to have an article on private property included. They failed again, however, to reach agreement on the manner in which private property might be expropriated and the terms of compensation in such cases. The commission finally decided to adjourn consideration of the question *sine die*.

Limitations on the Covenants

Part II of each covenant contains four articles defining the general obligation to ensure the substantive rights and stating certain limitations on them. These provisions—the result of many weeks of difficult drafting over the years—reflect the determination of the United States and of other Members that take a "narrow construction" of treaties to obtain certain overriding safeguards that would make it possible for them to ratify the covenants.

Each covenant contains, in its Article 2, a provision to ensure that it is non-self-executing. The Covenant on Civil and Political Rights states that where the rights are not already provided for by existing legislation or other measures, each party should undertake to take the necessary steps, in accordance with its constitutional processes, to adopt such legislative or other measures as might be necessary to give effect to the rights. The Covenant on Economic, Social, and Cultural Rights provides that each state party should

---

[32] U.N. Commission on Human Rights, *Report of Seventh Session*, Doc. E/1992 (May 24, 1951), p. 12.

undertake "to take steps, individually and through international co-operation, to the maximum of its available resources, with a view to achieving progressively the full realization of the rights recognized in this Covenant by legislative as well as by other means."

These two articles make clear that adherence to the covenants would not of itself automatically make their provisions effective. Each party would have to take affirmative action to give effect to the provisions of the covenants—immediately in the case of civil and political rights and progressively in the case of economic, social, and cultural rights. For the United States, this would mean that the provisions of the covenants would not, themselves, become enforceable in the courts as "supreme Law of the Land" under Article VI of the Constitution.

The question whether there might be a general limitation on the civil and political rights, under an "umbrella clause," or specific limitations on certain rights, occupied the commission at its early sessions. The result was a compromise. Specific limitations were written into the articles on freedom to manifest one's religion, freedom of expression, and the right of peaceful assembly. A general limitation was included in Article 4, which provided: "In time of public emergency which threatens the life of the nation and the existence of which is officially proclaimed, the States Parties hereto may take measures derogating from their obligations under this Covenant to the extent strictly required by the exigencies of the situation." No such derogation would be permitted, however, from the articles concerning arbitrary deprival of life, torture, slavery, imprisonment for indebtedness, freedom from *ex post facto* laws, recognition as a person before the law, and freedom of thought, conscience, and religion.

Provision was made in Article 5(2) of each covenant to make it expressly clear that the covenants could not be used to lower existing standards in a state. These clauses state that there should be no restriction on or derogation from any of the fundamental human rights recognized or existing in any contracting state pursuant to law, conventions, regulations, or custom "on the pretext that the present Covenant does not recognize such rights or that it recognizes them to a lesser extent." The United States, in particular, urged the inclusion of this clause and emphasized that the purpose of the covenants was to raise standards, not to lower them.

Self-Determination

Until the sixth session of the General Assembly in 1951-52, almost all of the rights set forth in the covenants were those of the individual. At that session, however, thirteen Arab-Asian delegations proposed the inclusion of the following article: "All peoples shall have the right of self-determination."[33] These delegations, supported by many of the Latin-American states and by the Soviet bloc, argued that the covenants would be incomplete unless the right of self-determination were included. They pointed out that Articles 1 and 55 of the Charter referred to "the principle of equal rights and self-determination of peoples," and that Article 21 of the Universal Declaration stated that "The will of the people shall be the basis of the authority of government." The Soviet Union introduced an amendment to the draft article providing that states that have responsibilities for non-self-governing territories shall promote the realization of this right. This attempt to include the right of self-determination in the covenants was closely related to the efforts of the Arab-Asian and Latin-American delegations, described later in this study, to have the General Assembly adopt recommendations on self-determination.[34] These efforts in turn were part of the general initiative taken by these delegations to focus attention on colonial and trusteeship issues in all forums of the United Nations.

The administering powers countered these arguments by replying that the right of self-determination of peoples was a group or territorial right and, as such, was of an entirely different character from the individual rights already in the covenants. They maintained that neither the phrase "right of self-determination" nor the word "peoples" could readily be defined. They also contended that the system of implementation being prepared for the covenants, including both reporting and the consideration of complaints, would not be applicable to this right. The United States emphasized that the right of self-determination should not be limited to non-self-governing peoples but should be equally applicable to all peoples, including those that had lost their independence in recent years.

This debate on the substantive issues was complicated by a series

[33] U. N. General Assembly, Sixth Session, Third Committee, Docs. A/C.3/L.186 (Dec. 7, 1951), and A/C.3/L.186/Add. 1 (Dec. 10, 1951).
[34] See below, Chap. III.

of procedural difficulties. The result was a resolution containing two different preambles and an almost incoherent operative paragraph, which first specified the exact wording of the article and then twice stipulated that the right should be promoted with regard to non-self-governing territories. The final vote, however, was overwhelming: 42 in favor, 7 against, with 5 abstentions.[35]

The Commission on Human Rights, at its session in 1952, carried out the mandate of the General Assembly by preparing an article on the right of self-determination for inclusion in both covenants. During the course of a long debate, the arguments made in the Assembly were repeated and amplified. The Soviet Union proposed, unsuccessfully, a new paragraph providing that the state should ensure to national minorities the right to use their native tongue and to possess their national schools, libraries, museums, and other cultural and educational institutions. The United States proposed an amendment, which eventually became the second paragraph of the article, broadening the reference to non-self-governing territories to include states "controlling in whatsoever manner the exercise of that right by another people." Another United States amendment, providing that the right of self-determination should be promoted and realized as provided in the Charter, in accordance with constitutional processes, and with proper regard for the rights of other states and peoples, was rejected by the commission.

The most significant development in this debate was the acceptance by the commission of a Chilean proposal for a new paragraph on the right of economic self-determination. This paragraph provided that the right of peoples to self-determination should also provide permanent sovereignty over their natural wealth and resources, and that in no case should a people be deprived of its own means of subsistence on the ground of any rights that might be claimed by other states. This new paragraph clearly reflected the historic conflict between the underdeveloped and developed countries over the issue of expropriation of private property—an issue that had frequently arisen in other debates in the United Nations not related to the subject of human rights.

The right of self-determination, which now stands as the first article of both covenants, adds a new and serious element of controversy in the human rights field. On the one hand, the administer-

---

[35] Opposed were Australia, Belgium, New Zealand, France, Luxembourg, the United Kingdom, and the United States.

ing powers have made it clear that they would find it virtually impossible to accept a covenant that contained this right. On the other hand, the nonadministering powers have insisted, by overwhelming majorities, that this right must be included. Suggestions have been made on occasion by both sides that the right of self-determination, because of its special character, belongs in a separate covenant. This question, which has so deeply divided the Members of the United Nations, may have a profound effect on the ultimate fate of the covenants.

Measures of Implementation

The early concept of an "International Bill of Rights," it will be recalled, comprised a declaration, a covenant, and measures of implementation. As the work of drafting the Covenant on Human Rights progressed, it was increasingly assumed that some kind of machinery should be included for implementing the rights contained in the covenant. Three points of view emerged: the United States, the United Kingdom, and others desired to limit the implementation to the examination of complaints by states parties to the covenant; India, Lebanon, the Philippines, Uruguay, and others favored provision for petitions from individuals and nongovernmental organizations; and the Soviet bloc was against implementation of any kind.

The majority of the Commission on Human Rights considered that a mere statement of rights would be of little use unless some provision were made for their implementation. The majority also considered, however, that it would be inadvisable to go beyond the traditional system of conciliation of differences between the parties to the treaty. Except for the Soviet bloc, this concept has had general support in the United Nations organs. The commission, at its session in 1950, prepared the essential elements of the elaborate machinery for state-to-state complaints that is now contained in Part IV of the Draft Covenant on Civil and Political Rights. In 1954, the commission considered applying this procedure to the Covenant on Economic, Social, and Cultural Rights, but took no action in this regard.

The Draft Covenant on Civil and Political Rights provides for the establishment of a Human Rights Committee, to be composed of nine persons, chosen for five-year terms by the International Court of Justice from nominations made by the states parties to the covenant. It provides that if one party to the covenant considers that another party is not giving effect to a provision of the covenant, the parties shall endeavor to adjust the matter through direct negotiations. If the matter is not satisfactorily adjusted within six months, either state may refer the matter to the Human Rights Committee. The committee is to ascertain the facts and make available its good offices to the states concerned, and to transmit a report on the case to the states concerned and to the Secretary-General for publication. If a solution is not reached, the committee is to state its opinion whether the facts disclose a breach by one of the states of its obligations under the covenant.

Many Members and nongovernmental organizations were not satisfied with the machinery to be provided for dealing with complaints. They felt that, because of political circumstances, a state would not often wish to offend another state by bringing a complaint under the covenant before the Human Rights Committee. They favored, therefore, machinery for the receipt and examination of petitions. At the session of the commission in 1949, a Philippine proposal that the covenant provide for petitions from individuals and groups was defeated by a vote of 8 to 7, with 1 abstention. One year later, the commission decided—by a vote of 7 to 4, with 3 abstentions—that the machinery for implementation should not apply to nongovernmental organizations, and—by a vote of 8 to 3, with 3 abstentions—that it should not apply to individuals. The pressure for petitions continued to mount, however, and the General Assembly, later in 1950, requested the commission "to proceed with the consideration of provisions, to be inserted in the draft Covenant or in separate protocols, for the receipt and examination of petitions from individuals and organizations with respect to alleged violations of the Covenant."[36] The vote was 31 in favor, 14 against, with 9 abstentions.

In the Commission on Human Rights, however, the opponents of petitions, which included all of the great powers, were able to negate this decision of the Assembly. Furthermore, the commission at several successive sessions rejected additional proposals concerning petitions. Most of these decisions were taken by very narrow majorities. As in the case of communications to the United Nations,

[36] Res. 421 F(V), Dec. 4, 1950.

which will be discussed later in this study, opposition to petitions has been one of the very few subjects on which the five great powers have been in agreement in the postwar years.[37]

As a device to keep machinery for petitions out of the covenant, the United States delegation submitted a draft protocol to the session of the commission in 1951, by which states might authorize the proposed Human Rights Committee to receive and examine petitions from individuals and certain nongovernmental organizations. By this means, machinery for petitions would be kept out of the covenant, but would be available to those states that wished to utilize it. The commission, however, did not have time to consider the protocol in 1951 and 1952. At the session in 1953, after the United States had declared its intention not to sign or ratify the covenants, its delegation withdrew the draft protocol.

Three other proposals for implementing civil and political rights have been submitted for consideration by the commission. In 1947 and subsequently, Australia proposed the establishment of an International Court of Human Rights, to consider cases brought by states, individuals, groups of individuals, and national or international associations and to render advisory opinions at the request of the Commission on Human Rights. In 1949, France proposed the establishment of a special commission to consider allegations by individuals and nongovernmental organizations of violations of human rights. In 1951, Uruguay submitted a proposal for the establishment of an Office of the United Nations High Commissioner (Attorney-General) for Human Rights, who would examine petitions and, if necessary, negotiate with the state concerned or bring the matter before the Human Rights Committee. However, none of these proposals, which represent the most extreme forms of possible implementation of the covenant, has been considered at any length by the commission.

Another form of implementation, to which the commission devoted much of its session in 1954, consists of provisions for reporting by parties to the covenants. The Covenant on Civil and Political Rights provides, in Part V, that the parties shall report on legislative or other measures, including judicial remedies, which they have adopted "(a) within one year of the entry into force of the Covenant for the State concerned and (b) thereafter whenever the Economic and Social Council so requests upon recommendation

[37] See below, Chap. III.

of the Commission on Human Rights." Another article provides, moreover, that states administering non-self-governing territories should report on measures taken concerning Article 1 on self-determination and on any violation of the right of economic determination contained in that article.

The Covenant on Economic, Social, and Cultural Rights provides also, in Part IV, a much more elaborate system of reporting on progress made in achieving the observance of these rights. Arrangements are provided for collaboration among the parties, the Economic and Social Council, and the specialized agencies for the preparation and consideration of these reports. The Council is authorized to submit to the General Assembly from time to time reports indicating the progress made in achieving general observance of these rights.

Federal-State Article

One of the most troublesome issues, involving a small number of Members, has been the question of a federal-state article. During the early years of drafting the covenants, the United States, Australia, Canada, and India maintained that some special provision should be made for federal states, where most of the matters covered by the treaty were within the jurisdiction of the states, provinces, or cantons and not of the federal government. They argued that their federal governments could not undertake all of the obligations contained in the covenants. To enable them to become parties to the covenants, this group contended, their federal governments should be required to assume obligations relating only to matters within their jurisdiction. Other federal states—such as Mexico, Brazil, and Venezuela—stated that they did not require a special article for their purposes, but they supported the general principle.

Many of the unitary states strongly objected, however, to any exception being made for the federal states. They maintained that it would be unfair to permit a small group of Members to accept a limited number of obligations, while the majority would have to accept all of them. The majority was consistently unable or unwilling to understand the constitutional problems of the minority, and insisted that the federal states, which had adhered to many different kinds of treaties in the past, should not insist on special privileges with respect to the covenants. The Soviet bloc did not hesitate to charge that it was primarily the problem of racial discrimination that led the United States to demand the special privileges, a charge that probably had some influence on many of the delegations that were especially color-conscious.

The text adopted by the commission in 1947 contained a rudimentary federal-state article, as follows:

> In the case of a Federal State, the following provisions shall apply:
> (a) With respect to any Articles of this Covenant which the federal government regards as wholly or in part appropriate for federal action, the obligations of the federal government shall, to this extent, be the same as those of parties which are not federal States;
> (b) In respect of Articles which the federal government regards as appropriate under its constitutional system, in whole or in part, for action by the constituent States, Provinces or Cantons, the federal government shall bring such provisions, with a favourable recommendation, to the notice of the appropriate authorities of the States, Provinces or Cantons.[38]

The commission, however, took no final action on this text or on alternative ones submitted during the next six sessions.

In 1950, when considering the four issues submitted to it by the Economic and Social Council, the General Assembly sought to reconcile the views of the federal states with the majority of unitary states. The Assembly, as a compromise, called upon the Council to request the Commission on Human Rights to prepare recommendations "which will have as their purpose the securing of the maximum extension of the Covenant to the constituent units of federal States, and the meeting of the constitutional problems of federal States."[39]

The commission did not take up this subject, however, until its session in 1952. At that time, Australia, India, and the United States introduced a new text, which gave greater precision to the first clause of the 1947 draft.[40] The new text took account of the directive of the General Assembly by expanding the second clause to provide that the federal government would not only bring the provisions of the covenant with favorable recommendations to the notice of the appropriate authorities of the constituent units, but

[38] U.N. Commission on Human Rights, *Report of the Second Session*, Doc. E/600 (Dec. 17, 1947), p. 29.

[39] Res. 421 C(V), Dec. 4, 1950.

[40] For text, see U. N. Commission on Human Rights, *Report of the Eighth Session*, Doc. E/2256 (June 27, 1952), pp. 55-56.

would also request information concerning the laws of the constituent units in relation to the covenant and transmit such information to the United Nations. The joint text also expressly provided that acceptance of the covenant would not alter the division
of powers within the federal state.

The showdown on the federal-state article did not come until the
session of the commission in 1954, after the United States, as will
be noted below, had announced that it would not sign or ratify
the covenants. Whether the commission would have retained a
federal-state article in the hope of ratification by the United States is
uncertain; but, with the United States no longer the most active
defender of this clause, the commission felt less need to do so.
Australia and India reintroduced the 1952 text, without co-sponsorship of the United States. Egypt also submitted an article providing that the covenants should not include provisions relating to
federal states; and the Soviet Union submitted a far more drastic
text: "The provisions of the Covenant shall extend to all parts of
federal States without any limitations or exceptions."[41] The Egyptian proposal was rejected by a tie vote of 8 to 8, with 2 abstentions,
after which the Soviet proposal was adopted by 8 to 7, with 3 abstentions.[42]

The decision of the commission, if sustained by the General
Assembly, will make it virtually impossible for at least certain federal states to adhere to the covenants. It is thus ironical that two
Members with some of the highest standards of freedom—Australia
and Canada—may be precluded from accepting the covenants by
reason of the votes of Members with far lower standards. It is also
ironical that another federal state, India, has been defending the
principle of the federal-state article against attacks by some of its
closest associates in the Arab-Asian world and by the Soviet bloc.

Territorial Clause

Whenever a treaty is being drafted in a United Nations organ,
one of the principal political issues is inevitably the "territorial
clause" or "colonial clause." The powers that do not administer

[41] U.N. Commission on Human Rights, *Report of the Tenth Session*, Doc.
E/2573 (April 1954), p. 26.
[42] The Soviet text became Article 52 of the Draft Covenant on Civil and Political Rights and Article 27 of the Draft Covenant on Economic, Social, and
Cultural Rights.

dependent territories feel strongly that a party to the treaty should apply its provisions automatically to all territories under its jurisdiction. The powers that administer such territories argue that each party to the treaty should have discretion concerning which territories should be covered by the treaty. The United Kingdom, in particular, contends that many of its territories have a large measure of self-government and that it would wish to consult the legislative organs of these territories to ascertain whether the treaty should apply to them. The United States is in a different position, because the provisions of a treaty, generally speaking, apply to all territories under American jurisdiction.

The early drafts of the covenant contained a territorial clause, similar in substance to those of many other treaties, that satisfied the administering powers. The article provided that (1) the covenant should apply to any colony, dependency, mandated territory, or trust territory administered by a state, when that state has acceded to the covenant on behalf of such colony or territory; (2) that the state concerned should, if necessary, seek the consent at the earliest possible moment of the governments of all such colonies and territories and accede to the covenant on their behalf as soon as their consent has been obtained. A somewhat more precise version of this article was prepared by a drafting committee at the session of the Commission on Human Rights in 1949; but no final action was taken on it during the next two sessions. In the meantime, alternative texts submitted by the Philippines and the Soviet Union proposed that the provisions of the covenant should extend to all territories administered by a state.

In 1950, the General Assembly took this matter out of the hands of the commission and dictated its own text. On the initiative of the Philippines and Syria, the Assembly requested the Commission on Human Rights to include the following article in the covenant: "The provisions of the present Covenant shall extend to or be applicable equally to a signatory metropolitan State and to all the territories, be they Non-Self-Governing, Trust or Colonial Territories, which are being administered or governed by such metropolitan State."[43] The article was vigorously opposed by the administering powers, which warned that inclusion of this provision would make it difficult for them to accept the covenant; but they were decisively defeated by a vote of 30 to 11, with 8 abstentions.

[43] Res. 422(V), Dec. 4, 1950.

This decision of the Assembly was accepted without debate by the Commission on Human Rights. At the session in 1954, the chairman ruled that the article would be incorporated in the text, and the commission agreed to include the article in both covenants. These decisions, like the inclusion of the article on self-determination, reflect the desire of the majority of nonadministering Members to write their own views of the colonial problem into the covenants even though this may make ratification impossible for the minority of administering Members. This would hardly seem to be the most satisfactory method of concluding a treaty that is supposed to represent the whole world community.

Reservations

The General Assembly at its sixth session in 1951-52, as a result of the confusion that had arisen over reservations to the Genocide Convention, recommended that organs of the United Nations and the specialized agencies, in preparing multilateral conventions, should consider the insertion of provisions relating to the admissibility or nonadmissibility of reservations.[44] Later in this session, the Assembly recommended that the Commission on Human Rights be instructed to prepare one or more clauses on this subject for inclusion in the two covenants.

Several different texts were submitted to the commission:[45]

1. A draft article proposed by the United Kingdom provided that any state may make a reservation "to the extent that any law in force in its territory is in conflict with, or to the extent that its law does not give effect to, a particular provision of Part III of this Covenant [containing the substantive rights]." A reservation would be deemed to be accepted "if not less than two-thirds of the States to whom copies have been circulated in accordance with this article accept or do not object to it within a period of three months following the date of circulation."

2. A draft article proposed by China, Egypt, Lebanon, and the Philippines provided that any state may make a reservation "compatible with the object and purpose of the Covenant." Any dispute on whether a reservation is compatible with the object and purpose of the covenant, if not settled by the parties concerned, would

---

[44] See below, Chap. III.
[45] For texts of these proposals, see U.N. Commission on Human Rights, *Report of the Tenth Session*, pp. 28-29.

be referred to the International Court of Justice. Unless a settlement is reached, "any State Party objecting to the reservation may
consider that the reserving State is not a party to the Covenant,
while any State Party which accepts the reservation may consider
that the reserving State is a party to the Covenant."

3. A Soviet amendment to the two preceding texts proposed that
any state may make a reservation to any provision in the covenant.
The Soviet Union also proposed, in accordance with the Soviet
opposition to any form of implementation, to delete the provisions
for settling a dispute. The covenant would be deemed to be in
force "in relations between the States which have made the reservations and all other Parties to the Covenant, in respect of all its
provisions except those with regard to which the reservations have
been made."

4. A draft article submitted by Chile and Uruguay disposed of
the matter much more simply: "No State Party to the Covenant
may make reservations in respect of its provisions."

These proposals were debated throughout eight meetings, during
which the whole complex issue of reservations was explored.[46] The
issue was especially difficult because of the nature of the covenants.
On the one hand, the rights contained in the covenants are supposed to be universal in scope and the civil and political rights to
be immediately applicable; hence it might be considered inappro-
priate for a state to make a reservation to one of these rights. On
the other hand, constitutions and laws vary so greatly that many
states might find it impossible to accept every provision of the covenants; hence it might be considered advisable to permit reservations,
in order to obtain as many ratifications as possible. Moreover, most
of the provisions of the covenants had been adopted by majority
votes, instead of unanimous votes, with the result that a state that
objected strongly to a particular article could not become a party
to the covenants unless it were able to make a reservation.

The debate was complicated by a Belgian proposal that any state
may "declare that, in accepting the present Covenant, it does not
assume any obligation in respect of all or any of the non-self-governing, trust or colonial territories which it administers or governs, and
the present Covenant shall not apply to territories named in such
declaration."[47] The Belgian delegation and others argued that this

[46] For a summary of this debate, see *ibid.*, pp. 29-33.
[47] *Ibid.*, p. 32.

form of reservation was essential in view of the widely varying conditions in the dependent territories. The nonadministering powers contended that such a reservation would negate the territorial clause that the General Assembly had inserted in the covenant.

The debate revealed no clear majority in favor of any one of the several approaches to the problem of reservations. Chile and Uruguay then introduced a draft resolution proposing that pertinent documents on the subject be transmitted to the General Assembly. Pakistan submitted an amendment to specify all of the pertinent documents *except* the Belgian proposal. Belgium protested this omission and submitted a sub-amendment to add the Belgian proposal to the others. The sub-amendment was defeated—by a vote of 10 in favor, 5 against, with 3 abstentions. This decision indicated the intention of the Commission on Human Rights that whatever system of reservations were ultimately adopted, it should not be permitted to limit the application of the covenants with respect to dependent territories.

The question of reservations was the only one on which the commission did not reach a conclusion. Otherwise, the two covenants, so far as the technical drafting was concerned, were complete by the time the General Assembly convened its ninth session in September 1954. At that session, the Assembly did not consider the texts but invited states Members and non-Members of the United Nations to communicate any amendments, additions, or observations to the Secretary-General and requested the Secretary-General to prepare a concise annotation of the draft covenants. The Assembly also recommended that, during the tenth session in 1955, the Third Committee should give priority to a discussion of the draft covenants, article by article.

The New United States Position

From 1948 onward, as organs of the United Nations turned their attention from the Universal Declaration of Human Rights to the proposed covenant, there were increasing indications in the United States that any treaty in the field of human rights might be rejected by the Senate. For example, the Genocide Convention, submitted in 1949 to the Senate for its consent to ratification, was never brought to a vote in the Committee on Foreign Relations. The Charter of the Organization of American States, also submitted in 1949, contained provisions for co-operation regarding economic, social, and cultural standards that caused the Senate to make a reservation. This reservation, which was adopted without debate when the Senate approved the Charter in August 1950, was as follows:

That the Senate give its advice and consent to ratification of the Charter with the reservation that none of its provisions shall be considered as enlarging the powers of the Federal Government of the United States or limiting the powers of the several states of the Federal Union with respect to any matters recognized under the Constitution as being within the reserved powers of the several States.[48]

The Japanese Peace Treaty, submitted for consent to ratification in 1952, provoked criticism in the Senate because its preamble stated the intention of Japan to realize objectives of the Universal Declaration of Human Rights. John Foster Dulles, who had negotiated the treaty as Special Assistant to the Secretary of State, and several Senators made clear that the safeguarding of human rights was a matter desired by Japan and not one dictated by the United States.[49]

[48] *Congressional Record,* Vol. 96, Pt. 10, 81 Cong. 2 sess., p. 13613.
[49] As a result of this criticism of the treaty, the Department of State submitted a "Memorandum Regarding the Reference in The Japanese Peace Treaty To The Universal Declaration of Human Rights," which was as follows:
"There is nothing in the peace treaty which makes human rights a matter of international contract or which gives any Allied nation the right to interfere in Japan's internal affairs on account of human rights. There is no article of the treaty which mentions human rights.
"The preamble of the treaty contains a number of declarations of intention as is customary and one of these is a statement by Japan that she intends 'to strive to realize the objectives of the universal declaration of human rights.' Some wanted the treaty to include a legal obligation to respect human rights and fundamental freedoms. This was done in the case of the Italian and satellite treaties. However, there has developed in the United States considerable objection to trying to make human rights a matter of enforceable treaty obligation because, under our Constitution, treaties become 'the supreme law of the land' and a treaty on human rights might perhaps impair states' rights in relation to this subject. Therefore, we did not make human rights a matter of treaty obligation.
"However, almost all of the nations of the world, except the Soviet bloc, have accepted the universal declaration of human rights as a statement of worthy objectives and the Japanese wanted to be in the same category. Also, almost all of the provisions of this declaration are already engrafted in the Japanese Constitution adopted during the occupation.
"It would be rather absurd for the United States to oppose Japan's making the kind of declaration of intent that she wanted and that other free nations have made." *Japanese Peace Treaty and Other Treaties Relating to Security in the Pacific,* Hearings before the Senate Committee on Foreign Relations, 82 Cong. 2 sess., p. 153.

Finally, in 1952 the new Constitution of Puerto Rico, as approved by the Constitutional Convention and forwarded to the United States Congress for approval, contained detailed provisions concerning economic and social rights. The Constitution was severely criticized in the Congress on the ground that these rights were "socialistic" in character and implied obligations that no government could fulfill. The Congress approved the Constitution subject to certain amendments, which the Constitutional Convention and later the Puerto Rican electorate accepted.

This significant trend of opinion in the Congress became more obvious after two actions were initiated by Senator John W. Bricker (Ohio) to restrict the participation of the executive branch in this area of foreign relations. In 1951, Senator Bricker introduced a resolution proposing that it be the sense of the Senate that: (1) the covenant, if ratified, would "prejudice those rights of the American people which are now protected by the Bill of Rights of the Constitution of the United States"; (2) the President should advise the United Nations that the proposed covenant would not be acceptable; and (3) the President should instruct United States representatives at the United Nations "to withdraw from further negotiations with respect to the Covenant on Human Rights, and all other covenants, treaties, and conventions which seek to prescribe restrictions on individual liberty which, if passed by Congress as domestic legislation, would be unconstitutional."[50] The Bricker resolution was not acted on, but it symbolized the growing public concern over the covenants. Subsequently, in February 1952, Senator Bricker and fifty-six other Senators introduced the first text of what came to be known as the "Bricker Amendment" to revise the treaty-making powers under the Constitution.

These indications of public and congressional anxiety over the role of treaties in the economic and social field became a matter of serious concern to the executive branch of the government. It was apparent that a situation was developing, like that in 1919 concerning the Treaty of Versailles, in which the executive branch might be staking American leadership and prestige on a treaty that would eventually be rejected by the Senate. However, so great was the determination of other Members of the United Nations to complete the covenants, and so important was the role of the United States in helping to ensure that the covenants reflected the democratic

[50] S. Res. 177, 82 Cong. 1 sess. (July 17, 1951).

way of life, that there seemed to be no alternative but to continue with active American participation in their drafting. At the same time, United States delegations to the United Nations repeatedly made clear that the covenants must be completely satisfactory from the American point of view if they were to be signed and ratified by the United States.

The forces behind the Bricker Amendment consisted of a wide variety of groups.[51] There were lawyers who were concerned about the use of the treaty power to effect domestic economic and social changes. Originally critical of the conventions adopted by the International Labour Organisation regarding labor and social matters, they later also took exception to the Genocide Convention and the proposed covenants. There were also those who were devoted to the concept of "States' Rights" and others who were opposed to any kind of international co-operation, especially through the United Nations. In addition to these groups, there were many civic groups, patriotic organizations, and newspapers and magazines that felt deeply about what they regarded as the misuse of executive agreements by President Roosevelt and President Truman —particularly the Yalta and Potsdam agreements, considered by them to be largely responsible for the spread of Soviet power in Asia and Europe. Many of the supporters of the Bricker Amendment were critical of the draft covenants, which they regarded as containing an "alien" philosophy, even though United States delegations had sought determinedly, and with considerable success, to keep the texts acceptable to the American point of view and in harmony with the Bill of Rights contained in the Constitution.[52]

[51] For an account of this movement by one of its leaders, a past President of the American Bar Association, see Frank E. Holman, *Story of the "Bricker" Amendment (First Phase)* (1954).

[52] At the end of the eighth session of the Commission on Human Rights, the last she attended as United States Representative, Mrs. Roosevelt issued a press statement that included the following: "In its approach to the economic and social articles, as well as the civil and political articles, the U. S. delegation has been guided by our Constitution and by existing statutes and policies approved by the legislative and executive branches of the Federal Government. . . . Neither of the Covenants as now drafted contains any provisions which depart from the American way of life in the direction of communism, socialism, syndicalism, or statism. When such provisions have been proposed, the United States has opposed them; every proposal by the Soviet Union and its satellites to write 'statism' into the Covenant has been defeated. Should such proposals gain acceptance, the United States will not sign or ratify the Covenants. The objective of the United States, and I am sure of the majority of the Commission, is greater freedom, not the limitation of its exercise." U. S. Department of State *Bulletin*, Vol. 26 (June 30, 1952), pp. 1024, 1026.

It was not until the winter of 1953, after the new administration had taken office, that this great debate came to a climax. In January 1953, Senator Bricker and sixty-three other senators (exactly the two-thirds vote required to adopt a constitutional amendment) introduced a revised text of the Bricker Amendment. The hearings before the Senate Committee on the Judiciary and the subsequent debate in the Senate over the Bricker Amendment and several alternative texts—together with the efforts of the executive branch to find a compromise that would satisfy the supporters of the Bricker Amendment and at the same time safeguard the prerogatives of the President in the conduct of foreign relations—represented a highly important chapter in the history of the United States Constitution. A substitute for the Bricker Amendment, submitted by Senator Walter George (Georgia), fell only one vote short of the two-thirds vote needed for passage in the Senate, after an amendment containing the original Bricker language had been defeated by 42 in favor and 50 against.[53]

On April 6, 1953, Secretary of State Dulles, in testifying on the Bricker Amendment before the Senate Committee on the Judiciary, stated the policy of the new administration toward the use of treaties in the social and human rights fields:

The present administration intends to encourage the promotion everywhere of human rights and individual freedoms, but to favor methods of persuasion, education, and example rather than formal undertakings which commit one part of the world to impose its particular social and moral standards upon another part of the world community, which has different standards. That is the point of view I expressed in 1951 in relation to the Japanese peace treaty. Therefore, while we shall not withhold our counsel from those who seek to draft a treaty or covenant on human rights, we do not ourselves look upon a treaty as the means which we would now select as the proper and most effective way to spread throughout the world the goals of human liberty to which this nation has been dedicated since its inception. We therefore do not intend to become a party to any such covenant or present it as a treaty for consideration by the Senate.[54]

In timing, this statement represented an effort to meet the basic concern of the advocates of the Bricker Amendment. In substance, it reflected the basic philosophy of President Eisenhower and Secretary of State Dulles that the promotion of human rights is essentially a

[53] The crucial vote on the Bricker amendment to the George resolution took place on February 25, 1954; the final vote on the George resolution, taken the next day, was 60 in favor and 31 against. *Congressional Record*, Vol. 100, Pt. 2, 83 Cong. 2 sess., pp. 2262, 2374-75.

[54] U. S. Department of State *Bulletin*, Vol. 28 (Apr. 20, 1953), p. 592.

matter for the state and local community in the United States and not ordinarily a matter for federal legislation or for international treaties. The repudiation of the covenants constituted, therefore, a complete reversal of this aspect of the foreign policy of the previous administration.

In a letter of instructions, dated April 3, 1953, to the new United States representative in the Commission on Human Rights (Mrs. Oswald B. Lord), Secretary of State Dulles reiterated the new position. After declaring that the covenants would probably not be as widely accepted by Members of the United Nations as initially anticipated and that "the areas where human rights are being persistently and flagrantly violated are those where the Covenants would most likely be ignored," the Secretary made the following statement:

In these circumstances, there is grave question whether the completion, signing and ratification of the Covenants at this time is the most desirable method of contributing to human betterment particularly in areas of greatest need. Furthermore, experience to date strongly suggests that even if it be assumed that this is a proper area for treaty action, a wider general acceptance of human rights goals must be attained before it seems useful to codify standards of human rights as binding international legal obligations in the Covenants.[55]

The Secretary again made clear, however, that as a loyal Member of the United Nations, the United States would continue to participate in the technical drafting of the covenants.

On April 8, two days after Secretary Dulles' declaration in Washington, the United States representative announced the new policy to the Commission on Human Rights meeting in Geneva. She then outlined, as will be explained in detail later in this study, three proposals for an action program in the field of human rights, based on the use of reporting, special studies, and technical assistance.[56]

[55] U.S. Department of State *Bulletin,* Vol. 28 (Apr. 20, 1953), p. 580. The same approach to the promotion of human rights has been expressed as follows by one of the leaders of the nongovernmental organizations concerned with the United Nations: "In looking forward to the continued activity of the United Nations in promoting the observance of human rights, one may venture to predict that progress will depend primarily upon the extent to which the four components of effective action are developed and called into play—a human rights conscience, education, publicity, and a standard voluntarily accepted by a sound majority of the people involved in any social situation. It is from a complex of such forces that laws are derived—at all events, laws that will be complied with and stand the test of time." O. Frederick Nolde, "Human Rights and the United Nations; Appraisal and Next Steps," *Proceedings of the Academy of Political Science,* Vol. 25 (January 1953), p. 178.

[56] See below, Chap. III.

The chairman of the commission (Dr. Mahmoud Azmi of Egypt) remarked that the United States announcement came as "a bomb-shell," and other speakers expressed disappointment and regret. However, the announcement did not deter the proponents of the covenants, and the commission continued at its sessions in 1953 and 1954 to complete the technical drafting. The United States delegation participated in the debates and restated many of its previous positions on major issues, especially those in which efforts were made to restrict a right or introduce the concept of state control. The delegation—as noted previously—introduced, unsuccessfully, an article on private property, but it withdrew the draft protocol on petitions that the United States had previously sponsored, as well as its co-sponsorship of a federal-state article.

Future of the Covenants

The repudiation in 1953 of the covenants by the United States Government reflected not only its preoccupation with the use of the treaty power in matters of domestic concern but also its view that the existing international atmosphere is not conducive to the conclusion of satisfactory treaties in the field of human rights. This latter view is of major significance, for it brings into question the value of the whole effort to complete the covenants. In fact, quite apart from the new position of the United States, there is growing evidence that it may prove extremely difficult, and perhaps impossible, for Members of the United Nations to reach any general agreement on the covenants.

The longer the work of drafting the covenants continues, the more apparent becomes the difficulty of finding precise texts that will reconcile the differing legal traditions, political systems, religious faiths, and economic and social standards represented by all of the Members of the United Nations. These differences are not merely those existing between democracy and communism, between Christianity and Islam, and between the Anglo-Saxon traditions of the common law and the continental traditions of Roman law. There are often differences of considerable importance between countries that have much in common—between the United States and the United Kingdom, and between countries of Western Europe, of the Arab world, and of Latin America. Consequently, the conclusion of the Universal Declaration of Human Rights in 1948 seems, in retrospect, to have been a real achievement. The efforts to translate human rights into treaty form was an inevitable and indeed a useful experiment, if only to expose the difficulties and dangers. Whether this effort can be successfully concluded on a world-wide scale—in contrast to the successful completion by the Council of Europe in 1950 of the Convention for the Protection of Human Rights and Fundamental Freedoms, including a European Court of Human Rights and provisions for examination of petitions—remains a major problem before the United Nations.[57]

Part of this problem relates to the character of the present text of the covenants. From the brief and simple definitions of civil rights submitted first by the United Kingdom and later by the United States, the early draft has grown into enormous twin texts. Each covenant is now so long, so detailed, and so complicated that presumably every Member of the United Nations can find some paragraph, some phrase, or some word objectionable. The very length and complexity of the two covenants will make it difficult—and perhaps impossible—for the final texts to receive the ratifications of any representative majority of the Members.

Finally, the practice in the United Nations of adopting separate articles of a treaty by a majority vote and of adopting the final text by a majority or even a two-thirds vote—in contrast to the rule of unanimity that often prevailed at international conferences in the past and is still characteristic of certain conferences—raises another serious question about the future of the covenants. Time after time, an article has been included in one of the covenants by a margin of only one or two votes in the Commission on Human Rights. The result is that one group of Members—sometimes from political motives and for purposes of propaganda—has inserted an article in the covenants over the vigorous protest of another group.

[57] The convention, which sets forth eleven civil rights, was signed by the fifteen Members of the Council of Europe and came into effect on September 3, 1953, when the necessary ten ratifications had been deposited. The European Commission on Human Rights was empowered to examine complaints by one Member against another and to consider petitions from individuals, non-governmental organizations, and groups of individuals when six Members recognized the competence of the commission to receive such petitions. Since July 5, 1955, the commission has had such competence as regards Belgium, Denmark, the Federal Republic of Germany, Iceland, Ireland, and Sweden. In September 1955, the commission gave preliminary examination to 63 of the 80 petitions thus far received; of these, 44 were rejected, 18 were reserved for further study, and 1 was transmitted to the Member concerned for observations. The European Court of Human Rights has not yet received the necessary eight ratifications.

The Members that do not administer dependent territories have included articles on self-determination and the territorial article over the protest of the eight administering Members. The unitary states have included a comprehensive article over the protest of the small minority of federal states. The large majority in favor of implementation have included elaborate machinery for complaints and reporting over the protest of the five Members in the Soviet bloc.

As a result, the two covenants now contain many highly controversial articles. Some of these reflect genuine differences of opinion over the nature of a particular right; others reflect the desire of one group of Members to embarrass another group rather than a general desire to find the highest common denominator of agreement. Few of these articles represent the unanimous or near-unanimous will of the Members of the Organization and many of them represent only a slight majority of its Members. Whether a treaty on human rights of this character will ultimately be worthy of the United Nations would seem to be doubtful.[58]

Thus the effort of the United Nations over the past ten years to define human rights has resulted in one success, the Universal Declaration, and one probable failure, the draft covenants. However, the very fact that this effort has been made is itself a testimony of the growing international concern with the rights of the individual.

[58] At the tenth session of the General Assembly in 1955, the Third Committee began its article-by-article consideration of the draft covenants but made relatively little progress. The committee tentatively adopted two almost identical preambles, after making minor modifications in them. It reserved the right, however, to consider additions to the preambles after completing Article 1, relating to self-determination. The committee postponed decision on Article 2 of the Draft Covenant on Economic, Social, and Cultural Rights, pending completion of Part III, containing the substantive articles. It devoted its primary attention, during twenty-six meetings, to Article 1 of the two covenants. The United States expressed vigorous opposition to paragraph 3, which referred to the right of peoples to "permanent sovereignty over their natural wealth and resources," while the other administering powers took special exception to paragraphs 1 and 2. The committee established a working party of nine members to consider the many amendments, comments, and suggestions. The revised text of the working party of Article 1, with several amendments, was adopted in the committee by a vote of 33 to 12, with 13 abstentions. It presumably will not be considered in plenary, however, until the remainder of the covenants are completed by the Third Committee. For the text as adopted, see Appendixes B and C.

CHAPTER III

Special Activities to Foster Human Rights

THE EFFORT to translate the general goals of the Charter into the more precise language of the Universal Declaration of Human Rights and the draft covenants has been only one aspect of the activity of the United Nations in the field of human rights. Although the drafting of international instruments has been the chief preoccupation of the Commission on Human Rights—some 400 of the 479 meetings of its first ten sessions having been devoted to this purpose—other organs of the United Nations have sought to promote respect for human rights in many different ways and in many different fields. In fact, a considerable number of the political issues considered by the Security Council and the General Assembly have involved, directly or indirectly, some aspect of human rights and fundamental freedoms. But only those issues and activities most directly related to the human rights field have been included in this study.

The activities of the United Nations in the field of human rights other than the drafting of the Universal Declaration and the covenants fall into two general groups. First are those that constitute efforts to foster one or another aspect of the rights and freedoms set forth in the Charter and the Universal Declaration. These activities reflect the widespread desire to develop effective means for promoting human rights and for safeguarding freedom of information. They also comprise efforts to prevent discrimination, to protect minorities, to prevent and punish the crime of genocide, to foster equal rights for women, and to advance the right of peoples and nations to self-determination. Second are those described later in this study, that deal with violations of human rights.[1] These activities include efforts to abolish slavery and forced labor and to safeguard trade union rights. They embrace attempts in the General Assembly to deal with violations of human rights in particular countries—the Union of South Africa as well as Bulgaria, Hungary, and

• [1] See below, Chap. IV.

Rumania—and with the failure of the Soviet Union and its satellites to repatriate, or otherwise account for, prisoners of war in the Second World War. Also included are a few attempts by one government to charge another government in a United Nations forum with violating the rights of a single individual or of a small group of individuals.

These two groups of activities have raised in acute form the interpretations to be placed on Articles 55 and 56 of the Charter, on the one hand, and on Article 2(7), on the other. In most of them the competence of the United Nations to take action has been questioned. In some instances, the competence of the General Assembly even to discuss the matter has been challenged. Many of the activities have aroused angry controversy in a United Nations forum— on some occasions, because they formed part of the "cold war" between the free world and the Communist bloc; in others, because they involved the "colonial question" or problems of racial discrimination. When viewed as a whole, they reveal the remarkable variety and extent of the pioneer work of the United Nations to express international concern over the rights of the individual.

Promotion of Human Rights

Ever since the San Francisco Conference, consideration has been given in many United Nations organs to measures for "promoting and encouraging respect for human rights and for fundamental freedoms for all without distinction as to race, sex, language, or religion." It has been recognized that the formulation of international instruments was only one of these measures, and that many others could and should be developed. For example, the compilation of information about the status of human rights in each of the states Members of the United Nations was regarded as an obvious first step. This and many other techniques for promoting respect for human rights and fundamental freedoms have been on the agenda of the Commission on Human Rights for many years; but the commission rarely has taken time to discuss them, and never in any thorough and comprehensive manner.

In June 1950, Secretary-General Lie circulated his "Twenty-Year Programme for Achieving Peace Through the United Nations," which included human rights as one of its ten points. The eighth point was as follows: "Vigorous and continued development of the work of the United Nations for wider observance and respect for human rights and fundamental freedoms throughout the world."[2] The Secretary-General later submitted a supplementary memorandum reviewing the work accomplished in the drafting of international instruments and outlining a number of other fields in which work might be undertaken in the future. The latter was largely a synthesis of several proposals previously made in the Commission on Human Rights, but never discussed there: education in and annual reports on human rights; communications concerning human rights; inquiry and conciliation; local human rights committees; and advisory services to governments.

As a result of action by the General Assembly and the Economic and Social Council, the Secretary-General's proposals concerning human rights were placed on the agenda of the Commission on Human Rights. The commission, because of its work on the draft covenants, deferred the item at its sessions in 1951 and 1952. It began consideration of the item, but in only a very brief and preliminary fashion, at its session in 1953 and in 1954, in connection with the United States proposals for a new action program in the field of human rights.

Yearbook on Human Rights

The compilation of basic material about human rights was one of the first activities in this field to be initiated by the United Nations. The "nuclear" Commission on Human Rights recommended the compilation and publication of a yearbook on law and usage relating to human rights. It further recommended that the first edition of this yearbook should include all declarations and bills on human rights now in force in the various countries. These recommendations were accepted by the Economic and Social Council at its second session in May-June 1946 and the Secretary-General was directed to make the necessary arrangements. The first issue of the *Yearbook on Human Rights* was published in August 1948.

The *Yearbook on Human Rights* represents the first attempt in history to bring together an official record of mankind's struggle to safeguard human liberty. The more recent volumes consist of four parts:

[2] U.N. General Assembly, Fifth Session, *Development of a Twenty-Year Programme for Achieving Peace Through the United Nations*, Doc. A/1304 (July 26, 1950).

Part I contains constitutional and legislative texts on human rights promulgated throughout the world in a given year. Since 1950, at the request of the Commission on Human Rights, the *Yearbook* has included summaries of significant decisions of national courts.

Part II is devoted to laws and other texts dealing with human rights in trust territories and non-self-governing territories. This section was first included, at the request of the Economic and Social Council, in the edition for 1949.

Part III records provisions on human rights in international treaties and agreements and in instruments adopted by specialized agencies, important regional and other multilateral treaties and agreements, and bilateral treaties.

Part IV surveys the activities of the United Nations throughout the whole field of human rights, noting in particular the efforts made to heighten the impact of the Universal Declaration of Human Rights and the progress made in drafting the covenants, and includes judgments and advisory opinions of the International Court of Justice.

Attention has been given on several occasions to improvement of the *Yearbook*. The Commission on Human Rights, at its sixth session in 1950 concluded that, without losing its present form and character as an annual work of reference, the *Yearbook* could be of greater use and could reach a wider public if it devoted less space to the reproduction of original texts and treated in each volume a particular right or group of rights. The Economic and Social Council subsequently adopted the recommendation of the commission and requested the Secretary-General to draw up a plan indicating, for a number of years ahead, which right or group of rights set forth in the Universal Declaration of Human Rights should be treated in each year. The Secretary-General prepared this plan, which proposed two lists—one containing personal and political rights and the other economic, social, and cultural rights that might be given priority over a five-year period. In the four succeeding years, the commission, however, never reached this item on its agenda.

Despite the inability of the commission to review the format of the *Yearbook*, this publication has become a comprehensive reference work. The volumes contain a vast collection of constitutional provisions, laws, regulations, court decisions, and summaries of current developments throughout the world. The 1951 edition, for example, contains contributions from 67 states, including 21 states not Members of the United Nations, and texts or notes relating to 5 trust territories and 20 non-self-governing territories. Some 1,775 copies of the English edition and 775 copies of the French edition were published, for distribution to governments or for sale to libraries and individuals.

The character of the contributions in the *Yearbook* varies considerably. These contributions, in accordance with procedures laid down by the Economic and Social Council, are received by the Secretary-General from governments or from correspondents approved by governments. For example, the United States contribution to the first *Yearbook*, which consisted of a collection of constitutional and legislative provisions, has been supplemented in later volumes by annual summaries of developments in the Federal Government, the states, and the territories administered by the United States. These summaries, initially prepared in the Department of State and reviewed by other interested departments and agencies, constitute an authoritative statement of action in the whole field of human rights. The contribution of the United Kingdom in recent years has consisted of a scholarly essay on the status of one right or group of rights at the present time. The contributions of the Soviet bloc, on the other hand, have comprised merely a collection of constitutional and legislative provisions that offer a superficial appearance of freedom.

The *Yearbook on Human Rights* is a unique reference work compiled at considerable expense of time and money by governments and by the Secretariat, but it has not yet been fully utilized by the United Nations. The Commission on Human Rights did not manage from 1950 to 1954 to discuss the format of these volumes, and both the commission and other organs neglected their substantive content. Now that the commission has completed the drafting of the covenants, it may be able to devise practical ways of making use of the vast wealth of material that has been accumulated in the *Yearbook*.[3]

[3] At its session in April 1955 the commission considered the *Yearbook* for the first time since 1950. The commission decided that, in addition to existing sections, the *Yearbook* for 1955 should include a section on the application and evolution of the right to freedom from arbitrary arrest, detention, or exile, as set forth in Article 9 of the Universal Declaration of Human Rights, and that the *Yearbook* for 1956 should include a section on motherhood and childhood, as set forth in Article 25(2) of the Declaration.

*Proposals for an Action
Program*

At the same time that Secretary Dulles, as recounted earlier in this study,[4] announced that the United States would not sign or ratify the draft covenants on human rights, he addressed a letter to the new United States Representative in the Commission on Human Rights, Mrs. Oswald B. Lord, instructing her to present a new program for action in this field:

. . . the United States Government asks you to present to the Commission on Human Rights at its forthcoming session a statement of American goals and policies in this field; to point out the need for re-examining the approach of the Human Rights Covenants as the method for furthering at this time the objectives of the Universal Declaration of Human Rights; and to put forward other suggestions of method, based on American experience,. for developing throughout the world a human rights conscience which will bring nearer the goals stated in the Charter. In making such suggestions, I am sure you will want to give special weight to the value of bringing the facts to the light of day, to the value of common discussion of problems in the international forum of the Commission on Human Rights, and to the value of each country drawing on the experience of other countries for inspiration and practical guidance in solving its own problems.[5]

At the session of the commission in 1953, Mrs. Lord introduced three proposals for a new action program. This was the first comprehensive program to be presented to the commission since the Secretary-General's twenty-year program of 1950. The United States representative emphasized that her proposals incorporated ideas from the twenty-year program and from many other proposals made by governments and nongovernmental organizations.[6] After extensive consultations during the session with other delegations, the Secretariat, several of the specialized agencies, and many nongovernmental organizations, she submitted three draft resolutions—on periodic reports, studies of specific aspects of human rights, and technical assistance.[7] At the suggestion of the commission, which took time for only a brief and inconclusive debate, the Economic

---

[4] See above, Chap. II.

[5] U. S. Department of State *Bulletin*, Vol. 28 (Apr. 20, 1953), p. 580.

[6] U. N. Commission on Human Rights, Ninth Session, *Summary Records*, 391st Meeting (May 19, 1953). For verbatim text of Mrs. Lord's statement, see U. S. Department of State *Bulletin*, Vol. 28 (June 15, 1953), pp. 842-47; reprinted in U. S. Department of State, *A New Human Rights Action Program*, Publication 5124 (July 1953).

[7] U. N. Commission on Human Rights, Ninth Session, Docs. E/CN.4/L.266, E/CN.4/L.268, and E/CN.4/L.267/Rev. 1 (May 7, 1953).

and Social Council forwarded the three proposals to Member governments and specialized agencies for comment.

The United States Government had hoped that the General Assembly, on the basis of the comments of governments and specialized agencies, would be able to consider, and perhaps to approve, the three proposals at its session in 1953. However, relatively few comments were received by that time—only six from governments, including the United States, and two from specialized agencies. The Third (Social, Humanitarian, and Cultural) Committee of the General Assembly undertook only a brief, general debate; and the Assembly requested the Commission on Human Rights to consider this program at its session in 1954. The commission, however, was again too preoccupied with the draft covenants to give any thorough consideration to these proposals, which the United States delegation had revised in the light of the comments it had received.

The three draft resolutions, in their revised form, may be summarized briefly as follows:

1. Each Member of the United Nations should transmit biennially a report on the results achieved and difficulties encountered in the promotion and development of human rights, for consideration by the commission; Member governments might be assisted in the preparation of their reports by an advisory body of experienced and competent persons; and the commission should consider these annual reports and submit to the Economic and Social Council such comments and conclusions thereon as it might deem appropriate.

2. The commission should initiate studies of specific aspects of human rights on a world-wide basis and at each session should select a specific subject or subjects for study, assisted by an expert adviser appointed by the Secretary-General. The expert adviser should have access to information from Member governments, specialized agencies, and nongovernmental organizations.

3. The United Nations and the specialized agencies should provide technical assistance and advisory services in the whole field of human rights.[8]

The debates in the General Assembly and the Commission on Human Rights, the comments submitted by governments and specialized agencies, and the observations of nongovernmental organizations reveal four major objections to the proposed action program.

[8] U. N. Commission on Human Rights, Tenth Session, Docs. E/CN.4/L.266/Rev.3, E/CN.4/L.268/Rev.1, and E/CN.4/L.267/Rev.2 (Apr. 13, 1954).

First, several representatives questioned the legal basis of the American proposals, and the Soviet representatives have asserted that they violated Article 2(7) of the Charter, concerning the domestic jurisdiction of Members. The United States representatives replied that the proposed action program is based on Articles 55 and 56 of the Charter, concerning the promotion of respect for and observance of human rights and fundamental freedoms. They have also noted that the proposals were consistent with Article 62, relating to the functions and powers of the Economic and Social Council.

Second, certain governments asked how Members of the United Nations could be requested to transmit reports on progress made in the promotion of human rights and how the commission could be expected to appraise that progress, without any criteria being established on what constitutes progress. The United States representatives replied that the goals and criteria were set forth in the Universal Declaration of Human Rights, and that the commission would not pass judgment on the governments submitting the reports but would merely use the reports as sources of information in its debates and studies.

Third, the negative tone of the comments of the United Kingdom Government and of several of the Western European governments suggest their concern that any kind of action program involving reporting, special studies, and debates on the observance of specific rights will lead to unnecessary controversy and to propagandistic attacks against the "good" states by the "bad" states. As the United Kingdom representative stated the problem in the General Assembly:

. . . Those countries in which many fundamental rights were disregarded would either not reply at all or would simply reply that the human rights situation in their country was as nearly perfect as possible. On the other hand, States which had the courage to admit to certain imperfections would lay themselves open to attack from countries whose record was far worse. The Commission on Human Rights was thus likely to become the forum for political recrimination to the detriment of the humanitarian functions which it ought to carry out.[9]

The United States reply was that this disadvantage, which pertains to many other activities in the economic and social fields, is outweighed by the advantage of developing a constructive program of exchange of information and discussion of common problems.

[9] U. N. General Assembly, Eighth Session, Third Committee, *Official Records,* 528th Meeting (Nov. 19, 1953), p. 262.

Fourth, the representatives of the Soviet bloc charged that the United States desired to "jettison" the draft covenants, just as they were nearing completion, in favor of its own proposals. The United States representatives replied that they had not tried to block the work on the covenants, that they had participated in that work, and that this new program was designed to supplement and expand the work of the United Nations in the field of human rights.

It may thus be surmised that a number of governments would have preferred to see the commission continue indefinitely with the technical drafting of the covenants rather than undertake surveys, appraisals, and comparisons of current developments. Other governments, however, have indicated support for the general principles of the United States program, although differing over some of the details.

These criticisms, it should be noted, relate not only to the United States proposals, but also to any similar proposals for new activities to be undertaken by the United Nations in the field of human rights. Now that the Commission on Human Rights has completed the technical drafting of the covenants, it will have to consider, beginning at its session in 1955, the nature and scope of its future activities.[10] The completion of the covenants will thus confront the United Nations with major decisions about its future work in this field. It will provoke a major controversy over interpretation of the Charter and another effort to reconcile the broad goals set forth in Articles 55 and 56 with the restrictions contained in Article 2(7).

Freedom of Information

In one of its early resolutions, adopted unanimously, the General Assembly declared: "Freedom of information is a fundamental human right and is the touchstone of all the freedoms to which the

[10] At its session in 1955 the commission adopted the third of the United States proposals, concerning technical assistance. This resolution was subsequently approved by the Economic and Social Council and the General Assembly, after the Council had modified it to consolidate all the technical assistance programs previously adopted by the Assembly (rights of women, discrimination and minorities, and freedom of information) under the title "Advisory Services in the Field of Human Rights." The commission, in adopting its program of work for future sessions, accepted the first two United States proposals in principle by including consideration of general developments, based in part on reports from Member governments, and studies of specific rights or groups of rights. Both of these activities would be carried on in accordance with further specific resolutions of the commission.

United Nations is consecrated."[11] This unanimous agreement on principle was short-lived, however, and the efforts of the General Assembly, the Economic and Social Council, and a series of *ad hoc* agencies to translate the principle into conventions and codes of ethics have been marked by frustration and failure. The mere existence of this stalemate, however, highlighted the basic issues involved, and the failure to conclude the Draft Convention on Freedom of Information—at least from the point of view of the United States, the United Kingdom, and others—advanced rather than retarded freedom of information. More recently, when the United Nations began to develop practical programs in this field, some of the earlier hopes of promoting freedom of information have begun to be realized.

In an endeavor to give effect to the recognition by the General Assembly of the importance of freedom of information, the "nuclear" Commission on Human Rights at its first meeting recommended the creation of a Subcommission on Freedom of Information and of the Press. The full commission, with the approval of the Economic and Social Council, established the subcommission in 1947, to consist of twelve experts. It was later arranged that the subcommission should report directly to the Council rather than to the commission.

Drafting of Conventions

The resolution of the General Assembly in 1946 authorized the Economic and Social Council to convene a conference to formulate "views concerning the rights, obligations and practices which should be included in the concept of freedom of information." The arrangements for the Conference on Freedom of Information were undertaken by the Council, including a detailed agenda proposed by the Subcommission on Freedom of Information and of the Press. Meeting in Geneva in March-April 1948, where fifty-four Member states and states not Members of the Organization were represented, the conference prepared three draft conventions, recommended articles for inclusion in the Universal Declaration of Human Rights and in the draft covenants, and adopted forty-three substantive and procedural resolutions.[12] This was perhaps the high point in

[11] Res. 59(I), Dec. 14, 1946.
[12] U. N. Conference on Freedom of Information, *Final Act*, Doc. E/Conf. 6/79 (Apr. 22, 1948).

efforts by the United Nations to reach agreement on general principles, but it revealed wide differences of opinion over the detailed application of those principles.[13]

The three draft conventions, accepted by very large majorities, were as follows:

1. The Draft Convention on the Gathering and International Transmission of News, sponsored by the United States, provided for facilitating the freest possible movement of foreign correspondents, protecting them from expulsion for any lawful exercise of their rights, and ensuring equitable treatment of their despatches.

2. The Draft Convention Concerning the Institution of an International Right of Correction, sponsored by France, was designed to afford protection against false or distorted reporting likely to injure relations between nations. It would apply to situations where a contracting state felt that a report sent from one country to another was false or distorted. The complaining government could send its version of the facts to the government of the other contracting state in which the report had been published, and the latter would be obliged to make this version available to its domestic information agencies.

3. The Draft Convention on Freedom of Information, sponsored by the United Kingdom, provided that the contracting states would secure to their nationals and to nationals of other contracting states certain broad rights—such as the right to seek, receive, and impart information and opinions—without governmental interference. The draft convention stated, however, that these rights "carry with them duties and responsibilities and may therefore be subject to necessary penalties, liabilities and restrictions clearly defined by law" on ten different grounds, ranging from "national safety" to "systematic diffusion of deliberately false or distorted reports which undermine friendly relations between peoples or States."[14] It would also forbid contracting states to regulate or control the use of media of in-

[13] "Taking into account the maladjusted world in which the Conference was held, the United States Delegation can point with confidence to the record of constructive achievement of the Conference on Freedom of Information. This was the case both in the positive sense of extending the concept and the practice of freedom and in the negative sense of combating incursions upon freedom." U. S. Department of State, *Report of the United States Delegates to the United Nations Conference on Freedom of Information,* Publication 3150 (1948), p. 11.

[14] U. N. Conference on Freedom of Information, *Final Act,* p. 15.

formation in any manner involving discrimination on political or personal grounds or on the basis of race, sex, language, or religion.

From this point onward, however, the fundamental divergencies of view became increasingly evident. The Economic and Social Council, after revising only the first of the three draft conventions in the summer of 1947, forwarded the recommendations of the conference to the General Assembly. The Assembly, at the second part of its third session in the spring of 1949, amalgamated the first and second conventions and approved this combined text as a Convention on the International Transmission of News and the Right of Correction. The Assembly, however, decided not to open this convention for signature until the third text, the Draft Convention on Freedom of Information, had been completed. The majority of delegations were determined that the rights of foreign correspondents contained in the completed convention should not become effective until the responsibilities contained in the still incomplete draft convention were also made effective.

A serious difference of opinion had arisen over the terms of the Draft Convention on Freedom of Information—ranging from the United States, with its insistence on virtually unrestricted freedom of the press, at the one extreme, and the Soviet Union, with its insistence on full state control and censorship, at the other. In between these two extremes, most other governments favor some form of limitations on freedom of the press. In particular, most of the Near Eastern, Asian, and Latin-American governments resent their dependence on the great news agencies of the United States, the United Kingdom, and France. They and their peoples are sensitive to the frankness, criticism, and at times even ridicule with which American newspapers and magazines occasionally report events in foreign countries. As a result, the original text became increasingly encumbered with qualifications permitting governmental controls. Yielding to these differences, the General Assembly decided at its fourth session in the autumn of 1949 to postpone action, after a long and bitter debate, in order to give the Commission on Human Rights an opportunity to include provisions concerning freedom of information in the draft covenant on human rights.

This decision gave the United States and other opponents of the Draft Convention on Freedom of Information a delay of a year. When the General Assembly, at its session in 1950, returned the draft covenant to the Commission on Human Rights, thus taking no decision on the text of the article dealing with freedom of information that it had prepared, these opponents argued for further postponement. They were defeated, however, by the supporters of the draft convention, who succeeded in establishing a special committee of fifteen members to prepare a new text.

The special committee revised the Draft Convention on Freedom of Information in January-February 1951 and recommended that the Economic and Social Council convene a plenipotentiary conference to open the treaty for signature. This time the opponents of the draft convention scored a series of victories that permanently pigeonholed it. The Council decided in the summer of 1951 not to convene the proposed conference. The General Assembly at its sixth session in 1951-52 did not deal with the matter; and, at its seventh session in the autumn of 1952, the Assembly rejected a sixteen-power proposal to proceed to an immediate detailed consideration of the draft convention. It is symbolical of the close split within the United Nations on the issue of governmental responsibility for information media that the final decision was taken by a tie vote—23 in favor of proceeding with the drafting, 23 against, with 8 abstentions.[15]

Shortly thereafter, the defeated supporters of the draft convention proposed that the Convention on the Transmission of News and the Right of Correction be split into two parts and that the provisions on the right of correction be opened for signature as a separate treaty. A draft resolution to this effect was introduced by Egypt, France, Lebanon, Uruguay, and Yugoslavia and was supported by many Arab, Asian, and Latin-American states. Despite strong opposition from the United States, the United Kingdom, and others, the Assembly approved the convention by 25 to 22, with 10 abstentions.[16]

[15] The vote also showed an unusual division among the major powers: France and the United States voted negatively because the draft convention went too far in the direction of government controls; the Soviet Union, because it did not go far enough; and the United Kingdom abstained. For recent developments, see below, note 23.

[16] U. N. General Assembly, Seventh Session, *Official Records*, 403rd Meeting (Dec. 16, 1952); Res. 630(VII), Dec. 16, 1952. It should be noted that if the convention had been considered an "important question" under Article 18 of the Charter, it would not have received the necessary two-thirds vote of the Assembly. The President did not so rule, however, and the opponents of the convention did not press for a decision on this matter. With the exception of resolutions concerning racial discrimination in South Africa and the Convention on Po-

The Convention on the International Right of Correction was opened for signature on March 31, 1953. It will come into force when six states have deposited instruments of ratification or accession. Thus far, few of the states that pressed most strongly for the convention in the General Assembly have signed or acceded to it.

Drafting of a Code of Ethics

Early in 1949, the Economic and Social Council, in accepting most of the recommendations of the Conference on Freedom of Information, decided that the Subcommission on Freedom of Information and of the Press should be continued for another three years and that its terms of reference should be considerably expanded; but that its existing members should be replaced by twelve new members elected by the Commission on Human Rights.

One of the principal tasks undertaken by the newly elected members of the subcommission was the preparation of an international code of ethics for journalists, which had been recommended by the conference. At its session in May 1950, the subcommission prepared a draft code, consisting of a preamble and four articles. The Economic and Social Council later requested the Secretary-General to transmit the draft code to information enterprises and national and international professional associations for comment. On the basis of comments received from some forty such enterprises and associations, the subcommission revised its text in March 1952, adding a fifth article covering the principle that responsibility rests on those engaged in the profession and not on any government.[17]

---

litical Rights of Women, the latter because an amendment provided for its application to trust and non-self-governing territories, all decisions in the field of human rights have been taken by an ordinary majority vote in the General Assembly.

[17] The general approach of the Draft International Code of Ethics is indicated in the following excerpts:

"The personnel of the Press and of all other media of information should do all in their power to ensure that the information the public receives is factually accurate." (Art. I, first sentence)

"Wilful calumny, slander, libel and unfounded accusations are serious professional offences; so also is plagiarism." (Art. II, third paragraph)

"The reputation of individuals should be respected and information and comment on their private lives likely to harm their reputation should not be published unless it serves the public interest, as distinguished from public curiosity. If charges against reputation or moral character are made, opportunity should be given for reply." (Art. III, third paragraph)

The Economic and Social Council then requested the Secretary-General to transmit the new text to informational enterprises and professional associations and to inform them that, if they thought it desirable, the United Nations might co-operate with them in organizing an international conference for the purpose of completing work on the code.

At the session of the General Assembly in 1952, it became clear that a division of opinion had developed comparable to that regarding the preparation of conventions. The Near Eastern, Asian, and Latin-American delegations favored the completion of a code of ethics under United Nations auspices. The United States, the older members of the British Commonwealth, and the Western European delegations took the position that the completion of such a code was a matter for the information media themselves, free of governmental interference. They were especially insistent that any conference on information media should be broadly representative of all points of view. The resolution adopted by the Assembly reflected this latter attitude: it noted the previous action of the Economic and Social Council but re-phrased it more precisely, requesting the Secretary-General, if a representative group of information enterprises and of national and international professional associations expressed a desire to organize an international professional conference to complete the draft code, to co-operate with the group.

The same division continued at the General Assembly in 1953. The proponents of a code of ethics urged that it be completed. The other group pointed out, however, that of the 500 enterprises and associations consulted by the Secretary-General, only fifty-four had replied. Of these, twenty-eight were favorable, twelve unfavorable, and fourteen uncertain. It was further noted that the group indicating an affirmative attitude was not geographically "repre-

"It is the duty of those who describe and comment upon events relating to a foreign country to acquire the necessary knowledge of such country which will enable them to report and comment accurately and fairly thereon." (Art. IV)

"This Code is based on the principle that the responsibility for ensuring the faithful observance of professional ethics rests upon those who are engaged in the profession, and not upon any government. Nothing herein may therefore be interpreted as implying any justification for intervention by a government in any manner whatsoever to enforce observance of the moral obligations set forth in this Code." (Art. V)

U.N. Subcommission on Freedom of Information and of the Press, *Report of the Fifth Session,* Doc. E/2190 (Mar. 31, 1952), p. 13.

sentative." The Assembly, therefore, merely invited the Secretary-General to address a further communication to the enterprises and associations that had not yet replied.

In August 1954, the Secretary-General reported to the General Assembly that his further consultations had resulted as follows: a total of fifty-one in favor, twenty-five against, and thirty-one uncertain. Some 367 enterprises and associations did not reply at all. The Secretary-General requested the Assembly itself to decide whether it wished him to co-operate in organizing the proposed conference. He pointed out that "wide and preponderantly favourable professional opinion is necessary if the conference is to achieve practical results and that, at present, there is no clear evidence of such preponderantly favourable opinion," and the Assembly later decided "to take no further action at the present time in regard to the organization of such a conference."[18]

Promoting a Freer Flow of Information

Special attention has been given by organs of the United Nations to measures for promoting a freer flow of information. This work began simultaneously with the efforts to draft conventions and a code of ethics, and has been accelerated as those efforts became stalemated.

The Subcommission on Freedom of Information and of the Press, during the course of its five sessions, considered a variety of barriers to the flow of news and possible remedies for removing these barriers. It adopted resolutions, some of which were approved by the Economic and Social Council and the General Assembly, on such matters as the following: jamming of radio broadcasts; restrictions on the gathering, transmission, and dissemination of news by means of newsreels; access of news personnel and their families to meetings of the United Nations and the specialized agencies; discriminatory treatment of foreign information personnel; governmental intervention in the sale and purchase of newsprint; and war-mongering and false and distorted reports.

Criticism of the work of the subcommission developed, however,

[18] U. N. General Assembly, Ninth Session, *Question of Organizing an International Professional Conference to Prepare the Final Text of an International Code of Ethics for the Use of Information Personnel*, Doc. A/2691 (Aug. 16, 1954), p. 11 and Res. 838(IX), Dec. 17, 1954.

in the Economic and Social Council and even among some of the members of the subcommission itself. It was asserted that the subcommission was attempting too many different projects at the same time, that its recommendations were often unrealistic and its work unfruitful, and that it neglected political barriers to freedom of information while concentrating on technical problems. As a result of this dissatisfaction, the Council in the summer of 1950, decided that the subcommission should not meet during 1951. At the session of the General Assembly in 1950, however, the Council was severely criticized by many of the Near Eastern, Asian, and Latin-American Members for this decision, and it was requested by the Assembly to reconsider its decision. After a long delay—involving one negative decision and one postponement—the Council finally decided in September 1951 to continue the subcommission for one more session in order that it might complete the Draft Code of Ethics. The long wrangle over the seemingly minor question of a meeting of a subcommission reflected a major clash of opinion over the value of the work of the subcommission and, to some extent, the value of the work of the United Nations generally in this field.

After the subcommission had submitted its final report in 1952, the Council considered several arrangements for continuing and strengthening its work in this field. It rejected the creation of an expert committee of twelve persons, as suggested by the subcommission, and a commission of inquiry of five persons to be appointed by the Secretary-General, as proposed by France. The Council ultimately adopted a United States proposal for a *rapporteur,* to be appointed in a personal capacity for an experimental period of one year. The *rapporteur* was requested to prepare for the session of the Council in mid-1953:

. . . a substantive report covering major contemporary problems and developments in the field of freedom of information, together with recommendations regarding practical action which might be taken by the Council in order to surmount those obstacles to the fuller enjoyment of freedom of information which can be surmounted at the present time.[19]

Even the choice of the *rapporteur* revealed the sharp division of opinion within the Council, the underdeveloped countries favoring Salvador P. López of the Philippines, and the developed countries favoring Robert Fenaux of Belgium. After two tie-votes, Fenaux withdrew and López was elected by acclamation.

[19] Res. 442 C(XIV), June 13, 1952.

In addition to appointing its *rapporteur,* the Council also approved a resolution calling for the development of information media. This resolution invited the Secretary-General, in conjunction with the United Nations Educational, Scientific, and Cultural Organization (UNESCO), to study "ways and means of encouraging and developing independent domestic information agencies."[20] The General Assembly, later in 1952, expanded this resolution to emphasize the need for information facilities in underdeveloped countries and requested the Secretary-General to elaborate a program of "concrete action" that would include such matters as the reduction of economic and financial obstacles, the exchange and training of information personnel, and measures in connection with the supply of newsprint.[21]

This new approach to the problem of freedom of information did not produce results until a year or more later. The Economic and Social Council, at its seventeenth session in March-April 1954 had before it both the *rapporteur's* report on contemporary problems and developments, which had been completed a year earlier, and the Secretary-General's report on the development of domestic information enterprises.[22] The *rapporteur's* report presented an analysis of national and international activities, the reasons for success and failure in reaching agreement in the United Nations, a statement of current practices and of the barriers to the free flow of news, and a series of recommendations for future action. The Secretary-General's report—prepared in collaboration with UNESCO —contained detailed suggestions for developing independent newspaper, radio, and film enterprises.

The *rapporteur's* report, the first document of its kind in the history of the United Nations, illustrated the advantages and disadvantages of this procedure for dealing with controversial problems. The very frankness of the report, which contained detailed statements about governmental controls and censorship, subjected the *rapporteur* to considerable abuse in the Council. Most delega-

[20] Res. 442 E(XIV), June 13, 1952.

[21] Res. 633(VII), Dec. 16, 1952.

[22] U.N. Economic and Social Council, Sixteenth Session, *Freedom of Information, 1953,* Report submitted by Salvador P. López, *Rapporteur* on Freedom of Information, Doc. E/2426 (May 6, 1953); *Freedom of Information: Supplementary Report,* submitted by *Rapporteur* on Freedom of Information, Doc. E/2426/Add. 1 (Feb. 1, 1954), and Additions 2-5 (Feb. 12, Apr. 9, Apr. 14, and May 24, 1954); U.N. Economic and Social Council, Seventeenth Session, *Freedom of Information: Encouragement and Development of Independent Domestic Information Enterprises,* Report by the Secretary-General, Doc. E/2534 (Jan. 14, 1954).

tions criticized some aspect of the report. Ironically, those delegations, especially the Soviet delegation, that had earlier fought for the election of the incumbent *rapporteur* were the most severe in denouncing his report. Indeed, these critics were so outraged by the report that they rejected his recommendation that the office of *rapporteur* be continued for another year!

The Council proceeded to give consideration to many of the recommendations contained in the *rapporteur's* report. It decisively rejected his recommendation that the General Assembly resume consideration of the Draft Convention on Freedom of Information. It also rejected his proposal to revitalize the Convention Concerning the Use of Broadcasting in the Cause of Peace concluded in 1936. Several of the parties to this treaty—including the United Kingdom—were doubtful about its current usefulness. This convention, which had been negotiated under the auspices of the League of Nations as a result of the misuse of radio broadcasting by Nazi Germany and Fascist Italy for purposes of propaganda, contains provisions for the control and censorship of radio that closely parallel the periodic Soviet proposals for the suppression of "war-mongering."[23]

[23] These two recommendations of the *rapporteur* fared better, however, in the ninth session (1954) of the General Assembly. On the initiative of Afghanistan, Costa Rica, Egypt, India, Indonesia, the Philippines, Saudi Arabia, and Yugoslavia, the Assembly adopted a resolution requesting the Economic and Social Council, at its nineteenth session (spring 1955), to discuss the Draft Convention on Freedom of Information and to formulate recommendations for the consideration of the General Assembly not later than at its eleventh session. The vote was 37 to 11, with 7 abstentions. The Council concluded, however, that "further action at this stage . . . would be unprofitable." (Res. 574 C(XIX), May 26, 1955.) On the initiative of the Soviet Union, the Assembly adopted a resolution requesting the states parties to the Convention Concerning the Use of Broadcasting in the Cause of Peace to state whether they wish to transfer to the United Nations the functions performed by the League of Nations and instructing the Secretary-General to prepare a draft protocol for this purpose. The Soviet draft resolution was amended by the Netherlands, Turkey, and the United Kingdom, however, so that the draft protocol would include new articles, based on an earlier resolution of the Assembly, to provide that each high contracting party "shall refrain from radio broadcasts that would mean unfair attacks or slanders against other peoples anywhere" and "shall not interfere with the reception, within its territory, of foreign radio broadcasts." Because of the addition of the latter clause about radio-jamming, the Soviet delegation felt obliged to abstain in the final vote on its own resolution, which was adopted by 38 to 0, with 17 abstentions.

The Council adopted, however, a series of resolutions, based on the *rapporteur's* report, on the following subjects: a concrete program of action to promote a wider knowledge of the work of the United Nations, of foreign countries, and of international affairs; a world-wide survey of censorship; a study of the legal aspects of the rights and responsibilities of information media; a study of the problem of protecting sources of information of news personnel; a study of public and private information monopolies; the transmission of news by telecommunications services; the status and movement of foreign correspondents; the relation of copyright to news and information media; the independence of information personnel; professional training for news personnel; press rates and priorities; better use of radio frequencies; the UNESCO Agreement on the Importation of Educational, Scientific, and Cultural Materials; technical assistance to promote freedom of information; and production and distribution of newsprint. The Council asked the Secretary-General, the United Nations Technical Assistance Administration, and several of the specialized agencies—especially UNESCO—to assume responsibility, as appropriate, for carrying out these programs.

The Secretary-General's recommendations were also put substantially into effect by the Council. The resolution of the Council invited governments of underdeveloped countries to study the possibility of developing independent information media; and it suggested that they consult with national, regional, or international professional associations, and drew their attention to the possibility of seeking technical assistance from the United Nations and the specialized agencies. It also recommended that UNESCO intensify its activities and encourage the development of independent enterprises in underdeveloped countries through research and technical assistance. In fact, the United Nations, which has had to deal with the political aspects of freedom of information, has tended increasingly to rely on UNESCO to deal with the technical problems.

This series of resolutions was adopted either unanimously or by overwhelming majorities—the first indication of any agreement on measures to promote freedom of information since the early years of the United Nations and certainly since the Geneva conference of 1948. The adoption of these resolutions, relating largely to programs for study and action, did not represent, however, any real agreement on the basic issue of what constitutes freedom of information. The underlying differences of opinion on the extent of governmental responsibility for the activities of information media remained unresolved.

Prevention of Discrimination

On few aspects of human rights do delegations in United Nations meetings feel more deeply than on racial discrimination. Race, the first of the four grounds of discrimination enumerated throughout the Charter, has become for many the crucial issue. This preoccupation with racial discrimination underlies much of the emotionalism in the debates on human rights, self-determination, the trusteeship system, and non-self-governing territories. It is in large part responsible for the debates on Indians in South Africa, on race relations in South Africa, and on Tunisia and Morocco, and for the importance that the whole "colonial" issue has attained in the United Nations. It has contributed to the "neutralism" of the Near Eastern and Asian delegations toward the conflict between democracy and communism, and has been used to advantage by spokesmen of the Soviet bloc for attacking the United States. It has caused the Subcommission on Prevention of Discrimination and Protection of Minorities to become an almost sacrosanct organ in the eyes of the underdeveloped countries.

Work of the Subcommission

The "nuclear" Commission on Human Rights, meeting in April-May 1946, agreed that the Secretariat should be asked to collect documentation on the prevention of discrimination and on the protection of minorities as a preliminary step to the consideration of establishing subcommissions on these subjects. One month later, the Economic and Social Council authorized the commission to establish two separate subcommissions. However, the full commission decided at its first session in January-February 1947, to create a single Subcommission on Prevention of Discrimination and Protection of Minorities, in view of the close relationship of the two subjects. The work of the subcommission fell into two parts: the first three sessions (1947, 1949, and 1950), followed by a prolonged controversy during which the subcommission was temporarily discontinued; and three later sessions (1951, 1952, and 1954), in which the subcommission reorganized and expanded its program of work.

During its first three sessions—in addition to its work on minorities, which will be described later—the subcommission initiated some rather limited and unco-ordinated work on the prevention of discrimination. It began with a definition of this term, which was approved by the Commission on Human Rights: "The Prevention of Discrimination is the prevention of any action which denies to individuals or groups of peoples equality of treatment which they may wish."[24] The principal accomplishment of the subcommission in this field was the adoption of a resolution on the prevention of discrimination in educational institutions. This resolution, as later approved by the commission and the Council, urged all Member states to take steps to eliminate all forms of discrimination in the schools. The resolution further invited UNESCO to give emphasis to practical activities that are likely to lead to the eradication of prejudice and discrimination, and recommended that it prepare and disseminate simple books and pamphlets explaining the fallacies of mistaken race theories and of religious and other prejudices.

By the summer of 1950, when the Economic and Social Council held its eleventh session, considerable dissatisfaction had developed over the work of the subcommission. Members of the Council, of the Commission on Human Rights, and even of the subcommission itself felt that the subcommission had not achieved positive results and that perhaps a new approach to the problem of discrimination and minorities was required. In particular, a division of opinion had arisen whether the subcommission should be concerned primarily with legislation and enforcement action, as emphasized by the Near Eastern, Asian, and Latin-American spokesmen, or with information and study programs, as preferred by the United States, the United Kingdom, and Western European representatives. The Council decided, therefore, that the subcommission should not meet in 1951.

This decision—like the related one concerning the Subcommission on Freedom of Information and of the Press, discussed earlier—provoked an angry controversy in the General Assembly in 1950. Many of the Near Eastern, Asian, and Latin American delegations charged the Council with lack of interest in this field. They made

[24] U. N. Commission on Human Rights, *Report of the Second Session*, Doc. E/600 (Dec. 17, 1947), p. 11.

clear they felt that the Council was dominated by the great powers and not representative of the organization as a whole. By an overwhelming vote, the Assembly requested the Council to reconsider its decision. The Council did so immediately thereafter, and a fourth session of the subcommission was ultimately scheduled for October 1951.

This did not end the controversy, however, for the Council in the summer of 1951 decided to discontinue the subcommission, its work to be taken over by the Council, the Commission on Human Rights, the Secretariat, or *ad hoc* agencies as appropriate. It requested the Secretary-General, after consultation with Member governments and the specialized agencies, particularly UNESCO, to report on future activities concerning discrimination and minorities. This decision set off another dispute in the General Assembly, this time at its session in 1951-52, with similar results. The Assembly, by another overwhelming vote, again reversed the Council by inviting it to continue the subcommission and to convene a session in 1952. The Council did so at its session in 1952.

Expansion of the Work
Program

More progress was made by the subcommission in its next three meetings. The reports of its sessions in 1951 and 1952 were not reviewed by the Commission on Human Rights, because of its work on the draft covenants, until 1953; but the report of its session in 1954 was reviewed promptly that year by the commission. In these three sessions, the subcommission produced a dozen or more resolutions dealing wholly or partly with the prevention of discrimination. These resolutions, which were considered by the commission and in certain instances by the Economic and Social Council, dealt with such matters as the following: a request that the Secretary-General collect documents containing provisions against discrimination to serve as precedents when constitutional or statutory provisions are to be elaborated; a recommendation that Members of the United Nations review their national legislation and administrative practices with a view to abolishing all measures of discrimination; arrangement for increased co-ordination of activities of international nongovernmental organizations in combating discrimination; and recommended action to eliminate discrimination against persons born out of wedlock.

During the period 1951-54, the subcommission also initiated a comprehensive program for the detailed study of specific areas of discrimination. At its session in 1952, the subcommission listed the following fields for future study: education (to be undertaken immediately with the aid of a *rapporteur*); employment and occupation; political rights; religious rights and practices; residence and movement, immigration and travel; the right to choose a spouse; enjoyment of family rights; and the cessation of any advocacy of national, racial, or religious hostility that constitutes an incitement to hatred and violence. The commission and the Council approved this program, but the latter stated that future studies that fall within the scope of specialized agencies or other bodies should normally be carried out by them.

This study program was reduced to more manageable proportions at the session of the subcommission in 1954. The study on education was outlined as a pilot project, to be undertaken in co-operation with UNESCO. It was assigned to a member of the subcommission—initially to M. R. Masani (India) and, later, to Charles D. Ammoun (Lebanon). The study on employment and occupation was referred, with the consent of the Economic and Social Council, to the International Labour Organisation. The subcommission then asked three of its members to prepare proposals for three other studies, one of which would be undertaken in 1955: political rights; religious rights; and emigration, immigration, and travel. In the Commission on Human Rights a few months later, the United States delegation sought to relate these three studies more closely to the corresponding articles of the Universal Declaration of Human Rights and, in particular, to replace "immigration, and travel" by "and the right to return to one's country as provided in paragraph 2 of Article 13 of the Universal Declaration of Human Rights."[25] Confronted by considerable opposition, the United States delegation submitted a new proposal merely calling the attention of the subcommission to the debate in the commission. The Economic and Social Council, however, later requested the subcommission to restrict the third study to the language of the Universal Declaration.[26]

[25] U.N. Commission on Human Rights, *Report of the Tenth Session*, Doc. E/2573 (April 1954), p. 58.
[26] This directive did not satisfy the subcommission, which, at its seventh session (January 1955), requested the Commission on Human Rights to invite the Council to decide that the subcommission is not precluded from undertaking a study of the question of discrimination in immigration. The commission approved this request by a vote of 10 to 5, with 2 abstentions. The Council rejected it, however, and revised the third study to read: "The right of everyone to leave any coun-

The use of a *rapporteur* or expert advisers for carrying on this type of study raises questions that have implications in the procedural realm for the whole field of human rights and freedom of information. Proponents of this device maintain that a *rapporteur,* with the assistance of the Secretariat, can usefully present embarrassing facts, frank comments, and critical conclusions that the Secretariat could not properly put forward. Opponents contend that the preparation of studies is a proper function of the Secretariat and that the use of *rapporteurs* may lead to irresponsible reports that will create unnecessary controversy.

The subcommission recommended at its session in 1952 that technical assistance services be extended to aid Members of the United Nations to eradicate prejudice or discrimination and to protect minorities. This proposal was approved, in turn, by the commission, the Economic and Social Council, and the General Assembly. It gave rise to searching debate in each of these organs, some Members arguing that no such resolution was necessary, that it might involve an undue burden on the budget, and that it might result in interference with the domestic jurisdiction of the states concerned. Others replied that the Secretary-General did require authority from the Assembly to grant this type of technical assistance, that little cost would be involved in the initial and experimental stage, and that the use of such technical assistance was a purely voluntary matter. Although the proposal of the subcommission was approved in October 1953, no states have yet requested technical assistance in the field of discrimination.

Protection of Minorities

The prevention of discrimination and the protection of minorities are two sides of the same coin—the safeguarding of the rights and

---

try, including his own, and to return to his country, as provided in article 13, paragraph 2, of the Universal Declaration of Human Rights." (Res. 586 C(XX), July 29, 1955.) The subcommission debated whether the first study of discrimination to be undertaken in 1955 should be in the field of political rights or of religious rights. It took no decision, however, after it was informed by the Secretary-General that, owing to budgetary limitations, no staff assistance could be provided until the first study, on discrimination in education, was completed. On the recommendation of the subcommission, revised and approved by the Commission on Human Rights, the Council authorized the subcommission to undertake one further study in the field of discrimination in 1956 and another, if possible, in 1957.

freedoms of individuals and groups. The first relates to persons who wish to become completely identified with the society in which they dwell and to enjoy equal rights and privileges, free of any discrimination on grounds of race, sex, language, or religion. The second relates to groups of persons who wish to remain distinct from others in their society and who wish special protection for their group. The prevention of discrimination thus requires "negative" action to prevent the denial of rights to individuals; the protection of minorities requires "positive" action to grant special privileges to groups that desire to preserve their own language, religion, and culture.

The Subcommission on Prevention of Discrimination and Protection of Minorities devoted much time to formulating a definition of the term "minority" and to preparing interim measures for the protection of minorities. The initial and relatively brief text drafted at the first session of the subcommission was submitted to the Commission on Human Rights, which did not have time to consider this text at its session in 1948. A recommendation concerning facilities that should be provided for the protection of minorities was forwarded to the commission in 1949. The commission in 1950 declined to forward either of these texts to the Economic and Social Council and returned them to the subcommission for further study. In 1951 the subcommission tried once again to submit revised texts for approval, but the commission, which did not consider the report of the subcommission until 1953, again returned them to the subcommission for further study.

The definition proposed by the subcommission, which was never approved by the commission, consisted of four parts: first, a general description of minorities that require special protection; second, a recognition that protection is not required when a group, though numerically inferior, is the dominant one in a population or when a group seeks complete identity of treatment with the rest of the population; third, a series of five "complex situations" that must be taken into account in any definition; and fourth, the definition itself. The text of the definition is as follows:

(i) the term minority includes only those non-dominant groups in a population which possess and wish to preserve stable ethnic, religious or linguistic traditions or characteristics markedly different from those of the rest of the population;

(ii) such minorities should properly include a number of persons sufficient by themselves to preserve such traditions or characteristics; and

(iii) such minorities must be loyal to the State of which they are nationals.[27]

With respect to interim measures for the protection of minorities the subcommission:

Recommends that, in the interest of enabling recognized minority groups to maintain their cultural heritage when they desire to do so, Member Governments should provide, as a minimum, adequate facilities, in districts, regions and territories where they represent a considerable proportion of the population, for:

(1) The use in judicial procedure of languages of such groups, in those cases where the member of the minority group does not speak or understand the language ordinarily used in the courts;

(2) The teaching in State-supported schools of languages of such groups, with due regard to the requirements of educational efficiency, provided that such groups request it and that the request in reality expresses the spontaneous desire of such groups.[28]

The debates in the Commission on Human Rights reveal a general disagreement over the basic elements in both the definition and the proposed interim measures. Almost every representative, viewing the definition in terms of his country or of experience with the minorities treaties under the League of Nations, found some serious flaw in it. Some considered the definition to be too broad; others, too narrow. Some questioned whether a minority should be granted a special status and special protection; and others asserted that too wide a degree of protection might create divisive elements that would destroy a state. Spokesmen for Latin America, mindful of their experience with Germans, Italians, and Japanese in the First and Second World Wars, were particularly concerned that immigrant groups settled in a new country not be regarded as a minority with special political rights.

In 1954, the subcommission, discouraged by the refusal of the commission to approve its proposals, tried a new approach—a study of "the present position as regards minorities throughout the world." Declaring that no further work on the problem of definition could serve any useful purpose, the subcommission nevertheless included, as "considerations" to be borne in mind, parts of its definition. It decided that "the study should be selective in character and should aim at presenting a concise account of the position of every minority in need of special protection measures, including consideration of

[27] U.N. Subcommission on Prevention of Discrimination and Protection of Minorities, *Report of the Fourth Session,* Doc. E/CN.4/641 (Oct. 25, 1951), p. 43.
[28] *Ibid.,* p. 45.

the present measures in force." The subcommission recommended the appointment of an expert to carry out this study.[29]

This substitute proposal aroused widespread opposition in the Commission on Human Rights. Some members objected to the tentative and incomplete definition that had been incorporated into the proposal. Others pointed to the political hazards in a selective study of specific minorities, especially in the absence of an agreed definition. Still others questioned the use of an expert who would belong to neither the subcommission nor the Secretariat. As a result, the commission rejected the proposal and requested the subcommission to give further study to the whole question, including the definition of the term "minority."

The effort of the United Nations to provide measures for the protection of minorities would thus appear to be a record of failure to find any basis for agreement. A few positive achievements, however, are to be found in the inconclusive work of the subcommission. At the request of the subcommission, the Secretariat prepared a comprehensive study of the legal validity of undertakings, including treaties supervised by the League of Nations, concerning minorities.[30] The subcommission also prepared a recommendation, endorsed by the commission and the Council, that special consideration be given to problems of minorities in the preparation of any international treaties, decisions of international organs, or other acts that establish new states or new boundary lines. Finally, as indicated earlier, the Secretariat was authorized by the General Assembly, on the initiative of the subcommission, to include the protection of minorities as one of the fields in which technical assistance may be rendered to Member states. Thus far, however, no requests have been received for technical assistance in this field.

Prevention and Punishment of Genocide

Throughout history there have been instances of massacres of whole groups of peoples—such as the destruction of Carthage by the Romans, the pogroms in Europe during the Middle Ages against the

---

[29] U.N. Subcommission on Prevention of Discrimination and Protection of Minorities, *Report of the Sixth Session*, Doc. E/CN.4/703 (Feb. 5, 1954), pp. 71-74.

[30] U.N. Commission on Human Rights, Seventh Session, *Study of the Legal Validity of the Undertakings Concerning Minorities*, Docs. E/CN.4/367 (Apr. 7, 1950); E/CN.4/367/Corr. 1 (Feb. 12, 1951); and E/CN.4/367/Add. 1 (Mar. 21, 1951).

Jews, the massacres of the Armenians under the Ottoman Empire, and the destruction of the Herreros in Africa by the German Empire. None of these atrocities, however, was executed on such a scale and with such dreadful efficiency as the mass slaughter of Jews and Poles by Adolf Hitler, whose determination to eliminate these populations from Europe sent millions of men, women, and children to death. Governments and peoples everywhere were shocked by the atrocities; and the word "genocide"—half Greek and half Latin—was invented to describe the kind of mass murder that had been perfected in the twentieth century.

The General Assembly
Resolution

The first action taken by the United Nations to deal with the kind of outrages that had been perpetrated by Hitler was the resolution of the General Assembly of December 11, 1946. The resolution—adopted on the initiative of Cuba, India, and Panama—began with this dramatic declaration:

Genocide is a denial of the right of existence of entire human groups, as homicide is the denial of the right to live of individual human beings; such denial of the right of existence shocks the conscience of mankind, results in great losses to humanity in the form of cultural and other contributions represented by these human groups, and is contrary to moral law and to the spirit and aims of the United Nations.[31]

The resolution went on to say that many instances of crimes of genocide have occurred and that the punishment of genocide is a matter of international concern. After affirming genocide "to be a crime under international law which the civilized world condemns," the Assembly invited Member states to enact legislation toward its prevention and punishment. It also requested the Economic and Social Council "to undertake the necessary studies" with a view to drawing up a draft convention on the crime of genocide.

Proponents of a convention felt strongly that the Nuremberg trials, which related only to "war crimes," had shown the necessity for defining as "a crime against humanity" an act of genocide that might occur not only during war but also during time of peace. This crime would be added to such previously established international crimes as the slave trade and piracy. However, other Members of

[31] Res. 96(I), Dec. 11, 1946.

the United Nations, particularly the United Kingdom, expressed doubt whether a convention was the best method to deal with this problem. Nevertheless, the resolution was adopted unanimously after a relatively brief debate in the Sixth (Legal) Committee of the Assembly and with no debate by the Assembly in its plenary.

The Genocide Convention

The drafting of the Genocide Convention, which was to deal with a single issue, required far less time than the Universal Declaration of Human Rights or the still incompleted covenants.[32] Under the direction of the Economic and Social Council, the Secretariat in 1947 prepared a first draft in consultation with three experts—Donnedieu de Vabres, Professor of the Paris Faculty of Law; Professor Raphael Lemkin, Professor of Family Law, Tachkmori College, Warsaw (1927-37); and Professor Vespasian V. Pella, President of the International Association for Penal Law.[33] Although neither the Commission on Human Rights nor the International Law Commission had time to review this draft, and although a majority of Member governments had not yet submitted observations on it, the General Assembly in November 1947 requested the Council to proceed as rapidly as possible with consideration of the subject. In the spring of 1948, the Council appointed an *ad hoc* committee of seven of its members to prepare a text of a draft convention on the basis of comments on the text prepared by the Secretariat that were received from Member governments and of the debates in the General Assembly and the Council. The text prepared by the *ad hoc* committee, under the chairmanship of the United States representative, was transmitted by the Council, without change, to the General Assembly.

The Convention on the Prevention and Punishment of the Crime of Genocide was adopted by the General Assembly, by a vote of 55 to 0, on December 9, 1948—one day before the proclamation by the Assembly of the Universal Declaration of Human Rights. The

[32] For a summary of the negotiations and analysis of the text, see Nehemiah Robinson, *The Genocide Convention: Its Origins and Interpretation* (1949).

[33] Professor Lemkin, whose family was destroyed in the Nazi massacres, has played a very active part during the past decade in stimulating interest in the subject of genocide among delegations at the United Nations and nongovernmental organizations. See Raphael Lemkin, "Genocide as a Crime under International Law," *American Journal of International Law*, Vol. 41 (1947), pp. 145-51.

juxtaposition of these two dates is significant, for it represents the high-water mark in the efforts of the United Nations to define human rights, both in general and in a single field. Both the Universal Declaration and the Genocide Convention were adopted without dissent—the former with eight abstentions and the latter with none. It is of interest to note, however, that in recent years the situation has become reversed, with most Members paying homage to the Universal Declaration and a number of Members, including the United States and the United Kingdom, withholding ratifications of the Genocide Convention.

The convention, after confirming that genocide is a crime under international law, sets forth the following definition:

In the present Convention, genocide means any of the following acts committed with intent to destroy, in whole or in part, a national, ethnical, racial or religious group, as such:
(a) Killing members of the group;
(b) Causing serious bodily or mental harm to members of the group;
(c) Deliberately inflicting on the group conditions of life calculated to bring about its physical destruction in whole or in part;
(d) Imposing measures intended to prevent births within the group;
(e) Forcibly transferring children of the group to another group.[34]

The convention defines certain acts as punishable: genocide, conspiracy to commit genocide, direct and public incitements to commit genocide, attempt to commit genocide, and complicity in genocide. It states that persons committing these acts "shall be punished, whether they are constitutionally responsible rulers, public officials or private individuals." The contracting parties undertake to provide effective penalties for persons guilty of these acts. They agree that persons charged with these acts "shall be tried by a competent tribunal of the State in the territory of which the act was committed, or by such international penal tribunal as may have jurisdiction with respect to those contracting parties which shall have accepted its jurisdiction."

The convention is open to signature and ratification or to adherence by Members of the United Nations or by any state not a Member of the Organization to which an invitation had been addressed by the General Assembly. In 1949, the Assembly extended invitations to those states not Members that had become active members of one or more specialized agencies or parties to the Statute of the Inter-

[34] Res. 260 A(III), Dec. 9, 1948.

national Court of Justice. Since that time, twenty-four of these states have been extended invitations. The convention came into force on January 12, 1951, after twenty instruments of ratification or adherence had been deposited.

During the long and often heated debates in 1948, the Assembly overwhelmingly rejected a number of Soviet proposals to extend the scope of the convention—to include a reference to "racial and national hatreds," to provide that contracting states should disband or prohibit in the future organizations whose aims are to incite racial, religious, or national hatred; to include "cultural genocide," such as destruction of schools and libraries and prohibitions on books and languages; and to include a "colonial clause" that would extend the application of the convention to all non-self-governing and trust territories administered by a contracting state. Several other issues considered at that time have become, however, objects of controversy.

Many critics have expressed regret that the definition of genocide does not include political groups. This question was discussed at great length in the Assembly. The Sixth (Legal) Committee first decided to retain this concept, which was contained in the draft convention prepared by the *ad hoc* committee. Later, when it became obvious that inclusion of the phrase might weaken support for the convention, the committee reconsidered the matter and deleted the phrase.

Considerable criticism has arisen over the inclusion of "causing . . . mental harm" as one of the acts constituting genocide. It has been frequently contended that it is impossible to define or limit this kind of action precisely enough for a treaty. The phrase was proposed by the Chinese delegation in the Assembly, because of the notorious efforts of the Japanese military authorities to increase the use of narcotic drugs in order to weaken the Chinese people. The "harm" must be of a serious nature and an act "committed with intent to destroy, in whole or part" a particular group as envisaged in the convention.

Much doubt and confusion has been created by the provision that persons may be tried by an international tribunal. The Soviet Union, in particular, strongly opposed this provision on the ground that it was contrary to Article 2(7) of the Charter; but the Soviet Union was defeated in both the committee and the plenary of the Assembly. It was the intent of the Assembly, however, that the convention itself would not establish such a tribunal or confer jurisdiction on it, but would merely enable contracting parties, through a supplementary instrument, to make such arrangements if they wished to do so. In fact, the Assembly, in the same resolution in which it approved the convention, invited the International Law Commission to study the desirability and possibility of establishing an international judicial organ for this purpose.

The fact that four states, Byelorussia, Czechoslovakia, the Ukraine, and the Soviet Union, signed the convention with reservations and that five others, Bulgaria, Hungary, the Philippines, Poland, and Rumania, later ratified or acceded with reservations raised the question whether such a state could be regarded as a party to the convention if its reservation were objected to by one or more parties but not by others. The General Assembly in 1950 referred this and related questions to the International Court of Justice for an advisory opinion. The Court replied, in an advisory opinion on May 28, 1951, that a state that made and maintained a reservation in these circumstances could be regarded as being a party if the purpose of the reservation were compatible with the purpose of the convention; but otherwise the states could not be regarded as being a party.[35]

In addition to its request for an opinion by the International Court of Justice regarding reservations to the Genocide Convention, the General Assembly in 1950 also requested the International Law Commission to give priority to a thorough study of the whole problem of reservations to multilateral conventions. At its session in 1951, the General Assembly considered both the advisory opinion of the International Court and the recommendations of the International Law Commission. The Assembly recommended that in the course of preparing multilateral conventions, drafters should "consider the insertion therein of provisions relating to the advisability or non-advisability of reservations and to the effect to be attributed to them." It further recommended, in regard to the Genocide Convention, that all states be guided by the advisory opinions of the International Court, and requested the Secretary-General, as depository, to conform his practice to that opinion. The Assembly also provided that, as depository of future conventions, the Secretary-General should not pass on the legal effect of reservations or objec-

---

[35] International Court of Justice, "Reservations to the Convention on Genocide," Advisory Opinion, May 28, 1951, *I.C.J. Reports, 1951*, p. 15.

tions thereto but should merely communicate these to the states concerned.[36]

Neither the resolution of the Assembly in 1946 nor the Genocide Convention has resulted in any definitive action in the United Nations. The only official charge of genocide brought by one Member against another was in connection with the Kashmir case in early 1948. Pakistan brought before the Security Council the charge that India was committing genocide against the Moslem populations; and this charge became one of the matters to be investigated by the good offices commission appointed by the Council. Pakistan also brought this charge before the president of the Economic and Social Council, but no action was taken on the matter. Allegations of genocide against one or another Member of the United Nations have been contained in communications from individuals and nongovernmental organizations, but these have never been considered by an organ of the United Nations.

A principal reason that charges of genocide have not been included in the periodic "cold war" debates in United Nations bodies has probably been the fact that, until only recently, none of the three great powers has been a party to the convention. The United Kingdom continued to remain skeptical about the need for a convention on this subject. The Soviet Union apparently remained dissatisfied with the convention until May 1954, when it suddenly deposited its ratification. One year before, the United States had also reversed its policy, but in the opposite direction.

The United States signed the convention on December 11, 1948; and the President transmitted it to the Senate six months later with a strong recommendation for its approval. However, the Genocide Convention, like the draft covenants on human rights, became a principal target of those who opposed the use of treaties in the field of human rights and who feared their effect on the jurisdiction of the states. It was the subject of numerous speeches and newspaper editorials throughout the country, some of which erroneously interpreted the provision of the convention concerning the possible jurisdiction of an international tribunal and charged that, if the United States ratified the convention, United States citizens could be tried in international courts on charges of committing the crime of genocide.

[36] Res. 598(VI), Jan. 12, 1951.

Under the chairmanship of the late Senator Brien McMahon (Connecticut), a subcommittee of the Senate Committee on Foreign Relations held hearings and recommended approval of the convention, subject to four reservations concerning the text and one stating that ratification would be an exercise of Federal authority to define and punish offenses against the law of nations and that the traditional jurisdiction of the several states with regard to crime was in no way abridged. The Committee on Foreign Relations took no action, however, on the report of its subcommittee. In April 1953, Secretary of States Dulles, in reply to a question during hearings on the Bricker Amendment, made the following statement:

I have some doubt as to whether in the [sic] view of the events that have intervened the Genocide Treaty is going to accomplish the purposes which were in the minds of those who drafted it. The Soviet Union and its satellites have either refused to ratify or ratified it with serious reservations. I believe that the solution of the problem which must be envisaged by that treaty could better be reconsidered at a later date. I would not press at the moment for its ratification.[37]

It is perhaps too early to appraise the merits of the resolution by the General Assembly in 1946 and the Genocide Convention. Together and for the first time in history, they make this kind of mass murder a crime under international law; and they make it more difficult for a future Hitler to attempt the destruction of large groups of people without the moral condemnation of all nations. Two questions, however, deserve consideration. Does a convention, especially one containing ambiguous or controversial clauses, detract from the moral authority of a resolution of the General Assembly? Does such a convention accomplish its purpose if it is not ratified by all of the great powers? It is not easy to answer these questions, but they are relevant to the whole effort of the United Nations to promote observance of human rights through the conclusion of treaties.

Equal Rights for Women

At the beginning of the Second World War, women still lacked the right to vote in one third of the countries of the world.[38] Equal

[37] *Treaties and Executive Agreements*, Hearings before a Subcommittee of the Senate Committee on the Judiciary, 83 Cong. 1 sess., p. 886.

[38] For the background of current United Nations action in this field, see U. S. Department of Labor, Women's Bureau, *International Documents on the Status of Women*, Publication 217 (1947); and U. N. Secretariat, Department of

suffrage existed generally in North America and Europe (except Switzerland); but in many countries in Latin America, the Near East, and Asia, women had only limited voting rights or none at all. The changes brought by the war greatly increased the area in which women could exercise suffrage, but at the time of the San Francisco Conference, there were still more than twenty countries in which women had no political rights and others in which women had not yet had an opportunity to use the franchise granted to them.

The San Francisco Conference took due account of this aspect of human rights. The Preamble of the Charter reaffirmed faith "in the equal rights of men and women." The phrase "without discrimination as to race, sex, language, or religion" was included in four different articles, largely at the insistence of those primarily concerned with the discrimination against women. Furthermore, Article 8 specified that the United Nations "shall place no restrictions on the eligibility of men and women to participate in any capacity and under conditions of equality in its principal organs."

The Conference committee on social and humanitarian questions discussed, moreover, a "declaration" on this subject, sponsored by the Brazilian delegation and supported by thirty-three others. This declaration recommended that the Economic and Social Council "set up a special commission of women to study conditions and prepare reports on the political, civil and economic status and opportunity of women with special reference to discrimination and limitations placed upon them on account of their sex."[39] The United States delegation and several others questioned the wisdom of a separate commission, suggesting that the work might better be conducted by the Commission on Human Rights or by a committee of the Council. The Conference took no decision, however, on this or other declarations of delegations.[40]

Work of the Commission on the Status of Women

The Economic and Social Council, at its first session in February

---

Social Affairs, *The Road to Equality: Political Rights of Women,* Doc. ST/SOA/ 13 (Dec. 17, 1952).

[39] U. N. Information Organizations and U. S. Library of Congress, *Documents of the United Nations Conference on International Organization,* Vol. 10 (1945), p. 189. For debate on the declaration, see pp. 212-14, 226; for report of the committee, see *ibid.,* Vol. 9, pp. 88-89.

[40] For a more detailed account see the volume in this Brookings series, *A History of the United Nations Charter.*

1946, established a Subcommission on the Status of Women, to be composed of nine members and to report to the Commission on Human Rights. When the report of this subcommission was presented to the Council at its second session in June 1946, the president of the subcommission (Mrs. Bodil Begtrup of Denmark) recommended that it be raised to the level of a full commission. A proposal to this effect, introduced by the United States representative, was adopted by the Council. The terms of reference of the commission on the Status of Women, as revised by the Council in 1947, provided that the commission shall "prepare recommendations and reports to the Economic and Social Council on promoting women's rights in political, economic, civil, social and educational fields" and "make recommendations to the Council on urgent problems requiring immediate attention in the field of women's rights with the object of implementing the principle that men and women shall have equal rights."[41]

The membership of the commission, which was originally fifteen, was increased to eighteen by the Council in 1951; and from the outset all of the representatives have been women. It would appear that membership in the commission is itself a stimulus toward equal rights for women: of the countries that have become members without women suffrage, only one has failed to grant women at least partial voting rights before its term of office expired.[42]

The commission has met annually, usually for a period of two weeks. In 1951, when the Council was reorganizing its structure, it decided that only the Narcotics Commission and the Commission on Human Rights should continue to meet annually and that the other functional commissions, including the Commission on the Status of Women, should meet biennially. At the following session of the General Assembly, this decision was strongly opposed by a number of the women delegates and women's organizations, on the ground that it would injure the work of the commission. The Assembly, despite the opposition of the United States and United Kingdom, which continued to favor biennial sessions in the interest of efficiency, voted by an overwhelming majority to request the Council to reconsider its decision. The Council did so at its next session and provided that the commission would continue to meet on an annual basis.

[41] Res. 48(IV), Mar. 29, 1947.
[42] Lorena B. Hahn, "The U. N.'s Role in Improving the Status of Women," U. S. Department of State *Bulletin,* Vol. 31 (July 5, 1954), p. 24.

In no organ of the United Nations do the nongovernmental organizations play a more active and influential role than in the Commission on the Status of Women. At each session, representatives of fifteen or twenty of these organizations attend the meetings, consult informally with the representatives, and—in many instances—formally present their views to the commission. As the commission regards exchange of information, development of public opinion, and education among its most potent weapons, it relies heavily on the cooperation of the private national and international organizations. Many of the representatives of these organizations have had long experience in promoting women's rights and are in close touch with women's organizations throughout the world. They have contributed significantly to the work of the United Nations in this field.

In the course of its nine sessions, the Commission on the Status of Women has considered a wide range of matters relating to women's rights. The commission has forwarded many recommendations for adoption by the Council and the Assembly; and, as indicated earlier in this study, it has transmitted several proposals to the Commission on Human Rights in connection with the Universal Declaration and the covenants.[43] Three of these subjects—political rights, nationality of married women, and status of women in private law—have raised issues that warrant special consideration. Others have included the status of women in public law, and the participation of women in the work of the United Nations and the specialized agencies. The commission has requested the International Labour Organisation to promote the principle of equal pay for equal work and to complete a convention and recommendation on this subject. The International Labour Organisation adopted these two instruments in 1951. Similarly, it has asked UNESCO to encourage equal opportunities for women in education. However, in debating such matters as improvement of the nursing profession, part-time work for women, and the problems of older women workers, the commission would seem to go somewhat beyond "promoting women's *rights*" as prescribed in its terms of reference.

Prolonged consideration has been given in United Nations organs to the use of technical assistance and advisory services to promote women's rights. In 1953, the General Assembly adopted a resolution, proposed by the commission and approved by the Council, authorizing the Secretary-General "to render, at the request of Member States, services which do not fall within the scope of existing techni-

[43] See above, Chap. II.

cal assistance programmes, in order to assist these States in promoting and safeguarding the rights of women."[44] As in the case of the similar resolutions in the field of discrimination and minorities and of freedom of information, mentioned earlier in this study, doubt was expressed concerning the need for such an authorization and the possible additional cost involved; but the final vote in the Assembly was without dissent—47 to 0, with 13 abstentions. To date, only two requests have been received by the Secretariat—one requesting that an expert on women's associations visit Pakistan, and one that an Egyptian woman leader attend a seminar outside that country.

Promotion of Political Rights

The Commission on the Status of Women and other organs have recognized from the outset that equality of political rights was the prerequisite for obtaining equality of rights in the economic, social, and cultural fields. The Economic and Social Council in June 1946 requested the Secretary-General to prepare "a complete and detailed study of the legislation concerning the status of women and the practical application of such legislation."[45] The Secretary-General accordingly sent to the Member governments, over a five-year period, detailed questionnaires on different aspects of this subject. A comparative analysis of these replies has provided a factual basis for discussion in the commission.

The first part of this questionnaire related to the franchise and the eligibility of women to public office. The information received from governments, supplemented by other authoritative sources, has formed the basis of an annual memorandum on the political rights of women in all countries. In 1948, the Council approved a suggestion of the commission that this information be revised and presented annually to the General Assembly "until all women throughout the world have the same political rights as men."[46]

This annual report by the Secretary-General has proved to be a useful document. It quotes constitutional and legislative provisions from each country, and it provides tables showing countries where women may vote in all elections on equal terms with men, countries

[44] Res. 729(VIII), Oct. 23, 1953.
[45] Res. 11(II), June 21, 1946.
[46] Res. 120(VI), Mar. 3, 1948.

where women may vote in all elections subject to certain qualifications not imposed on men, countries where women may vote in local elections only, and countries where women have no political rights. It also lists the date when women were first granted the vote in each country. The report provides the basic material for debates and recommendations of the commission and other organs, and a stimulus to governments and citizens to take action where necessary.

A recent edition of the report by the Secretary-General showed that women now vote on equal terms with men in sixty countries, and under certain limitations in six more; and that women are denied the vote altogether in seventeen countries.[47] Since the signing of the Charter in June 1945, twenty-four countries have extended full or limited political rights to women. This notable progress is surely due in part to the continuing efforts of United Nations organs to compile information, discuss developments, exchange experience, and exhort governments to take action.[48]

The General Assembly, usually acting on a recommendation of the commission approved by the Economic and Social Council, has adopted a number of recommendations concerning equal political rights for women. The Assembly, in one of its early resolutions adopted in December 1946, recommended that "all Member States, which have not already done so, adopt measures necessary to fulfill the purposes and aims of the Charter in this respect by granting to women the same political rights as to men."[49] This recommendation was reaffirmed by the Assembly at its session in 1952. In the following year, the General Assembly urged "States to take all necessary measures, particularly educational and legislative measures, leading to the development of the political rights of women in all Territories in which women do not enjoy full political rights, including Trust and Non-Self-Governing Territories."[50]

[47] U. N. General Assembly, Eighth Session, *Constitutions, Electoral Laws and Other Legal Instruments relating to Political Rights of Women*, Docs. A/2692 (Aug. 18, 1954) and A/2692/Corr.1(Sept. 7, 1954). Countries where women have no voting rights are Afghanistan, Cambodia, Colombia, Egypt, Ethiopia, Honduras, Iran, Iraq, Jordan, Laos, Libya, Lichtenstein, Nicaragua, Paraguay, Saudi Arabia, Switzerland, and Yemen. In Saudi Arabia and Yemen there are no electoral rights for either men or women.

[48] For an example of the efforts of the commission to promote education for citizenship, based on the experience of many different countries, see U. N. Department of Social Affairs, *Political Education of Women*, Doc. ST/SOA/6 (Oct. 1, 1951).

[49] Res. 56(I), Dec. 11, 1946.

[50] Res. 731(VIII), Oct. 23, 1953.

In 1949, the Mexican representative proposed in the commission that a United Nations convention on political rights of women be prepared, along the lines of the Inter-American Convention on the Granting of Political Rights to Women adopted at Bogotá in 1948 by the Organization of American States, the substantive article of which reads as follows: "The High Contracting Parties agree that the right to vote and to be elected to national office shall not be denied or abridged by reason of sex."[51] For several years the commission and the Council considered the text for a convention, taking into account the views received from governments. A number of Members, including the United States and the United Kingdom, questioned the need for a convention, inasmuch as a large majority of countries by that time had granted equal political rights; but many other Members considered that the adoption of an international standard would be useful, especially as a means for encouraging those governments that had not granted equal rights to do so.

The General Assembly in 1952 considered and approved the Convention on the Political Rights of Women. The first three articles of this convention are as follows:

Article I

Women shall be entitled to vote in all elections on equal terms with men, without any discrimination.

Article II

Women shall be eligible for election to all publicly elected bodies, established by national law, on equal terms with men, without any discrimination.

Article III

Women shall be entitled to hold public office and to exercise all public functions, established by national law, on equal terms with men, without any discrimination.[52]

Three issues arose during the debates in the Assembly on these substantive articles of the convention:

First, a number of delegations found it difficult to accept literally the phrase, "Women shall be entitled to hold public office." For example, in some countries where a state church exists, women are not permitted to hold office as priests or ministers. In the United States,

[51] U. S. Department of State, *Ninth International Conference of American States,* Publication 3263 (November 1948), p. 219.
[52] Res. 640(VII), Dec. 20, 1952.

women are forbidden by statute to hold the highest-ranking offices in the armed services. Thus it was generally agreed during the debates on the convention that this phrase implied only the ordinary public offices of a state and not such exceptional offices.

Second, the phrase "and to exercise all public functions," which is used in Europe, created difficulty for the United States and other countries where this phrase has no legal significance. The United States delegation stated that, in American usage, "public office" was coterminous with "public functions."

Third, the Soviet Union proposed, as it had done unsuccessfully in the commission and the Council, that each of the three articles end with the clause "without any discrimination on the grounds of race, colour, national or social origin, property status, language or religion." Other delegations, including the United States, pointed out that the proposed convention was supposed to deal with discrimination on the ground of *sex,* and that other forms of discrimination were hence extraneous; and that any such list of grounds would be incomplete, for this list omitted "political opinion." At the request of Indonesia, a separate vote was taken on the phrase "without any discrimination," which was retained in all three articles. The resulting language is somewhat ambiguous for purposes of a treaty.

The convention was adopted by the Assembly on December 20, 1952, without a dissenting vote—46 in favor, 0 against, with 11 abstentions, including the Soviet bloc. In October 1953, the General Assembly invited states that are members of one or more of the specialized agencies or parties to the Statute of the International Court of Justice to become parties to the convention, which came into force on July 7, 1954, ninety days after the sixth ratification had been deposited.[53] The United Kingdom, which abstained in the As-

[53] States that have ratified without reservations are China, Cuba, the Dominican Republic, Greece, Iceland, Israel, Sweden, Yugoslavia, and Thailand. States that have ratified with reservations are Bulgaria, Byelorussia, Denmark, Ecuador, Poland, Rumania, the Soviet Union, Albania, Czechoslovakia, Hungary, Pakistan, and the Ukraine. The Soviet bloc reservations relate to Article IX, which makes reference to the International Court of Justice compulsory at the request of either party to a dispute concerning the interpretation or application of the convention, and Article VII, which provides that the convention shall not enter into force as between a state making a reservation and other states that are or that become parties if those states notify the United Nations that they do not accept the reservation. A number of states have notified the United Nations that they do not accept the reservations of the Soviet bloc.

sembly vote, has not signed the convention, presumably because British law and practice do not accord literally with every provision of it. Also, the United States, which voted for the convention despite its misgivings over the phraseology, has not signed it, because of its recent opposition to treaties covering matters that traditionally have been within state and local jurisdiction in the United States. Secretary of State Dulles, appearing before the Senate Committee on Foreign Relations on the Bricker Amendment in April 1953, testified as follows about the convention:

This administration does not intend to sign the Convention on Political Rights of Women. This is not because we do not believe in the equal political status of men and women or because we shall not seek to promote that equality. Rather it is because we do not believe that this goal can be achieved by treaty coercion or that it constitutes a proper field for exercise of the treaty-making power. We do not now see any clear or necessary relation between the interest and welfare of the United States and the eligibility of women to political office in other nations.[54]

Nationality of Married Women

At the suggestion of the United States the Commission on the Status of Women began consideration, in 1948, of conflicts of law relating to the nationality of women who marry aliens. Information collected by the Secretariat revealed that in many states a woman who married an alien automatically acquired the nationality of the country of her husband even though she might retain her own. In some cases a woman might lose her nationality without acquiring the nationality of her husband.[55] In 1950, the Economic and Social Council approved, for incorporation into a United Nations convention on nationality, the principles agreed on by the commission— that there should be no distinction based on sex as regards nationality, and that neither marriage nor its dissolution should affect the nationality of either spouse.

The ratification of Denmark is subject to a reservation to Article III "in so far as it relates to the right of women to hold military appointments or to act as heads of recruitment services or to serve on recruitment boards." No other states have raised objections to this Danish reservation.

[54] U. S. Department of State *Bulletin*, Vol. 28 (Apr. 20, 1953), p. 592.

[55] U. N. Commission on the Status of Women, *Nationality of Married Women (Report Submitted by the Secretary-General)*, Docs. E/CN.6/126/Rev. 1 and E/CN.6/129/Rev. 1 (Nov. 29, 1950).

Controversy has arisen over the best procedure for putting these principles into effect. One group, including the United States, being skeptical about the value of a special United Nations convention, has maintained that the matter should be referred to the International Law Commission, which has been considering the general subject of nationality. Another group, including many Latin-American countries, has favored preparation of a convention by the Commission on the Status of Women, because of impatience at the slowness of the International Law Commission in dealing with the matter.

For several years, the former view was upheld by the Commission on the Status of Women and the Council; but in 1952 the International Law Commission decided not to proceed with drafting a convention. At its session in 1953, the Commission on the Status of Women, over the objection of the United States, recommended that its own draft convention be circulated to governments for comment. The Council circulated this draft without taking a position on its substance. In 1954, the commission, on the initiative of Cuba, recommended that a revised text of the convention be circulated to governments. At the same time, the commission adopted a proposal by the United States, which had abstained on the Cuban resolution, that the Council recommend to governments that "they take action, as necessary, to ensure that a woman have the same right as a man to retain her nationality on marriage to a person of different nationality."[56] The Council, in the summer of 1954, adopted both proposals, adding to the first a provision that the draft convention should go to the International Law Commission for its information.

The Commission on the Status of Women, at its session in 1955, forwarded to the Economic and Social Council a revised text of the preamble and the three substantive articles of the Draft Covenant on the Nationality of Married Women, together with the final articles submitted by Cuba and amendments thereto. The Council, in August 1955, recommended that the General Assembly adopt a convention and submitted the texts prepared by the commission. At the tenth session of the General Assembly in 1955, the Third Committee adopted a revised text of the preamble and the three substantive articles.[57] The committee referred the final articles to the Sixth

[56] U. N. Commission on the Status of Women, *Report of the Eighth Session*, Doc. E/2571 (April 1954), p. 8.

[57] For text, see U.N. General Assembly, Tenth Session, *Official Records*, Report by the Third Committee, Doc. A/3059 (Dec. 2, 1955).

(Legal) Committee for consideration. However, the latter committee, just before adjourning, returned the final articles to the Third Committee with the request that the terms of reference concerning those articles be formulated with greater precision.

Status of Women in Private Law

The Commission on the Status of Women has been giving attention to women's rights regarding marriage, the family, and property. After the Secretariat had compiled considerable information about women's rights under these aspects of private law in response to its questionnaires, the commission adopted in 1953, and the Council approved, a recommendation that governments:

(*a*) Take all possible measures to ensure equality of rights and duties of husband and wife in family matters;

(*b*) Take all possible measures to ensure to the wife full legal capacity, the right to engage in work outside the home and the right, on equal terms with her husband, to acquire, administer, enjoy and dispose of property.[58]

The commission also recommended that the Commission on Human Rights include Article 16 of the Universal Declaration, concerning equal rights in marriage, in the Draft Covenant on Civil and Political Rights. As related earlier in this study, the Commission on Human Rights later approved such an article in a revised form.[59]

In 1954, the commission went even further into the field of private law by adopting a series of five detailed resolutions recommending that:[60]

1. "Governments take all necessary measures to ensure the right of a married woman to undertake independent work, to carry it on, and to administer and dispose of her earnings without the necessity of securing her husband's authorization."

2. Member states should take all necessary steps to eliminate discriminatory legislation regarding property rights in marriage and drawing their attention to "the desirability of a statutory matrimonial regime which would provide for the separation of the property belonging to the spouses at the time of marriage and either

[58] Res. 504 D(XVI), July 23, 1953.
[59] See above, Chap. II.
[60] U. N. Commission on the Status of Women, *Report of the Eighth Session*, pp. 12-15.

for the separation of property acquired during marriage or for common ownership of property acquired by both spouses during marriage, such community property to be administered jointly by the spouses; and in either case, on dissolution of marriage, property acquired during marriage would be divided equally between them or their heirs."

3. The General Assembly and the Trusteeship Council, as appropriate, in collaboration with states including states administering trust and non-self-governing territories where customs, ancient laws, and practices contrary to the principles of the Charter and the Universal Declaration of Human Rights exist, should take "all appropriate measures to ensure complete freedom in the choice of a spouse; to abolish the practice of the bride-price; to guarantee the right of widows to the custody of their children and their freedom as to remarriage; to eliminate completely child marriages and the betrothal of young girls before the age of puberty, establishing appropriate penalties where necessary; to establish a civil register in which all marriages and divorces will be recorded; to ensure that all cases involving personal rights be tried before a duly appointed magistrate; to ensure also that family allowances, where these are provided, be administered in such a way as to benefit directly the wife and children."

4. The Economic and Social Council should revise the text on marriage and the family included by the Commission on Human Rights in the Draft Covenant on Civil and Political Rights, to conform more closely to Article 16 of the Universal Declaration of Human Rights.

5. The Council should arrange for the collection of further information on the status of women under private law.

These resolutions were adopted either unanimously or by overwhelming majorities. The United States delegation, which took the position that a United Nations organ should not adopt recommendations dealing with matters so closely related to national and local laws and practices and containing certain inaccuracies, voted for only the fifth resolution. The United Kingdom delegation voted against the second and fourth resolutions. Despite the continuing concern of the United States and the United Kingdom about the wisdom of the resolutions, all five of them were subsequently approved by the Economic and Social Council. The third of these resolutions, relating to customs, ancient laws, and practices, was adopted by the General Assembly at its ninth session in 1954. The vote was 48 to 0 with 5 abstentions.

In view of the widely differing systems of law, religious and cultural traditions, economic standards, and social practices existing among all the Members of the United Nations, and even within many of these countries, the question may well be asked whether United Nations organs should adopt specific recommendations in this field, at least until the reasons for national differences have been more carefully studied and other courses of action more fully explored. Resolutions on such controversial matters may in the long run subject the United Nations to resentment and even ridicule for attempting to prescribe uniform standards on subjects where the pattern is necessarily variegated.

The Right of Self-Determination

For the past four years, the majority of the Members of the United Nations have been showing an increasing concern over "the right of self-determination of peoples and nations." In fact, the current interest of the majority would appear to be ranged in this descending order: first, territorial rights; second, economic, social, and cultural rights; and third, civil and political rights. The steadily mounting tension over colonial problems has affected the deliberations of the United Nations organs on many other aspects of human rights.[61]

The present violent debate over self-determination had its beginning in a brief resolution adopted by the General Assembly in 1950, which called on the Economic and Social Council to request the Commission on Human Rights "to study ways and means which would ensure the right of peoples and nations to self-determination, and to prepare recommendations for consideration by the General Assembly at its sixth session."[62] The commission, however, did not have time to take up this matter. The Assembly, at its session in 1951-52, again requested the commission to prepare recommendations on international respect for the right of self-determination, and, as recounted earlier, adopted an article for inclusion in the draft covenants.[63]

[61] See Part Four of the volume in this Brookings series, *The United Nations and Promotion of the General Welfare.*
[62] Res. 421D(V), Dec. 4, 1950.
[63] See above, Chap. II.

The Commission on Human Rights devoted considerable attention, at its 1952 session, to revising the article for the draft covenants
and to preparing two draft resolutions for the General Assembly.
The first resolution began with a provocative preamble stating that
"it is as essential to abolish slavery of peoples and nations as of
human beings" and that "such slavery exists where an alien people
hold power over the destiny of a people." It recommended that
Members of the United Nations uphold the *principle* of self-
determination and that Members administering non-self-governing
and trust territories recognize and promote the *right* of self-
determination, "the popular wish being ascertained in particular
through a plebiscite held under the auspices of the United Nations."
The second resolution recommended that Members responsible for
non-self-governing territories voluntarily include in information
transmitted under Article 73(e) of the Charter "details regarding
the extent to which the right of peoples to self-determination is
exercised by the peoples of these territories."[64]

The debate on these two resolutions during the session of the
Assembly in 1952 repeated the debate on the article of the covenant
at the previous session. The non-administering powers, in a large
majority, emphasized the *right* of dependent territories to independence. The administering powers, in a small minority, accepted
the *principle* of self-determination for all peoples. The United States
attempted, unsuccessfully, to introduce a greater emphasis on the
universal character of the principle of self-determination, noting
that a number of nations had lost the right of self-determination
since the end of the Second World War; and to delete the reference
to plebiscites. Both this resolution and the second one concerning
Article 73(e) of the Charter were adopted by overwhelming majorities. The Assembly then proceeded to adopt a third resolution
asking the Commission on Human Rights to continue preparing
recommendations on international respect for the right of self-
determination, "and particularly recommendations relating to the
steps which might be taken, within the limits of their resources and
competence, by the various organs of the United Nations and the
specialized agencies."[65]

Inasmuch as the Commission on Human Rights did not consider

[64] U. N. Commission on Human Rights, *Report of the Eighth Session*, Doc.
E/2256 (June 27, 1952), p. 11.

[65] Res. 637C(VII), Dec. 16, 1952.

self-determination at its session in 1953, the non-administering powers raised that matter once again in the General Assembly later that year. The administering powers, regarding the debate as wholly unnecessary, maintained a silence that exasperated their opponents. The result was a procedural resolution in which the Assembly requested the commission to give "due priority" to the preparation of the recommendations on self-determination.[66]

At the end of the session in 1954 of the Commission on Human Rights, six of the non-administering powers—Chile, China, Egypt, India, Pakistan, and the Philippines—introduced a draft resolution containing proposals with far-reaching implications. The resolution proposed that the General Assembly establish two new commissions in this field. The first proposal, which noted that the right of self-determination as affirmed in the draft covenants included "permanent sovereignty over their natural wealth and resources," called for a commission to "conduct a full survey of the status of this basic constituent of the right to self-determination with recommendations, where necessary, for its strengthening." The second proposal provided for a good offices commission which, at the request of any ten Members of the United Nations, would "examine any situation resulting from alleged denial or inadequate realization of the right of self-determination."[67]

The sponsors of these proposals argued that they constituted a logical development and expansion of United Nations machinery for the promotion of the right of self-determination. Although the text of the covenants made no reference to non-self-governing and trust territories, the administering powers reacted vigorously. They pointed out that, with regard to the first proposed commission, it was improper to base a survey of this kind on an ambiguous and controversial provision of the uncompleted covenants. With regard to the second proposed commission, they objected that this type of machinery would conflict with the work of other organs and create dangerous confusion. They also protested that time was not available for careful consideration of the problem. The commission, nevertheless, adopted the resolution by 11 in favor and 6 against, with 1 absence.

In July 1954, the Council, where the administering powers have relatively more influence, subjected the two proposals to a critical

[66] Res. 738(VIII), Nov. 28, 1953.
[67] U. N. Commission on Human Rights, *Report of the Tenth Session*, pp. 37-38.

appraisal. The Egyptian representative, Dr. Mahmoud Azmi, who was also chairman of the Commission on Human Rights, argued that the Council should not block or alter recommendations prepared by the commission at the request of the Assembly. The United States and others replied that the Council was fully entitled to review the work of its subsidiary bodies. Australia, Belgium, France, and the United Kingdom argued strongly against the proposed new commissions. A motion to transmit the resolution to the Assembly was rejected in the Social Committee of the Council by a vote of 8 in favor and 10 against. The Council then adopted—by a vote of 9 in favor, 6 against, with 3 abstentions—a motion, made jointly by Ecuador and Cuba, to return the proposals to the commission for further study.

At its session in 1955, the commission reaffirmed its recommendations that the General Assembly establish two new commissions to deal with self-determination. The Council, in the summer of 1955, transmitted these two recommendations to the Assembly. However, it approved and also transmitted a third proposal, submitted by the United States, recommending that the Assembly establish an *ad hoc* commission to study the basic elements of the whole concept of self-determination. The Third Committee of the General Assembly did not reach this item until near the end of its tenth session in the autumn of 1955, after the long debate on Article 1 of the draft covenants on human rights. The committee decided without objection to recommend that consideration of this item be postponed to the eleventh session, and this recommendation was accepted by the plenary.

These annual debates on self-determination clearly reveal the ever-widening split between the administering powers and the non-administering powers in the United Nations.[68] Both sides are taking

[68] For analyses of the implications of these developments, see Clyde Eagleton, "Excesses of Self-Determination," *Foreign Affairs*, Vol. 31 (July 1953), pp. 592-604, and Benjamin Rivlin, "Self-Determination and Dependent Areas," *International Conciliation*, No. 501 (January 1955).

At the tenth session of the General Assembly in 1955, the relationship of self-determination to Article 2(7) was brought into controversy by the proposal of fourteen Arab-Asian delegations that "The question of Algeria" be added to the agenda (U.N. General Assembly, Tenth Session, Doc. A/2924, July 29, 1955). The recommendation of the General Committee that this item not be included on the agenda was rejected by 27 in favor to 28 against, with 5 abstentions; and the French Government immediately withdrew its entire delegation from the General Assembly. After prolonged negotiations with the Arab-Asian group and the

increasingly extreme and recalcitrant positions. Thus far, the efforts of the United States, the Scandinavian delegations, and a few others to find compromise formulas have not succeeded. In particular, their efforts to broaden the concept of self-determination to cover all territories, not just the non-self-governing and trust territories, have been resented by the Arab-Asian group. The resulting strain on the Organization is severe, and the threat to the unity of its Members is serious. Self-determination is one of many issues before the United Nations that needs a greater degree of good will, patience, and understanding than has been evident in recent years.

---

supporters of the French position, the Indian delegation introduced a procedural motion stating that the Assembly decides "not to consider further the item entitled 'The question of Algeria' and is therefore no longer seized of this item on the agenda of the tenth session." (U.N. General Assembly, Tenth Session, Doc. A/3044, Nov. 25, 1955.) The Indian motion was adopted without objection in both the First Committee and the plenary, and the French delegation then returned to the Assembly. It is of interest that the United States delegation invoked Article 2(7) for the first time in voting against the inscription of an agenda item. Ambassador Lodge, after quoting from the explanatory memorandum submitted by the fourteen Arab-Asian delegations, made the following statement:

"This memorandum indicates clearly that what is sought by the sponsors of the item is the sanction of the General Assembly to a course of action intended to bring about fundamental changes in the composition of one of the General Assembly's own Members—that is, the French Republic. If it does not mean that, it does not mean anything.

"The United States believes that the proposed item, viewed in the context of this action which it is suggested should be sought in the General Assembly, falls within the provision of Article 2(7) of the Charter." (U.N. General Assembly, Tenth Session, *Provisional Records*, 530th Meeting, Doc. A/PV.530, Sept. 30, 1955.)

CHAPTER IV

Efforts to Deal With Violations of Human Rights

IN ITS EFFORTS to deal with violations of human rights, even more than in its attempts to define and promote those rights, the United Nations has moved into new and controversial fields of activity. A few of these fields—slavery, forced labor, and prisoners of war—have been subjects of international concern and action in previous periods. Others—for example, racial discrimination in South Africa and violations of rights of individuals—mark a notable departure from the traditional activities of the League of Nations and earlier international organizations. In some instances, the fate of millions of persons condemned to forced labor camps has been studied and discussed; in others, the fate of a few hundred persons or even of a single individual has been debated. Some cases involve the interpretation of peace treaties or other international agreements; others involve an interpretation of Articles 55 and 56 of the Charter. Many of them have provoked angry disputes over the powers of organs of the United Nations to consider matters that one state or another has regarded as falling within its domestic jurisdiction.

Some of these cases—particularly those of the Greek prisoners and the Spanish prisoners—have been raised for purposes of propaganda or as part of the "cold war." Most of them, however, have reflected a genuine concern over human liberty and have constituted a unique experiment in attempting to turn the spotlight of world public opinion on violations of human rights in order to assure the victims of oppression that they have not been forgotten by the international community.

Only with respect to communications received from individuals and organizations, especially those alleging violations of human rights, has the United Nations—except for the arrangements in the trusteeship system for examining petitions—declined to take any real action. The Commission on Human Rights, with the approval of the Economic and Social Council, has declared that it has no power to deal with the numerous communications received by the Secretary-General from all over the world. This decision has been the subject of recurring dispute, but thus far it has not been modified.

One underlying issue in this whole area of activity is the extent to which United Nations organs should deal with alleged violations of human rights in view of the fact that the Charter contains no obligation on the part of Members to respect specific rights and that the Universal Declaration merely proclaims objectives and standards. The Convention on the Political Rights of Women defines an obligation, binding on parties to that convention, to respect one very limited group of rights; but, until the covenants are in force, there is no clear obligation on Members to respect all the other specific rights. As a result, it has been necessary for one delegation or another, with regard to a particular case, to take the position that, inasmuch as the purpose of the United Nations is to promote respect for human rights and fundamental freedoms, it is appropriate for organs of the United Nations to consider situations involving acts regarded by that delegation as violating human rights as understood by it, impairing friendly relations among nations, or endangering international peace and security.

Communications Concerning Human Rights

Since the Charter came into force, the United Nations has received tens of thousands of communications from individuals and organizations in practically every part of the world alleging violations of human rights or proposing measures to safeguard human liberty.[1] The question of what should be done with these communications has frequently been debated in the General Assembly, the Economic and Social Council, and the Commission on Human Rights.

[1] For the first seven sessions of the Commission on Human Rights (1946-51), when the confidential lists were not even summarized in the public records, no totals are available. The reports of the eighth, ninth, and tenth sessions of the commission (1952-54) reveal a total of 37,660 communications received. Of this total, 19,454, received in 1950-51, were mass communications of an almost identical character alleging political persecution in two countries. (Because of the confidential character of these lists, the names of countries accused are not revealed publicly.)

Two sharply divided schools of thought have developed over the disposition of these communications. On the one hand, many of the Near Eastern, Asian, and Latin-American Members as well as many of the nongovernmental organizations contend—as indicated earlier in this study, with regard to the draft covenants—that the right of petition is essential to the maintenance of freedom.[2] They consider that inasmuch as the United Nations is empowered to promote respect for the observance of human rights and fundamental freedoms, the Commission on Human Rights should have authority to receive and examine private communications relating to this purpose. They are not content to wait until the completion of the draft covenants, which would contain measures of implementation, including possibly even the right of petition; and they point out that, in any event, these procedures will affect only those states that become parties to the covenants. They feel, finally, that the failure to consider these complaints is damaging to the prestige of the United Nations and is discouraging to the peoples of the world.

On the other hand, the United States, the older members of the British Commonwealth, and the countries of Western Europe, as well as the Soviet bloc, maintain that the Charter made no provision, except in relation to the trusteeship system, for the consideration of communications from individuals and organizations. Consideration of communications, indeed, might constitute a violation of Article 2(7) of the Charter concerning domestic jurisdiction. These states insist that such provision could be made only by means of some special international convention like the draft covenants, or a protocol relating to them. Such an instrument, effective only as between the parties to it, would define the rights to be respected and the procedures for handling communications relating to these rights. They argue, furthermore, that if the Commission on Human Rights were authorized to consider communications, it might soon become swamped with the thousands of these documents, which would rapidly increase in number as soon as it became known that some action was being taken. Moreover, the commission would be at the mercy of propagandists, professional agitators, and irresponsible persons. The commission might easily be regarded as an appellate

[2] See above, Chap. I. Similar views were expressed by the former Secretary-General. See U. N. Commission on Human Rights, Fifth Session, *Report by the Secretary-General on the Present Situation with regard to Communications Concerning Human Rights*, Doc. E/CN.4/165 (May 2, 1949).

tribunal, reviewing decisions of the courts of the Member states. Finally, the governments of democratic countries realized that they would be subjected in international forums to continual criticism from their own citizens, especially opposition groups, whereas the totalitarian governments would be spared that embarrassment.

The "nuclear" Commission on Human Rights initially envisaged a significant role for the future body with respect to violations of human rights:

> Pending the eventual establishment of an agency of implementation the Commission on Human Rights might be recognized as qualified to aid the appropriate organs of the United Nations in the task defined for the General Assembly and the Economic and Social Council in Articles 13, 55, and 62 of the Charter, concerning the promotion and observance of human rights and fundamental freedoms for all, and to aid the Security Council in the task entrusted to it by Article 39 of the Charter, by pointing to cases where violation of human rights committed in one country may, by its gravity, its frequency, or its systematic nature, constitute a threat to the peace.[3]

However, the full commission recognized, at its first session, that "it has no power to take any action in regard to any complaints concerning human rights"; and this waiver of authority was promptly confirmed by the Council.[4] As a result, the present procedures are exceedingly restrictive. Under a resolution of the Council in 1947, subsequently amended, the Secretary-General compiles two lists of communications concerning human rights: a nonconfidential list containing a brief indication of the substance of each communication dealing with the principles involved in the promotion of universal respect for and observance of human rights, the identity of the authors to be divulged unless they indicated that they wished their names to remain confidential; and a confidential list contain-

---

[3] U. N. Commission on Human Rights, *Report of the Commission on Human Rights to the Second Session of the Economic and Social Council,* Doc. E/38/Rev.1 (May 21, 1946), p. 7. In view of the strong objection to any measures of implementation expressed in later years by representatives of the Soviet bloc, it is of interest that, in this initial discussion of the subject, the Soviet member was unable to support the position taken by his colleagues in the "nuclear" commission: "Mr. Borisov (U.S.S.R.) wished it to be recorded that he had not yet been able to study sufficiently the records of the Commission and the various documents and preferred, therefore, to abstain from voting on the question of the provisions for implementation."

[4] U. N. Commission on Human Rights, *Report of the First Session,* Doc. E/259 (1947), p. 6.

ing a brief indication of the substance of each communication alleging a violation of human rights in a particular country, to be furnished to members of the commission in a private meeting, without
divulging the identity of the authors except in cases where they
stated this had already been done or that they had no objection to
their names being divulged. The Secretary-General furnishes each
Member state concerned with a copy of any communication that
refers explicitly to that state or to territories under its jurisdiction,
without revealing the identity of the author except under the conditions noted above. The Secretary-General then circulates to members of the commission any observations made by governments concerning copies of the communications he had sent them.[5]

The Council later extended its arrangements to grant to the
Commission on the Status of Women, the Subcommission on Prevention of Discrimination and Protection of Minorities, and the
Rapporteur on Freedom of Information of the Economic and Social
Council the same authority to see the confidential list of communications. In 1952, the Council decided that its procedures for receiving
communications from nongovernmental organizations in consulta-
tive status would not apply to communications alleging violations
of human rights, on the ground that such communications would be
handled under the arrangements established for the Commission on
Human Rights. At the same time, the Council decided that communications containing complaints against governments on subjects
other than human rights would be distributed only after the government concerned had been notified by the Secretary-General. Any
reply from the government concerned, if received within six weeks,
would be circulated in the same document as the communication
from the nongovernmental organization. In this connection, the
Committee on Non-Governmental Organizations of the Council, in
hearing a statement by the representative of the World Jewish Congress on the commercial boycott of Jews in Saudi Arabia, ruled in
effect that it would not receive oral statements containing complaints
against governments; but it permitted the representative to discuss
the situation of Jews arising out of the Saudi-Arabian boycott of

[5] U. N. Economic and Social Council, Res. 75(V), Aug. 5, 1947; Res. 116A(VI),
Mar. 1-2, 1948; Res. 192A(VIII), Feb. 9, 1949; Res. 275B(X), Feb. 17, 1950. For
a consolidated text, see U. N. Economic and Social Council, Fourteenth Session,
Doc. E/2206 (Apr. 14, 1952), pp. 6-7.

Jewish merchants and of export firms with Jewish connections.[6] The Council, as will be indicated later, has also relaxed its restrictions regarding allegations against governments in the field of forced labor and of trade union rights.

The Secretary-General's two summaries for the year 1953 illustrate the volume and range of the communications received by the United Nations. The nonconfidential list contained summaries of 387 communications, received from April 1, 1953 to February 12, 1954, dealing with general principles concerning human rights. The confidential list contained summaries of or references to 9,524 communications received during the period March 13-December 31, 1953. Of this total, the great majority alleged violations of freedom of religion (7,850) and violations of human rights on political grounds (1,343). The remaining 331 communications related to the right to a fair trial, self-determination, trade union rights, minorities, and many others.

On four different occasions during the period 1951-53, efforts in United Nations organs to modify these arrangements—usually spearheaded by Egypt, India, and Uruguay—have been defeated. On the most recent occasion, at the General Assembly in 1953, the motion for a more flexible system was defeated by 11 in favor, 26 against, with 12 abstentions.

Thus these ever-increasing thousands of communications rest almost unnoticed in the archives of the Secretariat. The members of the Commission on Human Rights pay little attention to the Secretary-General's annual summaries. The commission each year merely takes note of the *distribution* of these summaries—not of the summaries themselves—because of strenuous Soviet objections. Governments also apparently pay little attention to those communications containing allegations against them, for in 1953 only thirteen of the 9,524 communications provoked a reply from the government

---

[6] The arrangements established by the Council for consultation with nongovernmental organizations are contained in Res. 288(X), Feb. 27, 1950. Its decisions concerning the handling of communications from nongovernmental organizations containing complaints against governments is contained in Res. 454(XIV), July 28, 1952. The Council's Committee on Non-Governmental Organizations did not agree to hear a statement from the World Jewish Congress until its representative had stated that the communication "contained neither accusations nor complaints against the Government of Saudi Arabia." U. N. Economic and Social Council, Council Committee on Non-Governmental Organizations, *Summary Records,* 116th Meeting (June 19, 1952), Doc. E/C.2/SR.117, p. 5.

that had been accused of violating human rights—an indication of the trivial or propagandistic character of many of the communications and perhaps of the fear of governments that replies would unduly dignify these documents and open the door to consideration of them in the commission. Neither the Council nor the commission has been willing to relax the barriers erected in 1947 to the consideration of communications. Despite the strong desire of many governments and nongovernmental organizations that the United Nations act on these private complaints, the unusual combination of the Western powers and the Soviet bloc has been able to prevent any action. Even in the General Assembly, the leading proponents have been unable to mobilize sufficient support in the Near Eastern, Asian, and Latin-American delegations to force a modification of policy.

Slavery, Forced Labor, and Trade Union Rights

Slavery and the slave trade, as indicated earlier in this study, were among the first subjects in the entire economic and social field to become matters of international concern.[7] The conclusion of the Slavery Convention in 1926, which was ratified by forty-five states, and the continuing efforts of the League of Nations to eliminate slavery were among the major contributions of that organization to the human rights field. The Slavery Convention prescribed certain conditions under which forced or compulsory labor might be permitted but required that this practice be put to an end progressively and as soon as possible.[8] The International Labour Organisation (ILO) in 1930 adopted a Convention Concerning Forced or Com-

[7] See above, Chap. I. For an historical account of the suppression of slavery and of the slave trade by means of international agreement, see U. N. Secretariat, *The Suppression of Slavery*, Doc. ST/SOA/4 (July 11, 1951).

[8] The parties to the Slavery Convention included the British Empire, France, Germany, Italy, and the United States among the principal powers of the period. The United States ratification was subject to the following reservation: "That the Government of the United States, adhering to its policy of opposition to forced or compulsory labor except as a punishment for crime of which the person concerned has been duly convicted, adheres to the Convention except as to the first subdivision of the second paragraph of article five, which reads as follows: ' (1) Subject to the transitional provisions laid down in paragraph (2) below, compulsory or forced labor may only be exacted for public purposes.' " Senate Committee on Foreign Relations, *Treaties, Conventions, International Acts, Protocols, and Agreements between the United States of America and Other Powers, 1923-1937*, S. Doc. 134, 75 Cong. 3 sess. (1938), p. 5030.

pulsory Labor, which was ratified by thirty states.[9] International action was confined largely to dependent territories in Africa and the Far East. For many years, especially after the Second World War, however, it became increasingly evident that a new form of forced labor was being maintained on a vast scale within the Soviet empire. A third subject—promoting trade union rights, or freedom of association—is a relatively new one, at least so far as international agreement is concerned. All three subjects—slavery, forced labor, and trade union rights—have been part of the effort of the United Nations to safeguard human rights.

Slavery

The United Nations did not deal with the problem of slavery until 1948, when the General Assembly provided in Article 4 of the Universal Declaration of Human Rights that: "No one shall be held in slavery or servitude; slavery and the slave trade shall be prohibited in all their forms." In May 1949, the Assembly, on the initiative of Belgium, unanimously requested the Economic and Social Council to study the problem. The Council, in turn, instructed the Secretary-General, after consultation with the organs and agencies having special competence in this field, to appoint a small *ad hoc* committee of experts to survey "the field of slavery and other institutions or customs resembling slavery," to assess the nature and extent of these several problems at the present time, to suggest methods of attacking them, and to suggest an appropriate division of responsibility among the various bodies within the United Nations system.[10] The Secretary-General appointed Moises Poblete Troncoso of Chile, Charles W. W. Greenidge of the United Kingdom, Bruno Lasker of the United States, and Mrs. Jane Vialle of France, to serve in their individual capacity as experts.

The *Ad Hoc* Committee on Slavery held two sessions, in February-March 1950 and April 1951. At its first session, the committee devised a detailed questionnaire, which—with the approval of the Council—it circulated to both Member States and states not Members of the Organization.[11] The committee also addressed inquiries

[9] The parties to the Forced Labor Convention included France, Germany, Italy, Japan, and the United Kingdom among the principal powers of that period.

[10] Res. 238 (IX), July 20, 1949.

[11] Res. 276 (X), Mar. 6, 1950; U. N. Doc. E/1617 (Feb. 21, 1950). Because the questionnaire included questions relating to forced labor and trade union rights,

to certain nongovernmental organizations having special competence in the field of slavery, and to a number of experts. It also requested the ILO to communicate all the information on slavery and other forms of servitude that it might have at its disposal.

The political hazards involved in the use of expert bodies by the United Nations were illustrated at the session of the General Assembly in 1950, when the representative of Peru in the Third (Social, Humanitarian, and Cultural) Committee violently assailed the *Ad Hoc* Committee on Slavery for accepting information from nongovernmental organizations and individuals alleging that conditions analogous to slavery existed in Latin America. The Peruvian representative introduced a draft resolution proposing that the committee be replaced by a commission of twelve governmental representatives. After a somewhat heated discussion, in which the United States and other delegations suggested that the committee should be allowed to finish its task, the proposal was defeated by a very narrow vote—17 in favor, 21 against, with 16 abstentions.

The committee reached the following conclusion:

. . . that slavery, even in its crudest form, still exists in the world today, and that it should continue to be a concern of the international community. Other forms of servitude exist in practically all regions of the world. They are rapidly subsiding in some, with favourable judicial or legislative action and an aroused public opinion; but in others they appear to be growing. The Committee felt that they should equally be a concern of the international community, particularly because the number of people affected and the suffering caused by these practices is much more significant at present than that resulting from crude slavery.[12]

It recommended, *inter alia,* the following: (1) that the United Nations should assume the powers and functions formerly exercised by the League of Nations under the Slavery Convention of 1926; (2) that the Economic and Social Council should establish a drafting committee to prepare a supplementary convention on slavery and other forms of servitude; (3) that governments should adopt legislative and administrative measures designed to end slavery and servitude without creating unnecessary social disorder, and that a standing body of experts on slavery should be created by the United

---

which—as is indicated later—the Council had referred to other bodies for action, the Council requested the *ad hoc* committee to revise the questionnaire. The committee accordingly revised the questionnaire before adjourning its first session.

[12] U. N. Economic and Social Council, Thirteenth Session, *Report of the Ad Hoc Committee on Slavery (Second Session),* Doc. E/1988 (May 4, 1951), p. 13.

Nations to perform tasks of a supervisory nature; (4) that regional conferences should be held under United Nations auspices; and (5) that the ILO should undertake a study of the implications of contracts of service for life or for a long period of years.

The report of the committee was less comprehensive and conclusive than most of those submitted by expert bodies. The committee received sixty-four replies from governments in response to its questionnaire and an even larger number from nongovernmental organizations and experts; but twelve governments made no reply, and much of the information received was incomplete, ambiguous, or contradictory. The committee did not have time to make a comprehensive survey of the existence of slavery and related institutions. Each of the four members prepared a study of conditions in the region with which he was especially familiar; but the committee merely drew these studies to the attention of the Economic and Social Council without assuming collective responsibility for their contents.[13] As a result, the Council in September 1951 found that the report was "not at present in such a form as to allow the Council to act upon it at this session" and requested the Secretary-General to supplement and complete it.[14]

The Secretary-General's report, amplifying the conclusions and recommendations of the committee, provided a more useful survey of the problem and an analysis of possible measures that might be taken, but furnished no new factual information about the existence of slavery.[15] After considering the report in April 1953, the Council recommended that the Secretary-General prepare a draft protocol for transferring to the United Nations the functions exercised under the Slavery Convention by the League of Nations; recommended that all states, which had not already done so, adhere as soon as

[13] U.N. Ad Hoc Committee on Slavery, Second Session, Memorandum on Slavery and Other Forms of Involuntary Servitude in Asia, Oceania, and Australasia (Submitted by Mr. Bruno Lasker), Doc. E/AC.33/R.11 (June 5, 1951); Memorandum on Slavery and Other Forms of Servitude in American Countries (Submitted by Mr. Moises Poblete Troncoso), Doc. E/AC.33/R.12 (June 7, 1951); Memorandum on Slavery in African Territories (Submitted by Mrs. Jane Vialle), Doc. E/AC.33/R.13 (June 13, 1951); and Minority Report of Mr. C. W. W. Greenidge, Member of the Ad Hoc Committee on Slavery, Doc. E/AC.33/R.14 (June 8, 1951).

[14] Res. 388 (XIII), Sept. 10, 1951.

[15] U.N. Economic and Social Council, Fifteenth Session, Slavery, the Slave Trade, and Other Forms of Servitude, Report by the Secretary-General, Doc. E/2357 (Jan. 27, 1953).

possible to the convention; and requested the Secretary-General to consult governments concerning the desirability of a supplementary convention. The protocol prepared by the Secretariat was adopted by the General Assembly in October 1953.[16] It has been either signed without reservation or accepted by twenty-five of the parties to the convention, including the United Kingdom; and it has been signed, subject to acceptance, by six others, including the United States and France.

The Economic and Social Council resumed consideration of the problem of slavery in April 1954. The Council noted that the information supplied in accordance with its previous resolution was still "not in such a form as to give a clear and concise statement as to the extent to which slavery and practices resembling slavery exist in the world today" and that all replies to the questionnaire had not yet been received.[17] It decided therefore, to appoint a *rapporteur*, Hans Engen, of Norway, to prepare a concise summary of the information received and any supplied by the ILO.

The Council also considered the report of the Secretary-General summarizing the replies of twenty governments on the desirability of concluding a supplementary convention. A number of these replies were negative or noncommittal in character; but others supported the idea of a supplementary convention and the United Kingdom submitted a draft text. The Council decided to transmit to all governments and to the ILO any draft supplementary convention submitted by governments, and accordingly circulated the United Kingdom text. The Council invited the comments of governments and of the ILO on the United Kingdom text and on any others, and requested the Secretary-General to prepare a report on the replies received for consideration at its nineteenth session, in the spring of 1955.[18]

Thus the United Nations, after a slow and stumbling start, has resumed the work previously carried on by the League of Nations in one field of human rights traditionally a subject of international concern. The compilation of information on a continuing basis

[16] Res. 794 (VIII), Oct. 24, 1953.

[17] Res. 525A (XVII), Apr. 29, 1954.

[18] In April 1955, the Council appointed a committee consisting of representatives of Australia, Ecuador, Egypt, France, India, the Netherlands, Turkey, the Soviet Union, and the United Kingdom to prepare a text of a draft supplementary convention for submission to the Council at its twenty-first session (April-May 1956).

about the existence of slavery and related conditions throughout the world is an especially urgent problem, for information is lacking about certain areas where the existence of slavery and conditions resembling slavery are suspected.

Forced Labor

For many years, informed public opinion had been aware of reports that the Soviet Union was condemning millions of persons to forced labor. It was not until February 1948, however, that the world community took official cognizance of an evil that in the past had been limited largely to tropical territories. In November 1947, the American Federation of Labor proposed that the Economic and Social Council ask the ILO to undertake a comprehensive survey of the extent of forced labor in all Member states of the United Nations and to suggest positive measures, including a revised convention and measures for its implementation, for eliminating forced labor. The item "Survey of Forced Labor and Measures for its Abolition," was placed on the agenda of the next session of the Council. However, the Council postponed consideration of the item at both of its sessions in 1948.

In February 1949, the Council began the first of a long series of debates on the problem of forced labor, involving some exceedingly vituperative exchanges between the Soviet Union and the Western powers. The United States proposed the establishment of a commission of inquiry to investigate the nature and scope of forced labor throughout the world. The Soviet Union, in one of the longest and most propagandistic draft resolutions in the annals of the United Nations, proposed the creation of a commission composed of the representatives of national and international trade union federations, on the basis of one representative for every million trade union workers, making a total of 110 to 125 representatives. The overwhelming majority of these representatives, by Soviet statistics, would have been drawn from Communist unions. The Council rejected the Soviet resolution, and adopted a revised version of the one proposed by the United States. The resolution requested the Secretary-General to co-operate closely with the ILO and "to approach all Governments and to enquire in what manner and to what extent they would be prepared to co-operate in an impartial inquiry into the extent of forced labor in their countries, including the reasons for which persons are made to perform forced labor and the treatment accorded them."[19]

Six months later, when the Council met at its summer session, only twenty-six Members had made substantive replies to the Secretary-General's inquiry, of which twenty stated that they were prepared to co-operate in an impartial survey. The Soviet Government merely endorsed the proposals it had made at the previous session. In the meantime, the Governing Body of the ILO in June had recognized forced labor as a "matter of grave and widespread concern" and offered its close co-operation with the United Nations in an impartial inquiry.[20] After another bitter debate, in which the Soviet Union again introduced its proposal for a large commission, the Council merely requested the Secretary-General to make a further inquiry of governments concerning their willingness to co-operate in a survey.

The year 1950 also went by without any definitive action being taken on the subject of forced labor. The Council postponed the item at its winter session and held an inconclusive debate at its summer session. At the latter, the United Kingdom and United States delegations introduced a draft resolution proposing that the Council invite the ILO to participate in the establishment of an *ad hoc* committee of inquiry. By this time thirty-one Member states and six states not Members had indicated their willingness to co-operate in an impartial inquiry; but the Soviet Union stood fast on its earlier proposal. As many members of the Council had misgivings about the creation of such a committee in the face of Soviet opposition, for fear that it might prove ineffective, the Council again deferred a decision.

It was not until February 1951 that the Council finally came to grips with the problem of forced labor. At the winter session, the United States and the United Kingdom once again charged the Soviet Union with maintaining an inhuman system of forced labor in territories under its control; and they—as well as the International Confederation of Free Trade Unions—introduced persuasive documentary evidence to this effect. The Council adopted their

[19] Res. 195 (VIII), Mar. 7, 1949.
[20] International Labour Organisation, Governing Body, *Minutes of the 109th Session* (June-July 1949), p. 148.

resolution by a vote of 15 to 3 (Soviet bloc) and then defeated the Soviet proposal by the same vote. In the resolution the Council stated that it was deeply moved "by the documents and evidence brought to its knowledge and revealing in law and in fact the existence in the world of systems of forced labour under which a large proportion of the populations of certain states are subjected to a penitentiary régime."[21] The resolution provided that the United Nations and the ILO establish an *ad hoc* committee of not more than five independent members, to be appointed jointly by the heads of the two organizations. It defined the terms of reference of the committee very precisely:

> To study the nature and extent of the problem raised by the existence in the world of systems of forced or "corrective" labour, which are employed as a means of political coercion or punishment for holding or expressing political views, and which are on such a scale as to constitute an important element in the economy of a given country, by examining the text of laws and regulations and their application in the light of the principles referred to above, and if the Committee thinks fit, by taking additional evidence into consideration.[22]

The Secretary-General and the Director-General of the International Labour Office appointed three distinguished persons to the committee: Sir Ramaswami Mudaliar of India; Justice Paul Berg, former President of the Supreme Court of Norway; and Enrique Garcia Sayan, former Minister for Foreign Affairs of Peru.[23] The committee held four sessions during 1951-53. It transmitted a questionnaire to all governments, whether or not Members of the United Nations and of the ILO. It received replies from forty-eight governments, but no reply from thirty-three others, including those of the Soviet bloc. The committee also made elaborate arrangements for receiving documentation—and, in some cases, oral statements—from nongovernmental organizations and individuals. After a preliminary examination of the information received, the committee decided to confine its study primarily to twenty-four of the countries, or territories under their administration, against which allegations had been made in the Council or subsequently. It communicated the allegations and related documentary material to the twenty-four

[21] Res. 350 (XII), Mar. 19, 1951.
[22] *Ibid.*
[23] Sayan replaced Felix Fulgencio Palavicini of Mexico, who died between the first and second sessions.

governments concerned, and received comments and observations from ten of them.[24]

The result of these intensive labors was an impressive report of 621 pages, remarkable for the volume of its factual material, the thoroughness of its analysis, and the objectivity of its conclusions. The committee concluded that direct or indirect forms of forced labor exist in a number of areas, and that legislation or administrative provisions might permit it to exist in others. It reached a far more sweeping condemnation of conditions in the Soviet Union and, to a lesser degree, of all its satellites:

. . . Soviet penal legislation . . . constitutes the basis of a system of forced labour employed as a means of political coercion or punishment for holding or expressing political views and it is evident from the many testimonies examined by the Committee that this legislation is in fact employed in such a way.

Persons sentenced to deprivation of liberty by a court of law or by an administrative authority, particularly political offenders, are for the most part employed in corrective labour camps or colonies on large-scale projects, on the development of mining areas or previously uncultivated regions, or on other activities of benefit to the community, and the system therefore seems to play a part of some significance in the national economy. . . .

Soviet legislation makes provision for various measures which involve a compulsion to work or place restrictions on the freedom of employment; these measures seem to be applied on a large scale in the interests of the national economy and, considered as a whole, they lead, in the Committee's view, to a system of forced or compulsory labour constituting an important element in the economy of the country.[25]

In June 1953, the Economic and Social Council deferred consideration of the report until its next session. Its reasons were ostensibly technical: the huge report had been circulated (in English

[24] A Soviet bureaucrat in either Moscow or New York provided, unintentionally, the only element of humor in this unhappy story. The Secretary-General's communication was returned with a letter which read as follows: "The Delegation of the Union of Soviet Socialist Republics to the United Nations presents its compliments to the United Nations Secretariat and herewith returns, *unexamined,* the documents attached to the Secretariat's letter of 22 November 1952, *since these documents contain slanderous fabrications concerning the Soviet Union.*" (Italics supplied.) U. N. Economic and Social Council, Sixteenth Session, *Official Records,* "Report of the *Ad Hoc* Committee on Forced Labour," Supplement No. 13 (1953); Doc. 36 in the Studies and Reports (New Series) of the International Labour Office, p. 519.

[25] U. N. Economic and Social Council, Sixteenth Session, *Official Records,* "Report of the *Ad Hoc* Committee on Forced Labour," Supplement No. 13 (1953), p. 98.

and French, but not in Spanish) only one week before the session opened with an already heavy agenda. Political motivations, however, were also present; for the United Kingdom, French, and other delegations preferred to avoid any unnecessary controversy with the Soviet Union, especially as the death of Stalin a few months previously had aroused hope in some quarters for more moderate Soviet policies. In the absence of any action by the Council, the United States Government later in the summer requested the inclusion of an item "Evidence of the Existence of Forced Labor" on the agenda of the eighth session of the General Assembly.

The debates in the Assembly on forced labor in the autumn of 1953 centered on the report of the *ad hoc* committee. The United States and other delegations quoted from the report to demonstrate the truth of their previous charges that forced labor existed in the Soviet Union, and urged the new regime there to co-operate with the committee. The Soviet delegation attacked the personal integrity of Sir Ramaswami Mudaliar and Justice Paul Berg, denied the existence of forced labor, and charged that forced labor could be found on a vast scale in the United States. Australia, Brazil, Chile, Costa Rica, Cuba, Greece, Pakistan, the United Kingdom, and the United States co-sponsored a draft resolution that, to win maximum support in the Assembly, did not condemn any state by name, but stated that "systems of forced labour constitute a serious threat to fundamental human rights and jeopardize the freedom and status of workers in contravention of the obligations and provisions of the Charter of the United Nations."[26] The resolution invited the Economic and Social Council and the ILO "as a matter of urgency," to give early consideration to the report. It also requested the Secretary-General to consult with governments that had not yet found it possible to provide information to the committee. This resolution was adopted by a vote of 39 in favor, 5 (the Soviet bloc) against, with 12 abstentions.

In the Economic and Social Council, which considered the report in the spring of 1954, there was no enthusiasm for continuing the *ad hoc* committee. The Council adopted a resolution that commended the *ad hoc* committee for its work and requested the Secretary-General and the Director-General of the International Labour Office to prepare jointly a report setting out whatever replies were received in response to the resolution of the Assembly and any

[26] Res. 740(VIII), Dec. 7, 1953.

new information on systems of forced labor submitted by Member states, specialized agencies, and nongovernmental organizations.[27]

The report of the *ad hoc* committee and the debates in the United Nations and the ILO have served to focus world-wide attention on one of the most shocking violations of human rights in the modern world. Indeed, the Soviet system of forced labor is more vicious than the remnants of slavery that still remain in the more backward areas of the world. The former represents a wholesale enslavement of millions of persons because of the deliberate policy of governments; the latter, the retail enslavement of persons because of the inability or unwillingness of governments to enforce their own laws against individual offenders.

The work of United Nations organs to condemn and expose forced labor has helped to promote human rights in accordance with the Charter; and the resolutions directed at systems of forced labor and not at specific countries would not appear to violate Article 2(7) on domestic jurisdiction. However, the fact that all the debates have seemed to be a "cold war" operation on the part of the great powers has seriously limited the appeal of this subject to the Near Eastern and Asian Members, and to some extent the Latin Americans. These states have come to regard forced labor as a subject that does not concern them (even though it may exist in their territories), and to remain aloof from the propaganda duels of the great powers. The result has been to isolate forced labor, so far as a large part of the United Nations is concerned, from the field of human rights as a whole. Future progress may well depend, therefore, on whether the United Nations will consider the question of forced labor within the general framework of human rights and whether the ILO, where the technical aspects of the subject can be explored more fully, will continue on a regular basis to collect and discuss information about forced labor throughout the world.

Trade Union Rights

Another area of human rights in which international concern has developed rapidly since the Second World War has been that of freedom of association, which in this period has related largely to

[27] In December 1954, the General Assembly expressed satisfaction with the action taken by the Council and requested the Council and the International Labour Organisation to continue their efforts toward the abolition of systems of forced labor.

trade union rights. In March 1947, both the pro-communist World Federation of Trade Unions and the pro-democratic American Federation of Labor submitted documents on trade union rights to the Economic and Social Council. Later in the year, this subject was considered in the United Nations by the Council, the Commission on Human Rights, and the General Assembly and in the ILO by the Governing Body and the International Labour Conference. By the end of 1948 trade union rights had been made the subject of an international convention and included in the Universal Declaration of Human Rights; and the United Nations and the ILO had started to develop joint machinery for safeguarding freedom of association.

The Convention on Freedom of Association and Protection of the Right to Organize gave international recognition, for the first time in history, to freedom of association for both workers and employers. Adopted by the International Labour Conference in July 1948, the convention defines the basic right as follows: "Workers and employers, without distinction whatsoever, shall have the right to establish and, subject only to the rules of the organisation concerned, to join organisations of their own choosing without previous authorisation."[28] Eight additional articles amplify this right and prescribe its exercise in detail. The convention contains no provisions for implementation of the right. In May 1949, the General Assembly expressed the "earnest hope" that governments would take prompt action for the early ratification of the convention. It has been ratified by seventeen countries.

The Universal Declaration of Human Rights, adopted in December 1948, included both the general principle of freedom of association, in Article 20, and the more specific right to join a trade union, in Article 23(4). The Draft Covenant on Civil and Political Rights contains similar provisions, together with provisions permitting certain necessary restrictions on the right of freedom of association. The covenant also makes reference in its Article 21 to the earlier convention of the ILO on this subject.[29]

After prolonged negotiations, the Economic and Social Council and the ILO established machinery in 1950 for the investigation of infringements of trade union rights in any state that is a Member of either the United Nations or the ILO. This machinery, as re-

[28] International Labour Office, *Official Bulletin*, Vol. 31 (Aug. 31, 1948), p. 2.
[29] See App. B.

vised later, provides for the creation by the Governing Body of the ILO of a Fact-Finding and Conciliation Commission on Freedom of Association. This commission, consisting of nine persons appointed by the Governing Body for their personal qualifications, is empowered to investigate the facts of any allegation made by a government, a trade union, or an employers' organization. However, the consent of the government concerned must be obtained by the Governing Body in the case of Members of the ILO, and by the Economic and Social Council in the case of states that are Members of the United Nations but not of the ILO. The Governing Body, because of the delicate political questions involved in handling these allegations, has created a small screening committee of nine of its members.

The creation of this machinery is significant in several respects. First, it constitutes the first standing international agency (outside the special fields of minorities, mandates, and the trusteeship system) ever empowered to examine allegations concerning violations of human rights. Second, this machinery has been created by the Economic and Social Council within the general framework of the Charter, and not as the result of a supplementary treaty. Indeed, it has not even received consideration and approval by the General Assembly. Third, this machinery has rarely provoked discussion of the question of domestic jurisdiction under Article 2(7) of the Charter. This is probably due both to the general recognition that low labor standards in one country tend to affect labor standards elsewhere, and to the provision that the consent of the government concerned must be obtained before an allegation is investigated. Fourth, the Economic and Social Council has relaxed its rigid restrictions on the handling of communications received by the United Nations, described earlier, in order that communications concerning trade union rights may be brought to the attention of the Council.

It is interesting that the two strongest supporters of these procedures—the United States and the United Kingdom—have been two of the strongest opponents of any implementation procedure in the draft covenants that permitted such a review of complaints from nongovernmental organizations and of any consideration by the Commission on Human Rights of communications from these organizations. In only this one aspect of human rights—perhaps because of the special interest of the trade unions in the subject and

the obvious advantage the procedure offered in the "cold war"—
have these two great powers deviated from their very rigid position
against the examination of communications.

From November 1951 to March 1954, the Governing Body of the
ILO and its screening committee completed preliminary action on
eighty-three cases. Of these, thirteen cases were dismissed without
being communicated to the governments concerned, in most instances because they were not substantiated by any evidence or
dealt with matters already considered in previous cases. Another
sixty-seven cases were, after an examination of the observations presented thereon by the governments concerned, dismissed as not
calling for further examination. In thirty-five of this group, however,
the Governing Body submitted observations or recommendations
to the government concerned. The remaining three cases were regarded as calling for further examination because the screening
committee had received no co-operation from the governments concerned—Czechoslovakia, Hungary, and Poland. In the case of Czechoslovakia, the Governing Body approved the finding of its screening
committee that the trade union organization established by the legislation at present in force in Czechoslovakia was contrary to the
principle of freedom of association.

During 1953-54, three important cases involving states not then
members of the ILO—Rumania, Spain, and the Soviet Union—arose
in which the governments concerned refused to co-operate with the
Economic and Social Council. In April 1954, the Council invited
both Rumania and Spain to reconsider their attitude and indicate
their willingness "to cooperate with the United Nations in its efforts
to safeguard trade union rights."[30] In July 1954, after the Soviet
Union had joined the ILO, the Council transferred to that organization the consideration of the allegations that the Council had previously been considering.

No case has yet gone to the Fact-Finding and Conciliation Commission of the ILO. This has resulted from two political factors:
the Soviet Union and its satellites, where the worst infringements
of trade union rights occur, refuse to co-operate; and the Governing Body and its screening committee are able to avoid a formal
investigation of the large number of cases by transmitting their
observations or recommendations to the governments concerned.
The refusal of the states of the Soviet bloc, as well as Spain, to

[30] Res. 523 (XVII), Apr. 29, 1954.

co-operate with others in the examination of these complaints demonstrates again the political difficulties inherent in any international system of promoting human rights.

Racial Discrimination in South Africa

The overriding importance of the issue of racial discrimination in contemporary affairs is nowhere more vividly illustrated than in the two items concerning the Union of South Africa that have been repeatedly debated in the General Assembly. The first, the status of the Indian population in South Africa, is one of the perennial items on the agenda of the Assembly; the second, the broader question of race relations in South Africa, has been on the agendas of the sessions since 1952.[31] Both items dramatize the political tensions involved in the human rights field; both highlight the basic issue under the Charter of the conflict between promotion of human rights and respect for the domestic jurisdiction of sovereign states.

Status of Indians in
South Africa

Only eight months after the Charter came into force, the Government of India asked the General Assembly to consider at its session in the autumn of 1946, the status of persons of Indian nationality or descent in the Union of South Africa. The debate at the session in 1946 was the first of a series of nine, for the question has been considered every year except in 1948.[32] Indeed, the Assembly on most occasions decided to place the item automatically on the provisional agenda of the next session.

In these debates, India and later Pakistan have charged that the Indian population in South Africa—numbering some 300,000—have suffered discrimination because of their race and were deprived of their essential political, economic, and social rights, in violation of the Charter and contrary to certain agreements concluded between the two governments in 1927 and 1932. This situation, it was

---

[31] The first item is commonly called "Indians in South Africa" because it refers to persons of Indian origin or descent in that country, even though many of them come from areas that now form part of Pakistan.

[32] The item was placed on the agenda of the first part (September-December 1948) of the third session but not discussed until the second part (April-May 1949). It was not considered at the fourth session (September-December 1949).

contended, impaired friendly relations between states and created tensions that might imperil international peace. To those charges, the Union of South Africa consistently replied that most of the persons concerned are its nationals and that, in any event, their status is a matter of proper concern to only the three states directly involved; that the Indian population is not mistreated; and that the whole subject is a matter of domestic jurisdiction under Article 2(7) of the Charter and therefore not a matter even for debate by the Assembly.

The resolution adopted at the session in 1953 contains a long preamble that summarizes the numerous actions taken by the General Assembly, in a steady crescendo, to bring pressure to bear on South Africa.[33] In summary, these have been:[34]

[33] Res. 719 (VIII), Nov. 11, 1953.
[34] Res. 44 (I), Dec. 8, 1946; Res. 265 (III), May 14, 1949; Res. 395 (V), Dec. 2, 1950; Res. 511 (VI), Jan. 12, 1952; Res. 615 (VII), Dec. 5, 1952.

The Good Offices Commission reported to the ninth session of the General Assembly in 1954 that, because of the unco-operative attitude of the Government of the Union of South Africa, it was unable to submit any proposal likely to lead to a peaceful settlement of the problem. The Assembly did not continue the commission; instead, it suggested to India, Pakistan, and South Africa that they seek a solution by direct negotiation and designate a government, agency, or person to facilitate, contacts between them and to assist them in settling the dispute. The Secretary-General was requested, if no agreement had been reached within six months concerning the designation of a "mediator," to designate a person for this purpose. This resolution was adopted by 45 in favor, 1 against, with 11 abstentions. Shortly thereafter, South Africa initiated preliminary consultations looking to resumption of direct negotiations but terminated them in April 1955 after Prime Minister Nehru of India delivered two speeches, one in Parliament, attacking South Africa.

In the absence of any agreement between the parties, the Secretary-General in June appointed Ambassador Luis de Faro, Jr. (Brazil) to serve as "mediator." Shortly thereafter, however, the Secretary-General received a letter from South Africa, which, after referring to the two speeches by Prime Minister Nehru, stated: "As far as the Union Government is concerned, the question of persons of Indian origin in the Union of South Africa must be regarded as definitely closed." (U.N. General Assembly, Tenth Session, Doc. A/3001/Add.1, Nov. 14, 1955, p. 3.) The South African Government declined to co-operate with Ambassador de Faro because this might prejudice its juridical position. Ambassador de Faro, after informal conversations with representatives of the three parties in New York, reported that there was nothing he could do to facilitate negotiations.

The Assembly later adopted an unusually brief resolution, which noted that the negotiations envisaged in the previous resolution had not been pursued, urged the parties to pursue negotiations, and requested the parties to report as appropriate, jointly or separately, to the next session. This was adopted by 43 to 0, with 8 abstentions; South Africa was absent because of its earlier withdrawal from the Assembly after the action taken in the *Ad Hoc* Political Committee with regard to the item on race relations in South Africa.

On four occasions, the Assembly has passed judgment on the substantive issue: in 1946, stating that the treatment of Indians in South Africa should be in conformity with agreements between the two governments and with relevant provisions of the Charter; in 1950 and 1951-52, declaring that a policy of "racial segregation" *(apartheid)* is necessarily based on doctrines of racial discrimination; and in 1953, expressing regret that the South African Government "is proceeding with further legislation contrary to the Charter and the Universal Declaration of Human Rights" and concluding that the actions of the South African Government "are not in keeping with its obligations and responsibilities under the Charter of the United Nations."

On five occasions, the Assembly has prescribed or re-prescribed measures for resolving the controversy: in 1946, requesting India and South Africa to report on measures taken to settle their dispute; in 1949, inviting India, Pakistan, and South Africa to enter into a round table conference; in 1950, recommending the establishment of a commission of three individuals, one nominated by South Africa, one by India and Pakistan, and a third by the other two members or, in default of an agreement, by the Secretary-General; in 1951-52, repeating the recommendation of 1950, and in the event of failure, requesting the Secretary-General or an individual appointed by him to render appropriate assistance; in 1952, establishing a Good Offices Commission of three states (Cuba, Syria, and Yugoslavia) appointed by the president of the Assembly to assist in negotiations; and in 1953, continuing the commission for another year and requesting it to report its own views on the problem and any proposals that might lead to a peaceful settlement.

On three occasions, the Assembly has directly or indirectly criticized South Africa for failure to co-operate: in 1951-52, 1952, and 1953, noting that South Africa has continued to implement its Group Areas Act, providing for segregation of the white and nonwhite populations, despite the request by the Assembly in 1950 to the contrary; and in 1953, regretting that South Africa has refused "to make use of the Commission's good offices or to utilize any of the alternative procedures for the settlement of the problem recommended by the four previous resolutions of the General Assembly."

The Union of South Africa, as the General Assembly concluded in 1953, has consistently refused to accept any of the measures put forward. South Africa, in particular, regarded the resolution by the

Assembly in 1952 as "unconstitutional" and refused to recognize the Good Offices Commission. The commission reported, therefore, that it had been unable to carry out its task. South Africa has repeatedly stated that it would negotiate with India and Pakistan outside the United Nations framework; and, in fact, it undertook preliminary talks in 1950 concerning an agenda for the proposed round table conference. South Africa—usually supported by Australia, Belgium, Greece, and the United Kingdom—has consistently contended that the General Assembly has no authority even to discuss this matter, much less to establish machinery for dealing with it. This challenge to the competence of the Assembly has been rejected in three different votes, with only a small minority agreeing with South Africa that the Assembly could not even discuss the matter.[35]

Few issues have so bitterly divided the General Assembly or so taxed the good will and ingenuity of the Member states favoring a middle-of-the-road approach. These Members—such as the United States and the Scandinavian States—wished neither to condone the racial policies of South Africa nor to condemn them in such extreme terms as to exacerbate the situation in South Africa and perhaps to drive that country out of the Organization. They preferred to avoid the issue of competence, to have the International Court decide the nature and extent of the international obligation involved in this case, to deal with the problem in as practical a manner as possible, to avoid a specific condemnation of South Africa, and to encourage direct negotiations among the three states concerned.

Because this subject was recognized from the outset as an "important matter" requiring a two-thirds majority, India and the Arab-Asian bloc were often prevented from obtaining adoption of their more extreme texts. For the same reason, the United States and others have failed to persuade the General Assembly to have the International Court determine the legal issues. In the session of 1947,

[35] Motions by South Africa that the General Assembly was not competent to consider the matter were defeated by votes of 5-33-12 in May 1949, and 6-45-8 during November 1952. A Syrian motion that the General Assembly was competent to do so was approved in November 1950 by 35-3-17. Toward the end of 1953, the South African representative proposed that the *Ad Hoc* Political Committee of the Assembly should decide that the committee had no competence to intervene, but this, together with a subsequent proposal along similar lines, was rejected by the Assembly in plenary meeting. U. N. General Assembly, Eighth Session, *Ad Hoc* Political Committee, *Official Records*, 42nd Meeting (Dec. 5, 1953), p. 228; U. N. General Assembly, Eighth Session, Plenary, *Official Records*, 469th Meeting (Dec. 8, 1953), p. 436.

the division of opinion was so sharp that three different resolutions failed to obtain a two-thirds majority, resulting in no action whatever; and in later sessions the Arab-Asian bloc found it necessary to eliminate many of the more provocative clauses from their proposals.

Race Relations in
South Africa

In September 1952, thirteen of the Near Eastern and Asian Members raised the issue of racial discrimination, and the Charter question involved in that issue, in an even more acute form. They asked that "the question of race conflict in South Africa resulting from the policies of *apartheid* of the Government of the Union of South Africa" be placed on the provisional agenda of the General Assembly. These Members declared that the race conflict in the Union was creating "a dangerous and explosive situation, which constitutes both a threat to international peace and a flagrant violation of the basic principles of human rights and fundamental freedoms which are enshrined in the Charter of the United Nations."[36]

During the session of the Assembly in 1952, this new item followed the same stormy path as the previous one on Indians in South Africa. The South African delegation denied that the United Nations, under Article 2(7) of the Charter, had any authority to deal with the matter; that Articles 55 and 56, relating to the promotion of respect for human rights, gave the General Assembly any jurisdiction; and that the situation constituted a threat to the peace. However, a South African motion that the Assembly was not competent to adopt proposals on the item was defeated by 6 in favor, 43 against, with 9 abstentions.

The division of opinion again was so sharp that, after long and bitter substantive debates and procedural wrangles, the Assembly ended by adopting two entirely different proposals with identical preambles. The first resolution—sponsored by eighteen Near Eastern, Asian, and Latin-American delegations—established a commission of three individuals to study the racial situation in South Africa. The second resolution—sponsored by Iceland, Denmark, Norway, and Sweden—omitted any specific reference to South Africa but

[36] U. N. General Assembly, Seventh Session, Doc. A/2183 (Sept. 15, 1952), pp. 1, 3.

condemned its laws and practices in unmistakable terms. It declared that:

> . . . in a multi-racial society harmony and respect for human rights and freedoms and the peaceful development of a unified community are best assured when patterns of legislation and practice are directed towards ensuring equality before the law of all persons regardless of race, creed or colour, and when economic, social, cultural and political participation of all racial groups is on a basis of equality.[37]

The deep split in the Assembly was apparent in the unusual votes: the first resolution was adopted by 35 to 1, with 23 abstentions; and the second by 24 to 1, with 34 abstentions.

The commission—composed of Hernán Santa Cruz (Chile), Henri Laugier (France), and Dantès Bellegarde (Haiti)—was completely boycotted by South Africa. Being prevented from visiting the Union of South Africa and communicating with its government, the commission based its report on published statements, legislation, and other secondary data. The report concluded that the racial policies of South Africa and their consequences are contrary to the Charter and the Universal Declaration of Human Rights.[38]

At the session of the General Assembly in 1953, the debate concerned the competence of the Assembly to consider the report rather than the substantive contents of it. Twice South Africa was defeated on motions concerning competence—first, in the *Ad Hoc* Political Committee by a vote of 7 in favor, 42 against, with 7 abstentions, on a motion that the committee had no right to intervene in the policies of a Member state in regard to such matters as land tenure, residency, immigration, social services, education, food subsidies, and local government; and, later, in the plenary by a vote of 8 in favor, 42 against, with 10 abstentions, on a motion that the General Assembly had no competence to adopt the draft resolution before it.[39] The Assembly ultimately adopted a sixteen-power resolution that continued the commission and requested it "to suggest measures

---

[37] Res. 616B (VII), Dec. 5, 1952.

[38] U. N. General Assembly, Eighth Session, *Report of the United Nations Commission on the Racial Situation in the Union of South Africa*, Doc. A/2505 (1953), p. 117. For the reports of the commission to the ninth and tenth sessions of the General Assembly, see Docs. A/2719 (1954) and A/2953 (1955).

[39] The negative votes were cast in the *Ad Hoc* Political Committee by Australia, Belgium, Colombia, France, Greece, the Union of South Africa, and the United Kingdom; in the plenary, by the same Members and Luxemburg.

which would help to alleviate the situation and promote a peaceful settlement."[40]

The debates in 1953 brought to a climax the developing controversy over the powers of the United Nations to "intervene in matters . . . essentially within the domestic jurisdiction" of a Member. The speeches of the Indian delegation, on the one hand, presented a broad interpretation of Articles 55 and 56 relating to the obligation of the Organization and its Members to promote respect for human rights. The speeches of the South African delegation, on the other hand, presented a limiting interpretation of Article 2(7), by taking the position that the General Assembly could not even discuss the subject of race relations in South Africa.

The United States, the Scandinavian states, and others took stands between these two positions. They maintained that, under Article 10, the General Assembly had the power to discuss these subjects and to adopt certain types of resolutions; but they urged the Assembly to confine itself to action that might have some practical results. At the same time, the United States declared it had observed with increasing concern the tendency of the Assembly to place on its agenda subjects the international character of which was doubtful, and that it believed the problem deserved most careful consideration by all Members in preparing for any conference on review of the Charter. During the debate in the committee, the United States

[40] Res. 721(VII), Dec. 8, 1953. At its ninth session in 1954, the General Assembly invited the Government of the Union of South Africa to reconsider its position and to take into consideration the suggestion of the commission for a peaceful settlement of the racial problem, and it requested the commission to keep the problem under review. The vote was 40 to 10, with 10 abstentions.

When the *Ad Hoc* Political Committee began consideration of this item at the tenth session in 1955, the South African delegation withdrew from the discussion, which it regarded in violation of Article 2(7), but reserved its right to take part in the vote on any draft resolution. The committee adopted a seventeen-power draft resolution, which, among other things, again requested the commission to keep the situation under review. The Union of South Africa immediately withdrew its entire delegation and its permanent representative to the United Nations for the duration of the session. In the plenary, however, the four paragraphs continuing the commission were eliminated from the resolution after the first of them failed—by a vote of 33 to 17, with 9 abstentions—to obtain the necessary two-thirds majority. A Costa Rican amendment, placing the item on the agenda of the eleventh session, also fell short—by a vote of 27 to 15, with 15 abstentions—of a two-thirds majority. The greatly abbreviated text was then adopted by a vote of 41 to 6, with 8 abstentions.

Thus, after four years of controversial debate, the General Assembly decided, in effect, that it was no longer seized of this item.

stated its opposition to addressing a recommendation to only one Member and to expressing regret over domestic legislation, and it abstained in the vote. Thus the United States appeared to return to the more cautious position of the earlier years: in 1946 and 1947, the United States voted against the Indian draft resolutions; later, it voted for most of the proposals on this subject; but in 1952 and 1953 it abstained on the more extreme resolutions on race relations.

The division between those favoring a "broad construction" of the Charter and those favoring a "strict construction" on the subject of race relations was revealed in 1953 in the vote of 38 in favor, 11 against, and 11 abstentions: the Near Eastern and Asian groups, the Soviet bloc, and most of the Latin-American States in favor; and the United States, the older members of the British Commonwealth, Western Europe (except Iceland), and several Latin-American States (Argentina, Colombia, the Dominican Republic, Panama, Peru, and Venezuela) against or abstaining.

Effect of United Nations Action

The impact on the Union of South Africa of these discussions in the United Nations is difficult to assess.[41]

On the one hand, the strong language of the Indian, Pakistani, and other delegations during the annual debate on the status of Indians has given ammunition to the leadership and press of that group in South Africa. Similarly, the debate on race relations during the past two years may have strengthened the efforts of certain Bantu, Indian, and Colored leaders to bring their organizations into a common front and may have encouraged the more moderate elements among them. On the other hand, the United Nations action may have antagonized the white population, embittered the National party leaders, and increased support for Prime Minister D. F. Malan from other sectors of the white population that have disagreed with some of his extreme measures.[42] Prime Minister Malan in May 1954, during a debate on foreign affairs in the South African Parliament,

[41] This appraisal is based in part on "The Impact of the United Nations on Africa," by Vernon McKay in Africa Today, ed. by C. Grove Haines (1955), pp. 366-85.

[42] In the election of 1953, the Nationalists were returned to power with greater strength than before. In 1954, J. G. Strydom, representing the more extreme wing, was chosen by the National party, over the more moderate N. C. Havenga, to succeed Prime Minister Malan.

while acknowledging the need of the world for an international organization, severely criticized the United Nations for stirring up unrest in Africa by giving backward peoples the idea that they were oppressed. On an earlier occasion, addressing a congress of his own Nationalist followers, he called the United Nations a failure and a cancer gnawing at world peace and tranquillity.

Perhaps it may be tentatively concluded, on the one hand, that the United Nations could not have ignored the existence of racial discrimination in the Union of South Africa and, in particular, the determination of the government to increase rather than decrease that discrimination. For the United Nations to overlook this situation entirely, while frequently debating the violations of human rights in the Soviet Union and its satellites, would have implied that the Organization was motivated more by considerations of "cold war" than those of humanitarian purposes and that the policies of the South African Government were condoned by the international community. Moreover, the fact that the South African Government has refused to submit a trusteeship agreement for the mandated territory of South West Africa may have increased the desire of a number of others to criticize and embarrass South Africa in United Nations forums.

On the other hand, the highly emotional character of the annual debates in the Assembly on South Africa and the adoption of condemnatory recommendations directed at a single Member, in possible contravention of Article 2(7) of the Charter, have proved to be unhelpful and possibly harmful. Most of the resolutions by the Assembly provide that the subject should automatically be on the agenda of the following session. This has helped lead to constant repetition of charges and countercharges and to an increasing sense of disillusionment and frustration. Whatever may have been the original value of turning the international spotlight on the violation of human rights in a single country, it would seem that the law of diminishing returns has begun to have its adverse effect, on both the United Nations and the Union of South Africa.

Violation of Human Rights in Bulgaria, Hungary, and Rumania

By the time of the First World War the right to worship according to the dictates of one's conscience had been secured throughout a large part of the world. In fact, the establishment of religious toleration had been considered one of the outstanding achievements of modern times. However, the postwar rise of communism and later of nazism brought into being a new era of religious persecutions that were equally ruthless and, because of the perfection of the police state in the twentieth century, even more efficient than any known in the past.

After the Second World War, three of the former enemy states—Bulgaria, Hungary, and Rumania—undertook in the peace treaties of 1947 to secure to all persons under their jurisdiction "without distinction as to race, sex, language or religion, the enjoyment of human rights and of fundamental freedoms, including freedom of expression, of press and publication, of religious worship, of public opinion and of public meeting."[43] The peace treaties contained complicated machinery for resolving any dispute over their interpretation or application. If direct negotiations failed, the dispute would be referred to the three heads of mission of the Soviet Union, the United Kingdom, and the United States in Bulgaria, Hungary, or Rumania, as the case might be. If the three heads of mission failed to settle the dispute, it would be referred to a commission composed of one representative of each party and a third member selected by agreement of the parties. In the absence of such agreement, the Secretary-General of the United Nations would appoint the third member at the request of either party.

In early 1949, world public opinion was shocked by the imprisonment and trial of Cardinal Mindszenty in Hungary and of Protestant churchmen in Bulgaria, and by the equally systematic but less dramatic suppression of religious liberty in Rumania. The United States and the United Kingdom, charging the three states with violation of the peace treaties, set in motion the machinery for settling the dispute. In March 1949, Australia and Bolivia asked the General Assembly to consider the violation of human rights in Bulgaria and Hungary. The Soviet Union and its satellites contended that consideration of this subject was precluded by both Article 2(7) of the Charter, concerning domestic jurisdiction, and Article 107, relating to action taken against former enemies. Australia, whose spokesman in the United Nations at that time was president of the Assembly, contended that these articles did not apply because another pro-

[43] U. S. Department of State, *Treaties of Peace with Italy, Bulgaria, Hungary, Roumania, and Finland,* Publication 2743 (1947).

vision of the Charter (Article 55) had not been observed and because Article 10 permitted discussion of any question or problem within the scope of the Charter.[44] The inclusion of this item on the agenda was by a relatively small vote, 30 to 7, with 20 abstentions, the unusual number of abstentions indicating a notable lack of enthusiasm on the part of many Members.

Many delegations took the position during the debate that the Assembly should not investigate the alleged violations of human rights for the present, in view of the fact that the parties to the peace treaties had already begun direct negotiations. The Assembly accordingly adopted a relatively brief resolution that expressed "its deep concern at the grave accusations made against the Governments of Bulgaria and Hungary," drew the attention of those governments to their obligations under the peace treaties, and retained the question on the agenda of the next session.[45] The vote was 34 in favor and 6 against, with 9 abstentions. All but one (Venezuela) of the abstentions came from the Near Eastern and Asian Members.

By the time the General Assembly convened in September 1949, the peace treaty machinery had become hopelessly stalled. Bulgaria, Hungary, and Rumania, as well as the Soviet Union, took the position that, as no violation of the treaties had occurred, no dispute had arisen to require settlement by either the heads of mission or a commission. A draft resolution was therefore introduced by Bolivia, Canada, and the United States requesting an advisory opinion from the International Court of Justice concerning the legal aspects of the case. After a long and bitter debate, the Assembly, by a vote of 47 to 5, with 7 abstentions, adopted a resolution submitting four questions to the Court.[46]

[44] Dr. Herbert Vere Evatt, presiding over the General Committee of the Assembly but speaking as representative of Australia, went on to take an unusually "broad construction" of the Charter: "If any question could be covered by an Article of the Charter, that question could no longer be held to be a matter essentially within domestic jurisdiction of a State." U. N. General Assembly, Third Session, Second Part, General Committee, *Official Records,* 58th Meeting (Apr. 6, 1949), pp. 15-16. It is of interest that Australia, under the Labour Government in which Dr. Evatt was Minister of External Affairs, often took a "broad construction" of the Charter, as in this debate, in its proposal for an International Court of Human Rights, and in matters relating to trust and non-self-governing territories; whereas since 1950, under the conservative coalition headed by Prime Minister Robert Gordon Menzies, Australia has consistently taken a "strict construction" of the Charter in these matters.

[45] Res. 272 (III), Apr. 30, 1949.

[46] Res. 294(IV), Oct. 22, 1949.

The first question was whether the diplomatic exchanges between the parties to the treaties disclosed disputes subject to the provisions for the settlement of disputes. In the event of an affirmative answer, the Court was then asked whether Bulgaria, Hungary, and Rumania were obligated to appoint representatives to the commission to settle the dispute. In the event of an affirmative answer to the second question and if the three governments failed to appoint their representatives, the Court was asked whether the Secretary-General was authorized to appoint the third member of the commission upon the request of the other party to the dispute. Finally, in the event of an affirmative answer to the third question, the Court was asked whether a commission composed of only the representatives of one party and the third member appointed by the Secretary-General was competent to make a definitive and binding decision.

The Court gave its answers to the first two questions in March 1950.[47] With regard to the first, the Court gave the opinion that, inasmuch as certain parties to the treaties had charged violations that other parties denied, this constituted a dispute within the meaning of the treaties. With regard to the second, the Court advised that Bulgaria, Hungary, and Rumania were obligated to carry out the provisions concerning the settlement of disputes, including the obligation to appoint their representatives to the commissions. After the three states failed to appoint their three representatives, the Court proceeded in July 1950 to render its opinion on the third question.[48] The Court this time gave a negative answer: if one party failed to appoint a representative, the Secretary-General was not authorized to appoint the third member on the request of the other party. The refusal to appoint commissioners, the Court concluded, made it impossible to constitute a valid commission. In view of its negative answer to the third question, the Court did not consider it necessary to answer the fourth question.

The General Assembly, at its session in 1950, once again considered the matter. After debating both its competence and the substance of the charges against the three states, the Assembly adopted, by a vote of 40 to 5, with 12 abstentions, its last resolution on this

[47] International Court of Justice, "Interpretation of Peace Treaties with Bulgaria, Hungary and Rumania," Advisory Opinion, Mar. 30, 1950, *I. C. J. Reports, 1950.*

[48] International Court of Justice, "Interpretation of Peace Treaties with Bulgaria, Hungary and Rumania (Second Phase)," Advisory Opinion, July 18, 1950, *I. C. J. Reports, 1950.*

subject. The resolution of the Assembly constitutes one of the most unequivocal condemnations of a state ever made by an international organization. In the three principal paragraphs of this condemnation, the Assembly stated that it:

> *Condemns* the wilful refusal of the Governments of Bulgaria, Hungary and Romania to fulfill their obligation under the provisions of the Treaties of Peace to appoint representatives to the Treaty Commissions, which obligation has been confirmed by the International Court of Justice;
>
> *Is of the opinion* that the conduct of the Governments of Bulgaria, Hungary and Romania in this matter is such as to indicate that they are aware of breaches being committed of those articles of the Treaties of Peace under which they are obligated to secure the enjoyment of human rights and fundamental freedoms in their countries; and that they are callously indifferent to the sentiments of the world community;
>
> *Notes* with anxiety the continuance of serious accusations on these matters against the Governments of Bulgaria, Hungary and Romania, and that the three Governments have made no satisfactory refutation of these accusations.[49]

The Assembly also invited Members of the United Nations, and in particular those that are parties to the peace treaties, to submit to the Secretary-General all evidence they held or that might become available in the future in relation to this question. The United States, in November 1951, submitted a large volume of evidence concerning the violation of human rights in Rumania; and the United Kingdom, one year later, submitted material on all three countries. No other Members, however, have responded to this request of the General Assembly.

This action by the Assembly, like the action taken on the charges against the Union of South Africa, demonstrates the political significance of the problem of human rights. These cases have all been considered by the political committees of the General Assembly, and not by its Third (Social, Humanitarian, and Cultural) Committee; nor have the Economic and Social Council and the Commission on Human Rights been asked to deal with the matters. They have been regarded as political disputes of the highest importance; yet they involve, like all other aspects of human rights considered by various organs of the United Nations, the rights of the individual.

The question of the competence of the General Assembly, with respect to Article 2(7) of the Charter, to consider this issue and to adopt a condemnatory resolution was somewhat blurred by the fact

[49] Res. 385 (V), Nov. 3, 1950.

that the peace treaties as well as the Charter were involved. The International Court of Justice was asked for an interpretation of the peace treaties, not of the Charter. It is noteworthy, however, that the *Ad Hoc* Political Committee of the Assembly twice rejected proposals that a committee of government representatives be established to study the situation in these countries of Eastern Europe.[50]

The position taken by the great powers on this subject had certain political overtones. The Soviet Union, which consistently voted that the General Assembly was competent to consider the items relating to South Africa, insisted that the Assembly was precluded by Article 2(7) from considering the alleged violation of human rights by its satellites. The United Kingdom, which has frequently voted that the Assembly could not consider the South African items, supported the competence of the Assembly in this case, on the ground that treaty obligations were involved.

The United States, which several years later began to be concerned about the excessive zeal of the Assembly in dealing with race relations in South Africa, took a categorical position, that, quite apart from the peace treaties, the Assembly was fully competent not only to discuss but also to adopt recommendations concerning the situation in Bulgaria, Hungary, and Rumania as a violation of the Charter, regardless of the restriction contained in Article 2(7). The position of the United States, which represented a very "broad construction" of the Charter, was reported in the summary record of the committee meeting to have been as follows:

Under Articles 55 and 56 of the Charter the field of human rights had been brought expressly within the scope of the Charter, and the General Assembly could exercise authority in this field under Articles 10 and 14. Article 2, paragraph 7 of the Charter regarding non-intervention in matters of domestic jurisdiction, was not intended to preclude, in appropriate cases, discussion in the Assembly on the promotion of human rights and fundamental freedoms. Nor was the Assembly barred, under appropriate circumstances, from expressing an opinion or making a recommendation when there was a persistent and wilful disregard for human rights in any particular country. Moreover, in determining the applicability of Article

[50] In April 1949, an amendment proposed by Australia and Cuba was defeated by 4 (Australia, Cuba, Lebanon, New Zealand)-30-18. In October 1949, a similar amendment proposed by Australia was defeated by 5 (Argentina, Australia, Lebanon, New Zealand, Uruguay)-29-22. Some of the opponents, such as the United States, preferred to complete the procedures under the peace treaties before undertaking a new approach; others, such as France, questioned the competence of the General Assembly, under Article 2(7), to take action.

2, paragraph 7, account had to be taken of the important fact that in the case under discussion, Bulgaria and Hungary had assumed in the peace treaties special obligations under international law to secure human rights and fundamental freedoms to all persons under their jurisdiction.[51]

Prisoners of War of the Second World War

"Of all the problems to come before this [Third] Committee—or, before the whole General Assembly," Governor James F. Byrnes told the session in 1953, "the failure of some Governments to repatriate the prisoners of war of World War II is one of the most tragic. Here is indeed a shocking example of 'man's inhumanity to man.' "[52] This is an accurate statement of one of the most callously deliberate violations of human rights in a century that is notable for such violations. The end of the Second World War left millions of prisoners, on all fronts, in the hands of the victors; but within a year or two, most of them had been either repatriated or otherwise accounted for. The Soviet Union and its satellites, however, had failed to repatriate or otherwise account for some hundreds of thousands of Germans, Japanese, Italians, and others whom they held. These prisoners simply vanished from the earth and, with some exceptions, their families and friends were left in heartbreaking ignorance of their fate.

For five years, the Western powers tried through diplomatic channels and through the control councils for Germany and Japan to persuade the Soviet Union to make some accounting for these missing prisoners. Undoubtedly, many of them had died; and the records of others were probably lost or destroyed. Yet any satisfactory accounting would have done much to meet the requirements of international practice and interests of the governments and the families concerned. In 1950, however, the Soviet Union announced, through its press agency, that with respect to German and Japanese prisoners, all but a few thousands of "war criminals" and seriously ill had been repatriated. This announcement provoked a storm of indignation in Germany and Japan, because first-hand accounts and even letters from the missing prisoners showed that a far larger number were still alive in Soviet custody.

[51] U. N. General Assembly, Third Session, Second Part, *Ad Hoc* Political Committee, *Official Records*, 35th Meeting (Apr. 19, 1949), p. 89.
[52] U. S. Delegation to the General Assembly, "Statement in the Third (Social, Humanitarian, and Cultural) Committee," Press Release 1842 (Dec. 1, 1953).

The governments of Australia, the United Kingdom, and the United States, having exhausted every other channel, asked the General Assembly to consider this problem in 1950. During the debates in the Assembly, they proposed the establishment of an impartial three-man commission to make an investigation concerning the situation with respect to prisoners of war of the Second World War. The Soviet Union, denying that it held any but the few "war criminals" and seriously ill, asserted that it was the United States, the United Kingdom, France, and others that were detaining large numbers of prisoners. It maintained that, in any case, Article 107 of the Charter prevented the United Nations from taking action in a matter that related to the enemy states of the war. The Indian and Iraqi delegations, reflecting the attitude of the Near Eastern and many of the Asian countries, proposed that the International Red Cross should make the investigation rather than the United Nations. The matter was referred to the International Committee of the Red Cross, which replied that it would undertake such a responsibility only if requested to do so by all the parties concerned.

As a result of this debate, the Assembly adopted a resolution expressing its concern "at the information presented to it tending to show that large numbers of prisoners taken in the course of the Second World War have neither been repatriated nor otherwise accounted for."[53] The resolution called on all governments having control of such persons to act in conformity with the recognized standards of international conduct and with the Geneva Convention of 1949 and the specific agreements between the Allied Powers; and to transmit to the Secretary-General full information about prisoners who were still held by them or who died while under their control.

It also established an *Ad Hoc* Commission on Prisoners of War to settle the question "in a purely humanitarian spirit and on terms acceptable to all the governments concerned." The commission was to be composed of three qualified and impartial persons chosen by the International Red Cross or, failing that, by the Secretary-General. After the International Committee of the Red Cross declined to select the members of the commission, the Secretary-General appointed them.[54]

[53] Res. 427(V), Dec. 14, 1950. The vote was 43 in favor, 5 (Soviet bloc) against, with 6 abstentions (including India, Iraq, and Venezuela).
[54] The following persons were appointed: J. G. Guerrero (El Salvador), Vice-President of the International Court of Justice, who was elected chairman and *rapporteur;* Countess Bernadotte (Sweden), widow of the late United Nations Mediator for Palestine; and U Aung Khine, Judge of the High Court of Burma.

The commission held six sessions during 1951-54, most of the meetings being private. In its report to the General Assembly in 1953, the commission emphasized that it had "scrupulously avoided the slightest gesture which might be given a political significance" and that it had "several times refused invitations to go to Japan and the Federal Republic of Germany in order to obtain information on the spot."[55] The commission requested information from the governments of eighty states, including both Members and states not Members of the Organization, and sought additional facts from many of them. Of the governments that replied, twenty-five indicated that at one time or another they had held prisoners of the Second World War in their custody. Of these, fourteen indicated that at the time of the establishment of the commission, they had completed the repatriation of all prisoners of war formerly in their custody. The commission reached the following conclusions:

> In sectors where the full co-operation of governments has been given, the problem of prisoners of war no longer exists.
> In sectors where that co-operation has been withheld, the problem remains in its entirety.[56]

After noting that it had received no official information from the Soviet Union, Communist China, Albania, Bulgaria, Czechoslovakia, Hungary, Poland, and Rumania and after stressing the complete refusal of the Soviet Union to respond in any way, the commission stated that it considered it its duty "to draw the attention of the General Assembly to the main obstacle through which its best efforts have been frustrated."[57]

By the time the General Assembly met in September 1953, Communist China, although ignoring the commission, had repatriated some 23,000 Japanese nationals, and there were news reports that the Malenkov regime in the Soviet Union was beginning to release small numbers of German and Japanese "war criminals." Most of the speakers in the Third Committee—including the representatives of Germany, Italy, and Japan, who were granted permission to state their views—voiced appreciation for the recent progress, however small, but expressed regret that the Soviet Union continued to refuse to collaborate in the humanitarian work of the commission.

[55] U. N. General Assembly, Eighth Session, *Progress Report to the Secretary-General on the Work of the Ad Hoc Commission on Prisoners of War*, Doc. A/2482 (Sept. 18, 1953), p. 8.
[56] *Ibid*, p. 24.
[57] *Ibid.*, p. 23.

The Assembly ultimately adopted, by a vote of 46 to 5, with 6 abstentions, a resolution sponsored by Australia, Brazil, Thailand, the United Kingdom, and the United States. The opening paragraph of the resolution, inserted as an amendment by Iraq, noted with satisfaction that some progress had taken place during the previous two years and expressed the hope "that those governments and Red Cross Societies which have contributed to that progress will continue their efforts."[58] The Assembly then reiterated "its grave and continuing concern at the evidence that large numbers of prisoners taken in the course of the Second World War have not yet been repatriated or otherwise accounted for." The Assembly, paraphrasing the conclusions of the *ad hoc* commission, also noted with concern "that certain governments and authorities mentioned in the report of the Commission have so far refused to co-operate with the Commission, which refusal represents the main obstacle by which the best efforts of the Commission have been frustrated." It requested the *ad hoc* commission to continue its work and urgently appealed to all governments and authorities that had not yet done so to co-operate with it.

The resolutions of both 1950 and 1953 contained, in almost identical paragraphs, a phrase that reflects a general principle of great significance in other activities of the United Nations. In these two paragraphs, the Assembly appealed to governments and authorities still having control of prisoners of war to act in conformity with the recognized standards of international conduct and with the general and specific agreements cited in the resolution "which require that, upon the cessation of active hostilities, all prisoners should, with the least possible delay, be given *an unrestricted opportunity of repatriation.*"[59] This phrase makes clear that prisoners of war are not to be forced to return to their homeland against their will, but are merely to be given full opportunity to do so. The Western powers have insisted on this principle in such matters as the treatment of refugees and in the treatment of prisoners of war in Korea, while the Soviet Union has demanded that every refugee and prisoner of war be compelled to return to his homeland. The United Nations has unequivocally upheld the concept of freedom of choice whenever the question has arisen.

During 1954, considerable progress was made in the repatriation

[58] Res. 741(VIII), Dec. 7, 1953.
[59] Res. 427(V), Dec. 14, 1950 and Res. 741(VIII), Dec. 7, 1953. Italics supplied.

of prisoners of war. At its fifth session, held during March and April 1954, the *ad hoc* commission issued a declaration, to be distributed to all governments, that began with the following statement:

It is time to end this problem—the problem of prisoners of war still unrepatriated or still unaccounted for. The Commission believes that this problem is not intrinsically insoluble. In fact, of all post-war problems, it perhaps lends itself most readily to peaceful solution. Recent actions have appreciably reduced its proportions. Steps left to be taken are not too difficult.[60]

After its sixth session, held in September, the commission made a relatively optimistic report:

The Commission is happy to report that the considerable amount of information it has received since its last report to the Secretary-General of the United Nations has shown that the majority of detaining governments have, in the meantime, released and repatriated the prisoners of war who had remained in their custody, while others have released large numbers of detainees; that the various Red Cross organizations and societies, international as well as national, which had co-operated in the past—with one another, with the Governments concerned, or with the Commission—to ameliorate the situation of prisoners of war and in particular to clarify the fates of thousands of missing persons have, in the course of the preceding year, continued to co-operate unto the same ends; and that their activities met with appreciable success.[61]

The commission also reported that, since its establishment, eight of the remaining eleven governments that had formerly held prisoners had completed their release and repatriation. Thus by late 1954, only three governments were still holding prisoners of war—France, the Soviet Union, and Communist China.[62] However, it was evident that the Soviet Union and Communist China were still holding thousands of prisoners and had not accounted for additional thou-

[60] U. N. *Ad Hoc* Commission on Prisoners of War, Fifth Session, *Declaration,* Doc. A/AC.46/15 (Apr. 2, 1954), p. 1.

[61] U. N. General Assembly, Ninth Session, *Progress Report to the Secretary-General on the Work of the Ad Hoc Commission on Prisoners of War,* Doc. A/AC.46/17 (Sept. 30, 1954), p. 2.

[62] France reported in September 1954 that only 145 German nationals were still being held in connection with war crimes. The commission emphasized that France had co-operated fully with it, in contrast to the Soviet Union and Communist China. Six other governments—Albania, Bulgaria, Czechoslovakia, Hungary, Poland, and Rumania—furnished no information whatever to the commission but were reported by other governments to be holding some of their nationals. The Federal Republic of Germany informed the commission that 1,386 German nationals were repatriated from Czechoslovakia, Hungary, and Poland during the year ending September 1954.

sands who had died while in their custody. The commission concluded its latest report by once more urging "the full co-operation of all governments and all agencies whose active participation is required to settle the problem of prisoners of war."[63]

It is impossible to judge to what extent the pressure of world public opinion, as reflected in these two debates of the General Assembly, and in the work of the *ad hoc* commission, persuaded the Soviet Union, its satellites, and Communist China to release some of the prisoners in their custody. The German, Italian, and Japanese spokesmen in the Assembly gave much credit to the United Nations for the progress, however limited, made thus far. At least, the United Nations strove to do all it could—through debate, use of its good offices, and solemn expression of its deep concern—to help relieve the plight of the missing prisoners and the anxiety of their families.

Violations of Rights of Individuals

The United Nations has been asked to consider alleged violations of the rights not only of large groups of peoples but also of individuals. No provision has been made, as indicated earlier in this study,[64] for consideration of the many thousands of communications received each year from organizations and individuals alleging violations of human rights. On several occasions, however, organs of the United Nations have been requested to consider complaints brought by one Member against another alleging violations of the rights of individuals. These occasions have revealed in dramatic fashion the degree to which the rights of the individual have become the concern of the international community and have raised in acute form the question how far an international organization should take action concerning matters traditionally within the domestic jurisdiction of states.

Three of these cases—those concerning the Soviet spouses of foreign nationals (1948), the Greek prisoners (1948-49), and the Spanish

[63] U. N. General Assembly, Ninth Session, *Progress Report . . . of the Ad Hoc Commission on Prisoners of War,* p. 23. The commission did not meet in 1955 but submitted a brief progress report. It noted "with satisfaction that during the year that has elapsed further progress has been made in the repatriation of prisoners of war and detained civilians, as well as in the clarification of the fate of hitherto missing persons." U.N. General Assembly, Tenth Session, *Progress Report to the Secretary-General,* Doc. A/AC.46/18 (Nov. 2, 1955), p. 1.

[64] See above, Chap. III.

prisoners (1952)—involved charges that a government was violating the rights of its own citizens. One other—that concerning the detention by Czechoslovakia of an American journalist in 1952—involved charges that a government was violating the rights of an alien. Each of these cases had obvious political overtones; and each throws some light on the crucial question whether the organs of the United Nations should consider alleged violations of rights of individuals and, if so, in what manner. This question is of continuing significance because Member governments are frequently under pressure of public opinion to bring into the United Nations charges of this kind against other Members.[65] The delay in the conclusion of the Draft Covenant on Civil and Political Rights, which would provide machinery for handling such complaints among parties to the Covenant, has probably increased this pressure on governments.

Soviet Spouses of Foreign Nationals

Until 1947, the Soviet Government recognized, at least in principle, the right of its citizens who married foreign nationals to leave the Soviet Union in order to accompany or join their spouses abroad. On February 15, 1947, however, the Soviet Government decreed that Soviet citizens could not marry foreign nationals, and it thereafter declined—by administrative action rather than by law or regulation —to permit citizens who had previously married foreigners to leave the country. This action resulted in obvious hardship to approximately one thousand foreign nationals, including members of the Allied armed services who had served in the Soviet Union during the Second World War, to their Soviet wives or husbands, and to children of these marriages. Among those refused permission to leave the Soviet Union were 350 Soviet wives and 65 Soviet husbands of United States citizens, as well as a Soviet woman who had married the son of the Chilean ambassador in Moscow.

In January 1948, the United Kingdom raised this matter, in rather general terms, in the Commission on the Status of Women. After a

[65] The Department of State and the United States Mission to the United Nations, for example, are frequently urged by members of the Congress, the press, organizations, and individuals to ask the United Nations to consider alleged violations of the rights of individuals, especially by the Soviet Union and its satellites. In particular, the United States representatives in the Commission on Human Rights—first, Mrs. Roosevelt and, later, Mrs. Lord—have received scores of letters each year from Americans and foreign nationals requesting the commission or other organs of the United Nations to deal with such complaints.

brief debate, the commission, calling the attention of the Economic and Social Council to the question of freedom of choice in marriage, made the following observation: "This right cannot be fully guaranteed unless it is recognized that individuals have the right to leave their country on marriage and to reside with the other partner in any country from which they cannot be lawfully excluded."[66]

In August 1948, when the Economic and Social Council considered the report of the Commission on the Status of Women, the representative of Chile proposed that the Council express its disapproval of legislative or administrative provisions that deny to persons the right to leave their country of origin and reside with their spouses elsewhere. Although Chile did not propose a specific condemnation of the Soviet Union, the Soviet representative reacted vigorously and proposed that the Chilean text be amended to provide that the Council recognized that its action referred "to solitary cases, in each of which the State refusing a visa to one of its citizens to leave the country may have entirely sufficient grounds connected with the maintenance of public order and State security." The Soviet amendment then went even further to propose the following paragraph:

The Economic and Social Council also understands that Article 2, paragraph 7, of the United Nations Charter does not entitle either the Council or any other organ of the United Nations to interfere in deciding the question of the departure from any State of its citizens, and that this is a matter entirely within the domestic competence of every State.[67]

Both parts of the Soviet amendment were defeated, the second paragraph—on the question of competence—by a vote of 3 in favor, 9 against, with 6 abstentions.[68]

At the conclusion of its debate, the Council decided to transmit to the Commission on Human Rights both the observations of the Commission on the Status of Women and the proposals submitted by Chile and the Soviet Union. In this resolution—adopted by a vote of 14 in favor, 3 against, with 1 abstention—the Council stated that it deplored

[66] U. N. Commission on the Status of Women, *Report of the Second Session*, Doc. E/615 (Jan. 26, 1948), p. 13.

[67] U. N. Economic and Social Council, Seventh Session, Doc. E/1003 (Aug. 23, 1948).

[68] In favor were Byelorussia, Poland, and the Soviet Union; against were Canada, Chile, China, Denmark, France, the Netherlands, Peru, the United Kingdom, and the United States; abstaining were Australia, Brazil, Lebanon, New Zealand, Turkey, and Venezuela.

. . . all legislative measures which forbid mixed marriages between persons differing as to colour, race, nationality, citizenship or religion, and in general such other legislative or administrative provisions as restrict the freedom to choose a spouse (with the exception of restrictions based on family relationships, age, the nature of the functions being exercised, or other similar reasons) as well as those legislative or administrative provisions which deny to a woman the right to leave her country of origin and reside with her husband in any other.[69]

At the third session of the General Assembly, after diplomatic negotiations had failed to remedy the situation, Chile proposed an item entitled "Violation by the Union of Soviet Socialist Republics of fundamental human rights, traditional diplomatic practices and other principles of the Charter." This was debated in the Sixth (Legal) Committee, where the spokesman for Chile was its former ambassador to the Soviet Union, whose daughter-in-law was one of the Soviet women who had been refused permission to leave the country. The Chilean delegation and others contended that the Soviet Union had violated its obligation, under Articles 55 and 56 of the Charter, to promote respect for human rights and, in the case of the ambassador's daughter-in-law, traditional diplomatic practices concerning members of foreign diplomatic missions, their families, and their retinue. The delegations of the Soviet bloc replied that the adult children of an ambassador had no special diplomatic privileges and that, in any case, the General Assembly, under Article 2(7) of the Charter, was not competent to consider this matter. On the latter point, the United States and others referred to the powers of discussion and recommendation that the General Assembly has under Articles 10 and 14.

The resolution adopted by the Sixth Committee was not considered by the Assembly in plenary until the second part of the third session, in April 1949. After another debate, in which the previous arguments were all reiterated, the Assembly adopted a resolution with the following conclusions:

The General Assembly . . .

Declares that the measures which prevent or coerce the wives of citizens of other nationalities from leaving their country of origin with their husbands or in order to join them abroad, are not in conformity with the Charter; and that when those measures refer to the wives of persons belonging to foreign diplomatic missions, or of members of their families or retinue, they are contrary to courtesy, to diplomatic practices and to the

[69] Res. 154D(VII), Aug. 23, 1948.

principle of reciprocity, and are likely to impair friendly relations among nations;

Recommends the Government of the Union of Soviet Socialist Republics to withdraw the measures of such a nature which have been adopted.[70]

This resolution is one of the few concerning human rights in which the General Assembly has made recommendations to a single country; but this aspect of the issue received virtually no attention during the debates.

The resolution adopted by the General Assembly apparently had no effect on the Soviet Government. Shortly after the death of Stalin, however, the Soviet Government permitted the daughter-in-law of the former Chilean ambassador to leave the country. In June 1953, following representations from the United States ambassador, it granted exit visas to the wives of six United States citizens of whom four were newspaper correspondents and two were employees of the United States Embassy. Two months later, the Soviet wife of a United Kingdom national was also granted permission to leave. With these few exceptions, it would appear that the Soviet Government has not relaxed its general refusal to permit Soviet citizens who have married foreigners to leave the Soviet Union in order to accompany or to join their spouses in other countries.

Greek Prisoners

On Saturday, November 6, 1948, when the First (Political and Security) Committee of the Assembly was considering the Greek problem during the third session of the General Assembly, the Yugoslav representative intervened on a point of order to say that he had received a telegram that morning to the effect that ten leaders of a Greek seamen's union had been sentenced to death on the previous day and were to be executed on the following Monday morning. The telegram, which urged that measures be taken to prevent the execution, was signed by the Federation of Greek Maritime Unions. The Yugoslav representative subsequently introduced a draft resolution that called upon the Greek government to take steps to see that the ten trade union leaders, listed by name, were not executed, and later in the meeting the Polish representative proposed that the Yugoslav draft resolution be given precedence over others dealing

---

[70] Res. 285(III), Apr. 25, 1949. The vote was 39 to 6 (the Soviet bloc), with 11 abstentions (Afghanistan, Burma, China, India, Iran, Iraq, Pakistan, Saudi Arabia, Syria, the Union of South Africa, and Yemen).

with the Greek problem. His proposal was supported by Czechoslovakia, the Soviet Union, and Yugoslavia; but Belgium, Ecuador, France, Syria, and the United Kingdom questioned the competence of the committee under Article 2(7) of the Charter to consider the matter.

During the discussion, the French delegation submitted a draft resolution that, after expressing confidence that the chairman of the committee would examine the matter with the Greek delegation, proposed that the committee proceed to the next item on the agenda. The Soviet delegation introduced an amendment proposing that the chairman take measures to save the lives of the trade unionists.

The French proposal was supported by El Salvador, Greece, and Venezuela. At the end of the debate, Poland requested that the question of the competence of the committee to deal with the Yugoslav proposal and the Soviet amendment be voted on separately. The committee decided by overwhelming majorities, with only the Soviet bloc in opposition, that it was not competent to entertain either the Yugoslav proposal or the Soviet amendment. The French draft resolution was then adopted by 41 to 0, with 9 abstentions. The chairman said that he had taken note of the difficult mission entrusted to him and that in his consultations with the Greek representatives he would not lose sight of the humanitarian aspects of the question. No further reference was made to the matter in that session of the Assembly.

During the fourth session of the General Assembly, in the autumn of 1949, the Soviet bloc undertook a new campaign in the First Committee on the question of death sentences passed by Greek military tribunals. The Polish delegation introduced a draft resolution by which the First Committee would appeal "to the Greek authorities to suspend all executions and all court martial procedures and in particular to set aside the death sentence issued by the Military Tribunal in Piraeus against Catherine Zevgos."[71] After a long debate, in which a number of delegates questioned the competence of the committee to interfere in the internal affairs of a sovereign state, the committee rejected the Polish draft resolution by 6 in favor, 41 against, with 9 abstentions.

The Soviet delegation, later in this session, introduced a draft

[71] U. N. General Assembly, Fourth Session, First Committee, Doc. A/C.1/483 (Sept. 28, 1949).

resolution by which the First Committee would call upon the Greek Government to suspend the carrying out of death sentences passed on eight named persons. During the course of a long debate, extending through several meetings, four additional draft resolutions were introduced, as follows: Paraguay, appealing to the Greek Government for leniency; Colombia, requesting all governments to suspend death sentences for crimes of a political nature; Uruguay, recommending the commutation of all death sentences and the elimination of the death penalty from legislation; and Ecuador, requesting the President of the Assembly to negotiate with the representatives of the Government of Greece concerning the suspension of death sentences passed by military courts for political reasons, so long as the Conciliation Committee of the General Assembly was in existence.

The First Committee decided, in a series of votes, that it was not competent to adopt the proposals of the Soviet Union, Paraguay, Colombia, and Uruguay. However, it decided, on a vote of 31 to 16, with 12 abstentions, that it was competent to vote on the Ecuadoran draft resolution. On the following day, the committee adopted, by a vote of 40 to 4, with 10 abstentions, the Ecuadoran resolution, which had been revised to request the President to "ascertain the views" of the Greek Government rather than "negotiate" with its representatives. At the last plenary meeting of the session, on December 10, the President of the Assembly, speaking as chairman of its Conciliation Committee, stated that he had been informed by representatives of Greece that no death sentences had been carried out since the enactment of the recent clemency legislation.

It should be noted that the issue here—in contrast to the initial debates on South Africa and on the peace treaties—was not whether the item should be placed on the agenda. Because the Greek problem was already on the agenda, the question of the Greek trials and executions was a relevant matter. The issue therefore was to what extent the Assembly could or should intervene.

The record of the third and fourth sessions of the Assembly shows clearly that the First Committee agreed that it was not competent, under Article 2(7) of the Charter, to intervene in the domestic affairs of a sovereign state by making a direct or indirect appeal to the Greek Government to suspend the death penalty against persons condemned by military courts for political crimes. Only one of the significant votes in this series (on the Polish resolution in 1949) was not specifically on the question of competence. In all its other votes, however, the committee dealt specifically with the question of competence and, in effect, ruled the several proposals out of order.

In neither 1948 nor 1949, however, did the First Committee refrain completely from attempting to influence the Greek Government. The circumstances of the case, the unceasing propaganda of the Soviet bloc, and the strong emotional objections to the death penalty on the part of the Latin-American delegations all combined to compel a compromise formula. This formula was similar in both sessions: in 1948, the chairman of the First Committee was to get in touch with the Greek delegation; and in 1949, the President of the Assembly was to ascertain the views of the Greek Government.

Spanish Prisoners

On December 28, 1951, during the sixth session of the General Assembly, the chairman of the Soviet delegation forwarded to the President of the Assembly a communication from a Belgian organization, "Notre Solidarité." The communication urged the General Assembly to take the necessary steps to save the lives of twenty-four Spanish "democrats" who had been arrested and imprisoned for taking part in the strike in Barcelona in March 1951 and who were subject to the death penalty after a trial, without benefit of counsel, by a military tribunal. The communication further requested the Assembly to invite the Spanish Government to abrogate the law of April 9, 1947, concerning the maintenance of public order, under which the twenty-four prisoners were to be tried. It denounced the Spanish Government for its suppression of civil liberties and the mistreatment of these and other prisoners. The letter and its enclosures were circulated by the Secretary-General to all delegations at the Assembly.

Two weeks later, while the Third Committee was considering the order in which it should discuss the various draft resolutions and amendments relating to the draft covenants on human rights, the Polish delegation proposed that the committee begin with a Polish draft resolution entitled "Defense of Twenty-four Inhabitants of Barcelona charged with a Capital Offense." This draft resolution requested the President of the General Assembly "to take the necessary steps in order that the appropriate authorities in Spain take measures to ensure the cessation of the persecution of the above-mentioned twenty-four inhabitants of Barcelona and their immediate release."[72]

[72] U. N. General Assembly, Sixth Session, Doc. A/C.3/203/Rev. 1 (Jan. 15, 1952).

The Polish draft resolution was supported by Guatemala, Haiti, and the Soviet Union. The United States contended, however, that the proposal constituted a new item and, in accordance with the rules of procedure, should be submitted first to the General Committee. Mexico subsequently proposed that consideration of the Polish draft resolution should be postponed for forty-eight hours in order to enable the committee to obtain factual information. After a long procedural wrangle, the committee, by a vote of 30 to 12, with 11 abstentions, adopted the Mexican proposal for postponement.

On January 17, 1952, the committee returned to the Polish draft resolution. In the meantime, Brazil, Colombia, Costa Rica, Honduras, the Netherlands, New Zealand, Nicaragua, Peru, the United Kingdom, the United States, and Venezuela had introduced a joint procedural motion to dispose of the matter. This motion provided that the *rapporteur* should include in his report a statement that the committee, without considering the substance of the draft resolution submitted by the Polish delegation, had decided that the subject matter was not within the item of the agenda concerning the draft covenants and that the committee was not authorized to consider this draft resolution as a new item on its own initiative. The debate on this motion, during which the Soviet bloc managed to refer frequently to the substance of the matter and to denounce the Spanish Government, lasted throughout two meetings. The Soviet bloc and others failed in their efforts to request the Secretariat to report any factual information it had been able to obtain about the case, because the sponsors of the procedural motion argued successfully that their motion had to be voted on first. Finally, after almost seven hours of debate, the motion was adopted by a vote of 28 to 13, with 13 abstentions. The total of 26 negative votes and abstentions revealed the humanitarian appeal of the Polish draft resolution as well as the attitude of some delegations toward the Spanish Government.

On July 3, 1952, during the fourteenth session of the Economic and Social Council, the Czechoslovak representative, speaking on a point of order, asserted that twenty-seven Spanish trade unionists, accused of leading the general strike in Barcelona in March 1951, were on trial by a military tribunal and were threatened by a summary death sentence or a long term of imprisonment. He submitted a draft resolution with the request that it be placed on the agenda of the Council and considered forthwith. The draft resolution, after noting that these trade unionists were "threatened shortly to be sentenced to death or to long term imprisonment," requested the President of the Economic and Social Council "to approach without delay the competent Spanish authorities with a view to obtaining the immediate discontinuance of this trial and the immediate release of the twenty-seven trade unionists now charged before the military tribunal."[73] The Czechoslovak draft resolution was supported by Mexico, Poland, and the Soviet Union and was opposed by Argentina. A United Kingdom motion to adjourn discussion until the afternoon of July 7, when more information would be available, was then adopted.

When the debate was resumed on July 7, the Czechoslovak representative renewed his demand that the Council include his item on its agenda under the revised title "Humanitarian Action on Behalf of Twenty-Seven Spanish Trade Unionists." He referred to communications about the case from the World Federation of Trade Unions and from trade union organizations in Norway, Mexico, and Finland. In view of the fact that the trial had already been completed, he submitted a revised draft resolution that omitted the earlier reference to the death penalty and requested the President of the Council to approach the Spanish authorities to obtain "the invalidation of the sentences and the immediate acquittal and release of the trade unionists convicted."[74]

The United Kingdom, the United States, Mexico, and Uruguay immediately pointed out that, as the death penalty was not involved, the case was no longer such an urgent matter. The French representative suggested that the Council postpone discussion until it came to the item on its agenda concerning trade union rights. After further debate, the Council rejected the Czechoslovak draft resolution by a vote of 3 in favor, 10 against, with 5 abstentions.

When the Council reached the item on trade union rights, it included the Czechoslovak draft resolution in its documentation, but the debate on the alleged violation of trade union rights in Spain was almost perfunctory. The Soviet Union, Czechoslovakia, and the World Federation of Trade Unions repeated all the earlier

[73] U. N. Economic and Social Council, Fourteenth Session, Doc. E/L.393 (July 3, 1952).

[74] U. N. Economic and Social Council, Fourteenth Session, Doc. E/L.393/Rev. 1 (July 7, 1952).

arguments; and Belgium, France, the United Kingdom, and the United States briefly opposed the Czechoslovak draft resolution in the course of the remarks on the general subject of trade union rights. The resolution was again rejected, this time by 3 in favor, 12 against, with 3 abstentions.

It may be noted that the question of competence, under Article 2(7) of the Charter, did not arise in connection with the case, except for an objection on this ground by Argentina to consideration of the subject. In the General Assembly, the debate centered solely on the question whether a draft resolution could be introduced under the established agenda. In the Economic and Social Council, the debate was devoted largely to the question whether the Council should take action on the matter; and later the subject was included in the regular debate on trade union rights. The Soviet bloc may have achieved its propaganda objectives, however, by airing the substance of the matter in the course of the debates on procedures.

Oatis Case

In April 1951, William Oatis, head of the Associated Press Bureau in Prague, was arrested, together with his three Czechoslovak employees, on a charge of espionage and conspiracy. After being held incommunicado for seventy-one days, he was brought to trial without benefit of defense counsel or the right to call witnesses in his defense. After Oatis had "confessed" to being guilty of the charges, he was sentenced to ten years in prison and to expulsion from the country after serving his term, which might be reduced to five years for good behavior. Neither before, during, nor after the trial was the American Embassy in Prague permitted to communicate with Oatis, although two of its representatives were permitted to attend the trial.

These events provoked a storm of protests in the American press and in the Congress. In August 1951, the United States raised the matter in the Economic and Social Council, during consideration by the Council of the question of freedom of information, and introduced a draft resolution on the treatment of foreign correspondents. This resolution, which the Council adopted by a vote of 14 to 3 (Soviet bloc), with 1 abstention, did not refer specifically to the Oatis case but dealt vigorously with the principles involved:

The Economic and Social Council . . .
Views with extreme concern all governmental action aimed at the

systematic exclusion of *bona fide* correspondents, the imposition of arbitrary personal restraints and the infliction of punishments upon such correspondents solely because of their attempts faithfully to perform their duties in gathering and transmitting news;

Urges strongly that personal restraints be removed and sentences imposing arbitrary punishments be revoked; and

Appeals to governments to do all within their power to safeguard the right of correspondents freely and faithfully to gather and transmit news.[75]

The resolution called for no action by the General Assembly and the annual report of the Council merely referred to the subject, without specifically mentioning the Oatis case, in two brief paragraphs in a summary of its activities in the field of freedom of information. When the Third Committee reached this item at the end of the sixth session, in January 1952, the United States used these two paragraphs in the report of the Council as the basis for another debate on the Oatis case. The United States delegation and others reviewed the circumstances of the imprisonment, trial, and conviction of Oatis and condemned both the restrictions on freedom of the press in Czechoslovakia and the violation of human rights in its judicial proceedings. They did not, however, submit a draft resolution for adoption, being content with a thorough airing of the case in the Third Committee.

The debates on the Oatis case were notable in two respects. First, the United States, despite the gross mistreatment of one of its citizens, consistently related the Oatis case to the general principles of freedom of information and did not ask for a condemnation of Czechoslovakia by either the Council or the Assembly. This procedure followed the pattern set with regard to forced labor and prisoners of war, but not with regard to South Africa, the peace treaties, and the Soviet spouses of foreign nationals. Second, Czechoslovakia, perhaps because of the broad approach taken by the United States, did not make the question of domestic jurisdiction a major issue in the debate. In the Council, however, the Czechoslovak delegation referred briefly to Article 2(7) of the Charter; and, in the General Assembly, its spokesman declared that the Oatis case "came solely within the competence of the Czechoslovak authorities, and it was contrary both to the United Nations Charter and to the principles of international law to contest the legitimacy of a verdict passed by the court of a sovereign State."[76]

[75] Res. 387B(XIII), Sept. 1, 1951. (Paragraph numbers omitted.)
[76] U. N. General Assembly, Sixth Session, Third Committee, *Official Records*, 414th Meeting (Jan. 31, 1952), p. 419.

The debates in the Council and the Assembly served to reaffirm the adherence of the United Nations to the basic principles of freedom of information and its concern over violations of those principles, without involving the Organization in a controversy over its competence to consider this subject. These debates apparently had no more impact on the Government of Czechoslovakia than the repeated diplomatic representations of the United States Government. In May 1953, however, the United States Ambassador in Prague was informed that the President of Czechoslovakia had pardoned Oatis on the basis of a petition received from Oatis's wife in November 1952. It is perhaps significant that the release of Oatis—like the granting of exit visas to a few Soviet spouses of foreign nationals, and the release of some of the prisoners of war and inmates of forced labor camps—took place after the death of Stalin, when the tactics of the Soviet bloc appeared to be shifting slightly to present a more "co-operative" attitude toward the rest of the world.

On balance, the pioneering work of the United Nations to promote respect for human rights and to remedy violations of those rights has been fruitful. It has helped to set national and local standards, to provide for the exchange of information and experience, to turn the spotlight of public opinion on violations of the rights of man, and to alert mankind to the evils of a Stalin or a Hitler. On the other hand, the line between the provisions of the Charter concerning the promotion of human rights and the domestic jurisdiction clause is an ill-defined one. Attempts to move too fast in this new area of international concern may antagonize some Members and prove self-defeating. Care will be required in the future to steer a proper course between excessive zeal and unjustified caution in order to prevent the various United Nations organs, on the one hand, from intervening in matters that are regarded as lying within the domestic jurisdiction of Member governments and, on the other hand, from failing effectively to promote the observance of human rights.

The record of the past ten years shows that the power of the General Assembly to discuss every aspect of the whole field of human rights, including allegations that the rights of large groups, or even of individuals, are being violated, is an essential one. The price of liberty today is in part eternal vigilance by the international community. The power of the Assembly to direct recommendations toward a particular state, however, raises legal questions and creates political difficulties; and it should be used with great caution and only as a last resort. The general objective, here as elsewhere in the field of human rights, should be to uphold the principles of the Charter, to reach a maximum degree of agreement, and to achieve practical results.[77]

[77] For a further appraisal of activities in the human rights field, see Part Five of the volume in this Brookings series, *The United Nations and Promotion of the General Welfare.*

APPENDIXES

APPENDIX A

Universal Declaration of Human Rights[1]

Preamble

Whereas recognition of the inherent dignity and of the equal and inalienable rights of all members of the human family is the foundation of freedom, justice and peace in the world,

Whereas disregard and contempt for human rights have resulted in barbarous acts which have outraged the conscience of mankind, and the advent of a world in which human beings shall enjoy freedom of speech and belief and freedom from fear and want has been proclaimed as the highest aspiration of the common people,

Whereas it is essential, if man is not to be compelled to have recourse, as a last resort, to rebellion against tyranny and oppression, that human rights should be protected by the rule of law,

Whereas it is essential to promote the development of friendly relations between nations,

Whereas the peoples of the United Nations have in the Charter reaffirmed their faith in fundamental human rights, in the dignity and worth of the human person and in the equal rights of men and women and have determined to promote social progress and better standards of life in larger freedom,

Whereas Member States have pledged themselves to achieve, in co-operation with the United Nations, the promotion of universal respect for and observance of human rights and fundamental freedoms,

Whereas a common understanding of these rights and freedoms is of the greatest importance for the full realization of this pledge,

Now, therefore,

The General Assembly

Proclaims this Universal Declaration of Human Rights as a common standard of achievement for all peoples and all nations, to the end that every individual and every organ of society, keeping this Declaration constantly in mind, shall strive by teaching and education to promote respect for these rights and freedoms and by progressive measures, national and international, to secure their universal and effective recognition and observance, both among the peoples of Member States themselves and among the peoples of territories under their jurisdiction.

Article 1

All human beings are born free and equal in dignity and rights. They are endowed with reason and conscience and should act towards one another in a spirit of brotherhood.

Article 2

Everyone is entitled to all the rights and freedoms set forth in this Declaration, without distinction of any kind, such as race, colour, sex, language, religion, political or other opinion, national or social origin, property, birth or other status.

Furthermore, no distinction shall be made on the basis of the political, jurisdictional or international status of the country or territory to which a person belongs, whether it be independent, trust, non-self-governing or under any other limitation of sovereignty.

Article 3

Everyone has the right to life, liberty and the security of person.

Article 4

No one shall be held in slavery or servitude; slavery and the slave trade shall be prohibited in all their forms.

Article 5

No one shall be subjected to torture or

[1] Source: Part A of Res. 217 (III), approved by the General Assembly on Dec. 10, 1948. Text as given in U.N. General Assembly, Third Session, First Part, *Official Records,* "Resolutions," pp. 71-77.

to cruel, inhuman or degrading treatment or punishment.

Article 6

Everyone has the right to recognition everywhere as a person before the law.

Article 7

All are equal before the law and are entitled without any discrimination to equal protection of the law. All are entitled to equal protection against any discrimination in violation of this Declaration and against any incitement to such discriminaton.

Article 8

Everyone has the right to an effective remedy by the competent national tribunals for acts violating the fundamental rights granted him by the constitution or by law.

Article 9

No one shall be subjected to arbitrary arrest, detention or exile.

Article 10

Everyone is entitled in full equality to a fair and public hearing by an independent and impartial tribunal, in the determination of his rights and obligations and of any criminal charge against him.

Article 11

1. Everyone charged with a penal offense has the right to be presumed innocent until proved guilty according to law in a public trial at which he has had all the guarantees necessary for his defence.

2. No one shall be held guilty of any penal offence on account of any act or omission which did not constitute a penal offence, under national or international law, at the time when it was committed. Nor shall a heavier penalty be imposed than the one that was applicable at the time the penal offence was committed.

Article 12

No one shall be subjected to arbitrary interference with his privacy, family, home or correspondence, nor to attacks upon his honour and reputation. Everyone has the right to the protection of the law against such interference or attacks.

Article 13

1. Everyone has the right to freedom of movement and residence within the borders of each State.

2. Everyone has the right to leave any country, including his own, and to return to his country.

Article 14

1. Everyone has the right to seek and to enjoy in other countries asylum from persecution.

2. This right may not be invoked in the case of prosecutions genuinely arising from nonpolitical crimes or from acts contrary to the purposes and principles of the United Nations.

Article 15

1. Everyone has the right to a nationality.

2. No one shall be arbitrarily deprived of his nationality nor denied the right to change his nationality.

Article 16

1. Men and women of full age, without any limitation due to race, nationality or religion, have the right to marry and to found a family. They are entitled to equal rights as to marriage, during marriage and at its dissolution.

2. Marriage shall be entered into only with the free and full consent of the intending spouses.

3. The family is the natural and fundamental group unit of society and is entitled to protection by society and the State.

Article 17

1. Everyone has the right to own property alone as well as in association with others.

2. No one shall be arbitrarily deprived of his property.

Article 18

Everyone has the right to freedom of thought, conscience and religion; this right includes freedom to change his religion or belief, and freedom, either alone or in community with others and in public or private, to manifest his religion or belief in teaching, practice, worship and observance.

Article 19

Everyone has the right to freedom of opinion and expression; this right includes freedom to hold opinions without interference and to seek, receive and impart information and ideas through any media and regardless of frontiers.

Article 20

1. Everyone has the right to freedom of peaceful assembly and association.

2. No one may be compelled to belong to an association.

Article 21

1. Everyone has the right to take part in the government of his country, directly or through freely chosen representatives.

2. Everyone has the right of equal access to public service in his country.

3. The will of the people shall be the basis of the authority of government; this will shall be expressed in periodic and genuine elections which shall be by universal and equal suffrage and shall be held by secret vote or by equivalent free voting procedures.

Article 22

Everyone, as a member of society, has the right to social security and is entitled to realization, through national effort and international co-operation and in accordance with the organization and resources of each state, of the economic, social and cultural rights indispensable for his dignity and the free development of his personality.

Article 23

1. Everyone has the right to work, to free choice of employment, to just and favourable conditions of work and to protection against unemployment.

2. Everyone, without any discrimination, has the right to equal pay for equal work.

3. Everyone who works has the right to just and favourable remuneration ensuring for himself and his family an existence worthy of human dignity, and supplemented, if necessary, by other means of social protection.

4. Everyone has the right to form and to join trade unions for the protection of his interests.

Article 24

Everyone has the right to rest and leisure, including reasonable limitation of working hours and periodic holidays with pay.

Article 25

1. Everyone has the right to a standard of living adequate for the health and well-being of himself and of his family, including food, clothing, housing and medical care and necessary social services, and the right to security in the event of unemployment, sickness, disability, widowhood, old age or other lack of livelihood in circumstances beyond his control.

2. Motherhood and childhood are entitled to special care and assistance. All children, whether born in or out of wedlock, shall enjoy the same social protection.

Article 26

1. Everyone has the right to education. Education shall be free, at least in the elementary and fundamental stages. Elementary education shall be compulsory. Technical and professional education shall be made generally available and higher education shall be equally accessible to all on the basis of merit.

2. Education shall be directed to the full development of the human personality and to the strengthening of respect for human rights and fundamental freedoms. It shall promote understanding, tolerance and friendship among all nations, racial or religious groups, and shall further the activities of the United Nations for the maintenance of peace.

3. Parents have a prior right to choose

UNITED NATIONS AND HUMAN RIGHTS

the kind of education that shall be given to their children.

Article 27

1. Everyone has the right freely to participate in the cultural life of the community, to enjoy the arts and to share in scientific advancement and its benefits.

2. Everyone has the right to the protection of the moral and material interests resulting from any scientific, literary or artistic production of which he is the author.

Article 28

Everyone is entitled to a social and international order in which the rights and freedoms set forth in this Declaration can be fully realized.

Article 29

1. Everyone has duties to the community in which alone the free and full development of his personality is possible.

2. In the exercise of his rights and freedoms, everyone shall be subject only to such limitations as are determined by law solely for the purpose of securing due recognition and respect for the rights and freedoms of others and of meeting the just requirements of morality, public order and the general welfare in a democratic society.

3. These rights and freedoms may in no case be exercised contrary to the purposes and principles of the United Nations.

Article 30

Nothing in this Declaration may be interpreted as implying for any State, group or person any right to engage in any activity or to perform any act aimed at the destruction of any of the rights and freedoms set forth herein.

Draft Covenant on Civil and Political Rights[1]

The States Parties hereto,

Considering that, in accordance with the principles in the Charter of the United Nations, recognition of the inherent dignity and of the equal and inalienable rights of all members of the human family is the foundation of freedom, justice and peace in the world,

Recognizing that these rights derive from the inherent dignity of the human person,

Recognizing that, in accordance with the Universal Declaration of Human Rights, the ideal of free men[2] enjoying civil and political freedom and freedom from fear and want can only be achieved if conditions are created whereby everyone may enjoy his civil and political rights, as well as his economic, social and cultural rights,

Considering the obligation of States under the Charter of the United Nations to promote universal respect for, and observance of, human rights and freedoms,

Realizing that the individual, having duties to other individuals and to the community to which he belongs, is under responsibility to strive for the promotion and observance of the rights recognized in this Convenant,

Agree upon the following articles:

PART I

Article 1[3]

1. All peoples and all nations shall have the right of self-determination, namely, the right freely to determine their political, economic, social and cultural status.

2. All States, including those having responsibility for the administration of Non-Self-Governing and Trust Territories and those controlling in whatsoever manner the exercise of that right by another people, shall promote the realization of that right in all their territories, and shall respect the maintenance of that right in other States, in conformity with the provisions of the United Nations Charter.

3. The right of peoples to self-determination shall also include permanent sovereignty over their natural wealth and resources. In no case may a people be deprived of its own means of subsistence on the grounds of any rights that may be claimed by other States.

PART II

Article 2

1. Each State Party hereto undertakes to respect and to ensure to all individuals within its territory and subject to its jurisdiction the rights recognized in this Covenant, without distinction of any kind, such as race, colour, sex, language, religion, political or other opinion, national or social origin, property, birth or other status.

[1] Source: Text as given in U.N. Economic and Social Council, Eighteenth Session, *Official Records*, Supplement No. 7, pp. 65-72.

[2] At the tenth session of the General Assembly in 1955, the Third Committee changed the phrase "free men" to "free human beings."

[3] During the tenth session of the General Assembly in 1955, the Third Committee adopted the following text for Article 1:

"1. All peoples have the right of self-determination. By virtue of this right they freely determine their political status and freely pursue their economic, social and cultural development.

"2. The peoples may, for their own ends, freely dispose of their natural wealth and resources without prejudice to any obligations arising out of international economic cooperation, based upon the principle of mutual benefit, and international law. In no case may a people be deprived of its own means of subsistence.

"3. All the States Parties to the Covenant, including those having responsibility for the administration of Non-Self-Governing and Trust Territories, shall promote the realization of the right of self-determination, and shall respect that right, in conformity with the provisions of the United Nations Charter."

2. Where not already provided for by existing legislative or other measures, each State undertakes to take the necessary steps, in accordance with its constitutional processes and with the provisions of this Covenant, to adopt such legislative or other measures as may be necessary to give effect to the rights recognized in this Covenant.

3. Each State Party hereto undertakes:

(a) To ensure that any person whose rights or freedoms as herein recognized are violated shall have an effective remedy, notwithstanding that the violation has been committed by persons acting in an official capacity;

(b) To develop the possibilities of judicial remedy and to ensure that any person claiming such a remedy shall have his right thereto determined by competent authorities, political, administrative or judicial;

(c) To ensure that the competent authorities shall enforce such remedies when granted.

Article 3

The States Parties to the Covenant undertake to ensure the equal right of men and women to the enjoyment of all civil and political rights set forth in this Covenant.

Article 4

1. In time of public emergency which threatens the life of the nation and the existence of which is officially proclaimed, the States Parties hereto may take measures derogating from their obligations under this Covenant to the extent strictly required by the exigencies of the situation, provided that such measures are not inconsistent with their other obligations under international law and do not involve discrimination solely on the ground of race, colour, sex, language, religion or social origin.

2. No derogation from articles 6, 7, 8 (paragraphs 1 and 2), 11, 15, 16 and 18 may be made under this provision.

3. Any State Party to the Covenant availing itself of the right of derogation shall inform immediately the other States Parties to the Covenant, through the intermediary of the Secretary-General, of the provisions from which it has derogated, the reasons by which it was actuated and the date on which it has terminated such derogation.

Article 5

1. Nothing in this Covenant may be interpreted as implying for any State, group or person any right to engage in any activity or perform any act aimed at the destruction of any of the rights and freedoms recognized herein or at their limitation to a greater extent than is provided for in this Covenant.

2. There shall be no restriction upon or derogation from any of the fundamental human rights recognized or existing in any Contracting State pursuant to law, conventions, regulations or custom on the pretext that the present Covenant does not recognize such rights or that it recognizes them to a lesser extent.

PART III

Article 6

1. No one shall be arbitrarily deprived of his life. Everyone's right to life shall be protected by law.

2. In countries where capital punishment exists, sentence of death may be imposed only as a penalty for the most serious crimes pursuant to the sentence of a competent court and in accordance with law not contrary to the principles of the Universal Declaration of Human Rights or the Convention on the Prevention and Punishment of the Crime of Genocide.

3. Any one sentenced to death shall have the right to seek pardon or commutation of the sentence. Amnesty, pardon or commutation of the sentence of death may be granted in all cases.

4. Sentence of death shall not be carried out on a pregnant woman.

Article 7

No one shall be subjected to torture or to cruel, inhuman or degrading treatment or punishment. In particular, no one shall be subjected without his free consent to medical or scientific experimentation involving risk, where such is not required by his state of physical or mental health.

Article 8

1. No one shall be held in slavery; slavery and the slave trade in all their forms shall be prohibited.

2. No one shall be held in servitude.

3. (*a*) No one shall be required to perform forced or compulsory labour;

(*b*) The preceding sub-paragraph shall not be held to preclude, in countries where imprisonment with hard labour may be imposed as a punishment for a crime, the performance of hard labour in pursuance of a sentence to such punishment by a competent court;

(*c*) For the purpose of this paragraph the term "forced or compulsory labour" shall not include:

(i) Any work or service, not referred to in sub-paragraph (*b*), normally required of a person who is under detention in consequence of a lawful order of a court;

(ii) Any service of a military character and, in countries where conscientious objection is recognized, any national service required by law of conscientious objectors;

(iii) Any service exacted in cases of emergency or calamity threatening the life or well-being of the community;

(iv) Any work or service which forms part of normal civic obligations.

Article 9

1. Everyone has the right to liberty and security of person. No one shall be subjected to arbitrary arrest or detention. No one shall be deprived of his liberty except on such grounds and in accordance with such procedure as are established by law.

2. Anyone who is arrested shall be informed, at the time of arrest, of the reasons for his arrest and shall be promptly informed of any charges against him.

3. Anyone arrested or detained on a criminal charge shall be brought promptly before a judge or other officer authorized by law to exercise judicial power and shall be entitled to trial within a reasonable time or to release. It shall not be the general rule that persons awaiting trial shall be detained in custody, but release may be subject to guarantees to appear for trial, at any other stage of the judicial proceedings, and, should occasion arise, for execution of the judgment.

4. Anyone who is deprived of his liberty by arrest or detention shall be entitled to take proceedings before a court, in order that such court may decide without delay on the lawfulness of his detention and order his release if the detention is not lawful.

5. Anyone who has been the victim of unlawful arrest or deprivation of liberty shall have an enforceable right to compensation.

Article 10

1. All persons deprived of their liberty shall be treated with humanity.

2. Accused persons shall be segregated from convicted persons, and shall be subject to separate treatment appropriate to their status as unconvicted persons.

3. The penitentiary system shall comprise treatment directed to the fullest possible extent towards the reformation and social rehabilitation of prisoners.

Article 11

No one shall be imprisoned merely on the ground of inability to fulfil a contractual obligation.

Article 12

1. Subject to any general law of the State concerned which provides for such reasonable restrictions as may be necessary to protect national security, public safety, health or morals or the rights and freedoms of others, consistent with the other rights recognized in this Covenant:

(*a*) Everyone legally within the territory of a State shall, within that territory, have the right to (i) liberty of movement and (ii) freedom to choose his residence;

(*b*) Everyone shall be free to leave any country, including his own.

2. (*a*) No one shall be subjected to

arbitrary exile;

(*b*) Subject to the preceding sub-paragraph, anyone shall be free to enter his own country.

Article 13

An alien lawfully in the territory of a State Party to the Covenant may be expelled therefrom only in pursuance of a decision reached in accordance with law and shall, except where compelling reasons of national security otherwise require, be allowed to submit the reasons against his expulsion and to have his case reviewed by and be represented for the purpose before the competent authority or a person or persons especially designated by the competent authority.

Article 14

1. All persons shall be equal before the courts and tribunals. In the determination of any criminal charge against him, or of his rights and obligations in a suit at law, everyone shall be entitled to a fair and public hearing by a competent, independent and impartial tribunal established by law. The Press and public may be excluded from all or part of a trial for reasons of morals, public order or national security in a democratic society, or when the interest of the private lives of the parties so requires, or to the extent strictly necessary in the opinion of the Court in special circumstances where publicity would prejudice the interest of justice; but any judgment rendered in a criminal case or in a suit at law shall be pronounced publicly except where the interest of juveniles otherwise requires or the proceedings concern matrimonial disputes or the guardianship of children.

2. Everyone charged with a criminal offence shall have the right to be presumed innocent until proved guilty according to law. In the determination of any criminal charge against him, everyone shall be entitled to the following minimum guarantees, in full equality:

(*a*) To be informed promptly in a language which he understands and in detail of the nature and cause of the accusation against him;

(*b*) To have adequate time and facilities for the preparation of his defence;

(*c*) To defend himself in person or through legal assistance of his own choosing; to be informed, if he does not have legal assistance, of this right; and to have legal assistance assigned to him, in any case where the interests of justice so require, and without payment by him in any such case where he does not have sufficient means to pay for it;

(*d*) To examine, or have examined, the witnesses against him and to obtain the attendance and examination of witnesses on his behalf under the same conditions as witnesses against him;

(*e*) To have the free assistance of an interpreter if he cannot understand or speak the language used in court;

(*f*) Not to be compelled to testify against himself, or to confess guilt.

3. In the case of juveniles, the procedure shall be such as will take account of their age and the desirability of promoting their rehabilitation.

4. In any case where by a final decision a person has been convicted of a criminal offence and where subsequently his conviction has been reversed or he has been pardoned on the ground that a new or newly-discovered fact shows conclusively that there has been a miscarriage of justice, the person who has suffered punishment as a result of such conviction shall be compensated unless it is proved that the non-disclosure of the unknown fact in time is wholly or partly attributable to him.

Article 15

1. No one shall be held guilty of any criminal offence on account of any act or omission which did not constitute a criminal offence, under national or international law, at the time when it was committed. Nor shall a heavier penalty be imposed than the one that was applicable at the time when the criminal offence was committed. If, subsequently to the commission of the offence, provision is made by law for the imposition of a lighter penalty, the offender shall benefit thereby.

2. Nothing in this article shall prejudice

the trial and punishment of any person for any act or omission which, at the time when it was committed, was criminal according to the general principles of law recognized by the community of nations.

Article 16

Everyone shall have the right to recognition everywhere as a person before the law.

Article 17

1. No one shall be subjected to arbitrary or unlawful interference with his privacy, home or correspondence, nor to unlawful attacks on his honour and reputation.

2. Everyone has the right to the protection of the law against such interference or attacks.

Article 18

1. Everyone shall have the right to freedom of thought, conscience and religion. This right shall include freedom to maintain or to change his religion, or belief, and freedom, either individually or in community with others and in public or private, to manifest his religion or belief in worship, observance, practice and teaching.

2. No one shall be subject to coercion which would impair his freedom to maintain or to change his religion or belief.

3. Freedom to manifest one's religion or beliefs may be subject only to such limitations as are prescribed by law and are necessary to protect public safety, order, health, or morals or the fundamental rights and freedoms of others.

Article 19

1. Everyone shall have the right to hold opinions without interference.

2. Everyone shall have the right to freedom of expression; this right shall include freedom to seek, receive and impart information and ideas of all kinds, regardless of frontiers, either orally, in writing or in print, in the form of art, or through any other media of his choice.

3. The exercise of the rights provided for in the foregoing paragraph carries with it special duties and responsibilities. It

may therefore be subject to certain restrictions, but these shall be such only as are provided by law and are necessary, (1) for respect of the rights or reputations of others, (2) for the protection of national security or of public order, or of public health or morals.

Article 20

The right of peaceful assembly shall be recognized. No restrictions may be placed on the exercise of this right other than those imposed in conformity with the law and which are necessary in a democratic society in the interests of national security or public safety, public order, the protection of public health or morals or the protection of the rights and freedoms of others.

Article 21

1. Everyone shall have the right to freedom of association with others, including the right to form and join trade unions for the protection of his interests.

2. No restrictions may be placed on the exercise of this right other than those prescribed by law and which are necessary in a democratic society in the interests of national security or public safety, public order, the protection of public health or morals or the protection of the rights and freedoms of others. This article shall not prevent the imposition of lawful restrictions on the exercise of this right by members of the armed forces or of the police.

3. Nothing in this article shall authorize States Parties to the International Labour Convention of 1948 on Freedom of Association and Protection of the Right to Organize, to take legislative measures which would prejudice, or to apply the law in such a manner as to prejudice, the guarantees provided for in that Convention.

Article 22

1. The family is the natural and fundamental group unit of society and is entitled to protection by society and the State.

2. The right of men and women of

marriageable age to marry and to found a family shall be recognized.

3. No marriage shall be entered into without the free and full consent of the intending spouses.

4. The legislation of the States Parties to this Covenant shall be directed towards equality of rights and responsibilities for the spouses as to marriage, during marriage and at its dissolution. In the last-mentioned case the law shall lay down special measures for the protection of any children of the marriage.

Article 23

Every citizen shall have the right and the opportunity, without any of the distinctions mentioned in article 2 of this Covenant and without unreasonable restrictions:

(a) To take part in the conduct of public affairs, directly or through freely chosen representatives;

(b) To vote and to be elected at genuine periodic elections which shall be by universal and equal suffrage and shall be held by secret ballot, guaranteeing the free expression of the will of the electors;

(c) Of access, on general terms of equality, to public service in his country.

Article 24

All persons are equal before the law. The law shall prohibit any discrimination and guarantee to all persons equal and effective protection against discrimination on any ground such as race, colour, sex, language, religion, political or other opinion, national or social origin, property, birth or other status.

Article 25

In those States in which ethnic, religious or linguistic minorities exist, persons belonging to such minorities shall not be denied the right, in community with the other members of their group, to enjoy their own culture, to profess and practice their own religion, or to use their own language.

Article 26

Any advocacy of national, racial or religious hostility that constitutes an incitement to hatred and violence shall be prohibited by the law of the State.

PART IV

Article 27

1. There shall be established a Human Rights Committee (hereinafter referred to as "the Committee"). It shall consist of nine members and shall carry out the functions hereinafter provided.

2. The Committee shall be composed of nationals of the States Parties to the Covenant who shall be persons of high moral standing and recognized competence in the field of human rights, consideration being given to the usefulness of the participation of some persons having a judicial or legal experience.

3. The members of the Committee shall be elected and shall serve in their personal capacity.

Article 28

1. The members of the Committee shall be elected from a list of persons possessing the qualifications prescribed in article 27 and nominated for the purpose by the States Parties to the Covenant.

2. Each State Party to the Covenant shall nominate at least two and not more than four persons. These persons may be nationals of the nominating State or of any other State Party to the Covenant.

3. A person shall be eligible to be renominated.

Article 29

1. At least three months before the date of each election of the Committee, other than an election to fill a vacancy declared in accordance with article 33, the Secretary-General of the United Nations shall address a written request to the States Parties to the Covenant inviting them to submit their nominations within two months.

2. The Secretary-General of the United Nations shall prepare a list in alphabetical order of all the persons thus nominated, and shall submit it to the International Court of Justice and to the States Parties to the Covenant.

3. The Secretary-General of the United Nations shall request the International Court of Justice to fix the time of elections for members of the Committee and to elect such members from the list referred to in the preceding paragraph and in accordance with the conditions set out in this part of the Covenant.

Article 30

1. The Committee may not include more than one national of the same State.

2. In the election of the Committee consideration shall be given to equitable geographical distribution of membership and to the representation of the different forms of civilization.

3. The quorum laid down in article 25, paragraph 3, of the Statute of the International Court of Justice shall apply for the holding of the elections.

4. The persons elected shall be those who obtain the largest number of votes and an absolute majority of the votes of all the members of the International Court of Justice.

Article 31

1. The members of the Committee shall be elected for a term of five years. They shall be eligible for reelection if renominated. However, the terms of five of the members elected at the first election shall expire at the end of two years; immediately after the first election the names of these five members shall be chosen by lot by the President of the International Court of Justice.

2. Elections at the expiry of office shall be held in accordance with the preceding articles of this part of this Covenant.

Article 32

1. If, in the unanimous opinion of the other members, a member of the Committee has ceased to carry out his functions for any cause other than absence of a temporary character, the Chairman of the Committee shall notify the Secretary-General of the United Nations who shall then declare the seat of such member to be vacant.

2. In the event of the death or the resignation of a member of the Committee, the Chairman shall immediately notify the Secretary-General of the United Nations who shall declare the seat vacant from the date of death or the date on which the resignation takes effect.

Article 33

1. When a vacancy is declared in accordance with article 32 the Secretary-General of the United Nations shall notify each State Party to the Covenant, which may, if it is necessary, within one month, with a view to election to the vacant seat on the Committee, complete its list of available nominees to four persons.

2. The Secretary-General of the United Nations shall prepare a list in alphabetical order of the persons thus nominated and shall submit it to the International Court of Justice and the States Parties to the Covenant. The election for the vacancy shall then proceed in accordance with articles 29 and 30.

3. A member of the Committee elected to replace a member whose term of office has not expired, shall hold office for the remainder of that term. Provided that if such term of office will expire within six months after declaration of the vacancy in accordance with article 32, no nomination shall be requested and no election shall be held to fill that vacancy.

Article 34

1. Subject to the provisions of article 32, a member of the Committee shall remain in office until a successor has been elected. But if the Committee has, prior to the election of his successor, begun to consider a case, he shall continue to act in that case, and his successor shall not act in it.

2. A member of the Committee elected to fill a vacancy declared in accordance with article 32 shall not act in any case in which his predecessor had acted, unless the quorum provided in article 39 cannot be obtained.

Article 35

The members of the Committee shall, with the approval of the General Assembly of the United Nations, receive emoluments from United Nations resources on such terms and conditions as the General Assembly may decide having regard to the importance of the Committee's responsibilities.

Article 36

1. The Secretary of the Committee shall be a high official of the United Nations, elected by the Committee from a list of three names submitted by the Secretary-General of the United Nations.

2. The candidate obtaining the largest number of votes and an absolute majority of the votes of all the members of the Committee shall be declared elected.

3. The Secretary-General of the United Nations shall provide the necessary staff and facilities for the Committee and its members; the staff shall be part of the United Nations Secretariat.

Article 37

1. The Secretary-General of the United Nations shall convene the initial meeting of the Committee at the Headquarters of the United Nations.

2. After its initial meeting, the Committee shall meet:

(*a*) At such times as it deems necessary;

(*b*) When any matter is referred to it under article 40;

(*c*) When convened by its Chairman or at the request of not less than five of its members.

3. The Committee shall meet at the Headquarters of the United Nations or at Geneva.

Article 38

Every member of the Committee shall, before taking up his duties, make a solemn declaration in open committee that he will exercise his powers impartially and conscientiously.

Article 39

1. The Committee shall elect its Chairman and Vice-Chairman for the period of one year. They may be re-elected. The first Chairman and the first Vice-Chairman shall be elected at the initial meeting of the Committee.

2. The Committee shall establish its own rules of procedure, but these rules shall provide, *inter alia*, that:

(*a*) Seven members shall constitute a quorum;

(*b*) Decisions of the Committee shall be made by a majority vote of the members present; if the votes are equally divided the Chairman shall have a casting vote;

(*c*) If a State refers a matter to the Committee under article 40,

(i) Such State, the State complained against, and any State Party to this Covenant whose national is concerned in such matter may make submissions in writing to the Committee;

(ii) Such State and the State complained against shall have the right to be represented at the hearing of the matter and to make submissions orally;

(*d*) The Committee shall hold hearings and other meetings in closed session.

Article 40

1. If a State Party to the Covenant considers that another State Party is not giving effect to a provision of the Covenant, it may, by written communication, bring the matter to the attention of that State. Within three months after the receipt of the communication, the receiving State shall afford the complaining State an explanation or statement in writing concerning the matter, which should include, to the extent possible and pertinent, references to domestic procedures and remedies taken, or pending, or available in the matter.

2. If the matter is not adjusted to the satisfaction of both Parties within six months after the receipt by the receiving State of the initial communication, either State shall have the right to refer the matter to the Committee, by notice given to the Secretary of the Committee, and to the other Sate.

3. Subject to the provisions of article 41 below, in serious and urgent cases the Committee may, at the request of the complaining State, deal expeditiously with the matter on receipt of that request in accordance with the powers conferred on

it by this part of the Covenant and after notifying the States concerned.

Article 41

Normally, the Committee shall deal with a matter referred to it only if available domestic remedies have been invoked and exhausted in the case. This shall not be the rule where the application of the remedies is unreasonably prolonged.

Article 42

In any matter referred to it the Committee may call upon the States concerned to supply any relevant information.

Article 43

1. Subject to the provisions of article 41, the Committee shall ascertain the facts and make available its good offices to the States concerned with a view to a friendly solution of the matter on the basis of respect for human rights as recognized in this **Covenant.**

2. The Committee shall in every case, and in no event later than eighteen months after the date of receipt of the notice under article 40, draw up a report which will be sent to the States concerned and then communicated to the Secretary-General of the United Nations for publication.

3. If a solution within the terms of paragraph 1 of this article is reached the Committee shall confine its report to a brief statement of the facts and of the solution reached. If such a solution is not reached the Committee shall draw up a report on the facts and state its opinion as to whether the facts found disclose a breach by the State concerned of its obligations under the Covenant. If the report does not represent in whole or in part the unanimous opinion of the members of the Committee, any member of the Committee shall be entitled to attach to it a separate opinion. The written and oral submissions made by the Parties to the case in accordance with article 39, paragraph 2(c), shall be attached to the report.

Article 44

The Committee may recommend to the Economic and Social Council that the Council request the International Court of Justice to give an advisory opinion on any legal question connected with a matter of which the Committee is seized.

Article 45

The Committee shall submit to the General Assembly, through the Secretary-General or the United Nations, an annual report on its activities.

Article 46

The States Parties to this Covenant agree that any State Party complained of or lodging a complaint may, if no solution has been reached within the terms of article 43, paragraph 1, bring the case before the International Court of Justice after the report provided for in article 43, paragraph 3, has been drawn up.

Article 47

The provisions of this Covenant shall not prevent the States Parties to the Covenant from submitting to the International Court of Justice any dispute arising out of the interpretation or application of the Covenant in a matter within the competence of the Committee.

Article 48

1. The States Parties to this Covenant, including those who are responsible for the administration of any Non-Self-Governing Territory undertake to submit reports annually to the Committee on the measures taken by them to meet the obligations set forth in article 1 of this Covenant.

2. The States Parties to this Covenant who are responsible for the administration of any Non-Self-Governing Territory, undertake, through elections, plebiscites or other recognized democratic means, preferably under the auspices of the United Nations, to determine the political status of such territory, should the Committee make a proposal to that effect and such proposal be adopted by the General Assembly. Such decision shall be based on

evidence of the desire of the inhabitants of such territory as expressed through their political institutions or parties.

3. The States Parties to this Covenant shall report to the Committee any violation of the right laid down in paragraph 3 of article 1.

PART V

Article 49

1. The States Parties to this Covenant undertake to submit a report on the legislative or other measures, including judicial remedies, which they have adopted and which give effect to the rights recognized herein (a) within one year of the entry into force of the Covenant for the State concerned and (b) thereafter whenever the Economic and Social Council so requests upon recommendation of the Commission on Human Rights and after consultation with the State Parties.

2. Reports shall indicate factors and difficulties, if any, affecting the progressive implementation of article 22, paragraph 4, of this Covenant.

3. All reports shall be submitted to the Secretary-General of the United Nations for the Economic and Social Council which may transmit them to the Commission on Human Rights for information, study and, if necessary, general recommendations.

4. The specialized agencies shall receive such parts of the reports concerning the rights as fall within their respective fields of activity.

5. The States Parties directly concerned, and the above agencies may submit to the Economic and Social Council observations on any general recommendation that may be made in accordance with paragraph 3 of this article.

Article 50

Nothing in this Covenant shall be interpreted as impairing the provisions of the Charter of the United Nations and of the constitutions of the specialized agencies, which define the respective responsibilities of the various organs of the United Nations and of the specialized agencies in regard to the matters dealt with in this Covenant.

PART VI

Article 51

1. This Covenant shall be open for signature and ratification or accession on behalf of any State Member of the United Nations or of any non-member State to which an invitation has been extended by the General Assembly.

2. Ratification of or accession to this Covenant shall be effected by the deposit of an instrument of ratification or accession with the Secretary-General of the United Nations, and as soon as twenty States have deposited such instruments, the Covenant shall come into force among them. As regards any State which ratifies or accedes thereafter the Covenant shall come into force on the date of the deposit of its instrument of ratification or accession.

3. The Secretary-General of the United Nations shall inform all Members of the United Nations, and other States which have signed or acceded, of the deposit of each instrument of ratification or accession.

Article 52

The provisions of the Covenant shall extend to all parts of federal States without any limitations or exceptions.

Article 53

The provisions of the present Covenant shall extend to or be applicable equally to a signatory metropolitan State and to all the territories, be they Non-Self-Governing, Trust or Colonial Territories, which are being administered or governed by such metropolitan State.

Article 54

1. Any State Party to the Covenant may propose an amendment and file it with the Secretary-General of the United Nations. The Secretary-General shall thereupon communicate the proposed amendments to the States Parties to the Covenant with a request that they notify him

whether they favour a conference of States Parties for the purpose of considering and voting upon the proposal. In the event that at least one-third of the States favours such a conference the Secretary-General shall convene the conference under the auspices of the United Nations. Any amendment adopted by a majority of States present and voting at the conference shall be submitted to the General Assembly of the United Nations for approval.

2. Such amendments shall come into force when they have been approved by the General Assembly and accepted by a two-thirds majority of the States Parties to the Covenant in accordance with their respective constitutional processes.

3. When such amendments come into force they shall be binding on those Parties which have accepted them, other Parties being still bound by the provisions of the Covenant and any earlier amendment which they have accepted.

APPENDIX C

Draft Covenant on Economic, Social and Cultural Rights[1]

The States Parties hereto,

Considering that, in accordance with the principles proclaimed in the Charter of the United Nations, recognition of the inherent dignity and of the equal and inalienable rights of all members of the human family is the foundation of freedom, justice and peace in the world,

Recognizing that these rights derive from the inherent dignity of the human person,

Recognizing that, in accordance with the Universal Declaration of Human Rights, the ideal of free men[2] enjoying freedom from fear and want can only be achieved if conditions are created whereby everyone may enjoy his economic, social and cultural rights, as well as his civil and political rights,

Considering the obligation of States under the Charter of the United Nations to promote universal respect for, and observance of, human rights and freedoms,

Realizing that the individual, having duties to other individuals and to the community to which he belongs, is under responsibility to strive for the promotion and observance of the rights recognized in this Covenant,

Agree upon the following articles:

PART I

Article 1[3]

1. All peoples and all nations shall have the right of self-determination, namely, the right freely to determine their political economic, social and cultural status.

2. All States, including those having responsibility for the administration of Non-Self-Governing and Trust Territories and those controlling in whatsoever manner the exercise of that right by another people, shall promote the realization of that right in all their territories, and shall respect the maintenance of that right in other States, in conformity with the provisions of the United Nations Charter.

3. The right of peoples to self-determination shall also include permanent sovereignty over their natural wealth and resources. In no case may a people be deprived of its own means of subsistence on the grounds of any rights that may be claimed by other States.

PART II

Article 2

1. Each State Party hereto undertakes to take steps, individually and through international co-operation, to the maximum of its available resources, with a view to achieving progressively the full realization of the rights recognized in this Covenant by legislative as well as by other means.

2. The State Parties hereto undertake to guarantee that the rights enunciated in this Covenant will be exercised without

[1] Source: Text as given in U.N. Economic and Social Council, Eighteenth Session, *Official Records*, Supplement No. 7, pp. 62-65.

[2] At the tenth session of the General Assembly in 1955, the Third Committee changed the phrase "free men" to "free human beings."

[3] During the tenth session of the General Assembly in 1955, the Third Committee adopted the following text for Article 1:

"1. All peoples have the right of self-determination. By virtue of this right they freely determine their political status and freely pursue their economic, social and cultural development.

"2. The peoples may, for their own ends, freely dispose of their natural wealth and resources without prejudice to any obligations arising out of international economic cooperation, based upon the principle of mutual benefit, and international law. In no case may a people be deprived of its own means of subsistence.

"3. All the States Parties to the Covenant, including those having responsibility for the administration of Non-Self-Governing and Trust Territories, shall promote the realization of the right of self-determination, and shall respect that right, in conformity with the provisions of the United Nations Charter."

distinction of any kind, such as race, colour, sex, language, religion, political or other opinion, national or social origin, property, birth or other status.

Article 3

The States Parties to the Covenant undertake to ensure the equal right of men and women to the enjoyment of all economic, social and cultural rights set forth in this Covenant.

Article 4

The State Parties to this Covenant recognize that in the enjoyment of those rights provided by the State in conformity with this Covenant, the State may subject such rights only to such limitations as are determined by law only in so far as this may be compatible with the nature of these rights and solely for the purpose of promoting the general welfare in a democratic society.

Article 5

1. Nothing in this Covenant may be interpreted as implying for any State, group or person, any right to engage in any activity or to perform any act aimed at the destruction of any of the rights or freedoms recognized herein, or at their limitation to a greater extent than is provided for in this Covenant.

2. No restriction upon or derogation from any of the fundamental human rights recognized or existing in any country in virtue of law, conventions, regulations or custom shall be admitted on the pretext that the present Covenant does not recognize such rights or that it recognizes them to a lesser extent.

PART III

Article 6

1. Work being at the basis of all human endeavour, the States Parties to the Covenant recognize the right to work, that is to say, the fundamental right of everyone to the opportunity, if he so desires, to gain his living by work which he freely accepts.

2. The steps to be taken by a State Party to this Covenant to achieve the full realization of this right shall include programmes, policies and techniques to achieve steady economic development and full and productive employment under conditions safeguarding fundamental political and economic freedoms to the individual.

Article 7

The States Parties to the Covenant recognize the right of everyone to just and favourable conditions of work, including:

(a) Safe and healthy working conditions;

(b) Remuneration which provides all workers as a minimum with:

(i) Fair wages and equal remuneration for work of equal value without distinction of any kind, in particular, women being guaranteed conditions of work not inferior to those enjoyed by men, with equal pay for equal work; and

(ii) A decent living for themselves and their families; and

(c) Rest, leisure and reasonable limitation of working hours and periodic holidays with pay.

Article 8

The States Parties to the Covenant undertake to ensure the free exercise of the right of everyone to form and join local, national and international trade unions of his choice for the protection of his economic and social interests.

Article 9

The States Parties to the Covenant recognize the right of everyone to social security.

Article 10

The States Parties to the Covenant recognize that:

1. Special protection should be accorded to motherhood and particularly to maternity during reasonable periods before and after childbirth; and

2. Special measures of protection, to be applied in all appropriate cases, within and with the help of the family, should be taken on behalf of children and young

persons, and in particular they should not be required to do work likely to hamper their normal development. To protect children from exploitation, the unlawful use of child labour and the employment of young persons in work harmful to health or dangerous to life should be made legally actionable; and

3. The family, which is the basis of society, is entitled to the widest possible protection. It is based on marriage, which must be entered into with the free consent of the intending spouses.

Article 11

The States Parties to the Covenant recognize the right of everyone to adequate food, clothing and housing.

Article 12

The States Parties to the Covenant recognize the right of everyone to an adequate standard of living and the continuous improvement of living conditions.

Article 13

1. The States Parties to the Covenant, realizing that health is a state of complete physical, mental and social well-being, and not merely the absence of disease or infirmity, recognize the right of everyone to the enjoyment of the highest attainable standard of health.

2. The steps to be taken by the States Parties to the Covenant to achieve the full realization of this right shall include those necessary for:

(a) The reduction of infant mortality and the provision for healthy development of the child;

(b) The improvement of nutrition, housing, sanitation, recreation, economic and working conditions and other aspects of environmental hygiene;

(c) The prevention, treatment and control of epidemic, endemic and other diseases;

(d) The creation of conditions which would assure to all medical service and medical attention in the event of sickness.

Article 14

1. The States Parties to the Covenant

recognize the right of everyone to education, and recognize that education shall encourage the full development of the human personality, the strengthening of respect for human rights and fundamental freedoms and the suppression of all incitement to racial and other hatred. It shall promote understanding, tolerance and friendship among all nations, racial, ethnic or religious groups, and shall further the activities of the United Nations for the maintenance of peace and enable all persons to participate effectively in a free society.

2. It is understood:

(a) That primary education shall be compulsory and available free to all;

(b) That secondary education, in its different forms, including technical and professional secondary education, shall be generally available and shall be made progressively free;

(c) That higher education shall be equally accessible to all on the basis of merit and shall be made progressively free;

(d) That fundamental education for those persons who have not received or completed the whole period of their primary education shall be encouraged as far as possible.

3. In the exercise of any functions which they assume in the field of education, the States Parties to the Covenant undertake to have respect for the liberty of parents and, when applicable, legal guardians, to choose for their children schools other than those established by the public authorities which conform to such minimum educational standards as may be laid down or approved by the State and to ensure the religious education of their children in conformity with their own convictions.

Article 15

Each State Party to the Covenant which, at the time of becoming a party to this Covenant, has not been able to secure in its metropolitan territory or other territories under its jurisdiction compulsory primary education, free of charge, undertakes, within two years, to work out and adopt a detailed plan of action for the progressive implementation, within a reasonable number of years, to be fixed in the plan, of the principle of compulsory primary education free of charge for all.

Article 16

1. The States Parties to the Covenant recognize the right of everyone:

(a) To take part in cultural life;

(b) To enjoy the benefits of scientific progress and its applications.

2. The steps to be taken by the States Parties to this Covenant to achieve the full realization of this right shall include those necessary for the conservation, the development and the diffusion of science and culture.

3. The States Parties to the Covenant undertake to respect the freedom indispensable for scientific research and creative activity.

PART IV

Article 17

1. The States Parties to this Covenant undertake to submit in conformity with this part of the Covenant reports concerning the progress made in achieving the observance of the rights recognized herein.

2. (a) All reports shall be submitted to the Secretary-General of the United Nations for the Economic and Social Council;

(b) Any State Party which is also a member of a specialized agency shall at the same time transmit, in respect of matters falling within the purview of that agency, a copy of its report, or relevant extracts therefrom, as appropriate, to that agency.

Article 18

1. The States Parties shall furnish their reports in stages, in accordance with a programme to be established by the Economic and Social Council after consultation with the States Parties to this Covenant and the specialized agencies concerned.

2. Reports may indicate factors and difficulties affecting the degree of fulfilment of obligations under this Covenant.

3. Where relevant information has already previously been furnished to the United Nations or to any specialized agency by any State Party it will not be necessary to reproduce that information but a precise reference to the information so furnished will suffice.

Article 19

Pursuant to its responsibilities under the Charter in the field of human rights, the Economic and Social Council may make arrangements with the specialized agencies in respect of their reporting to it on the progress made in achieving the observance of the provisions of this Covenant falling within the scope of their activities. These reports may include particulars of decisions and recommendations on such implementation adopted by their competent organs.

Article 20

The Economic and Social Council may transmit to the Commission on Human Rights for study and general recommendation or as appropriate for information the reports concerning human rights submitted by States, and those concerning human rights submitted by the specialized agencies.

Article 21

The States Parties directly concerned and the specialized agencies may submit comments to the Economic and Social Council on any general recommendation under article 20 or reference to such general recommendation in any report of the Commission or any documentation referred to therein.

Article 22

The Economic and Social Council may submit from time to time to the General Assembly, with its own reports, reports summarizing the information made available by the States Parties to the Covenant directly to the Secretary-General and by the specialized agencies under Article . . . indicating the progress made in achieving general observance of these rights.

Article 23

The Economic and Social Council may

bring to the attention of the international organs concerned with technical assistance or of any other appropriate international organ any matters arising out of the reports referred to in this part of the Covenant which may assist such organs in deciding each within its competence, on the advisability of international measures likely to contribute to the progressive implementation of this Covenant.

Article 24

The States Parties to the Covenant agree that international action for the achievement of these rights includes such methods as conventions, recommendations, technical assistance, regional meetings and technical meetings and studies with governments.

Article 25

Nothing in this Covenant shall be interpreted as impairing the provisions of the Charter of the United Nations and of the constitutions of the specialized agencies, which define the respective responsibilities of the various organs of the United Nations and of the specialized agencies in regard to the matters dealt with in this Covenant.

PART V

Article 26

1. This Covenant shall be open for signature and ratification or accession on behalf of any State Member of the United Nations or of any non-member State to which an invitation has been extended by the General Assembly.

2. Ratification of or accession to this Covenant shall be effected by the deposit of an instrument of ratification or accession with the Secretary-General of the United Nations, and as soon as twenty States have deposited such instruments, the Covenant shall come into force among them. As regards any State which ratifies or accedes thereafter the Covenant shall come into force on the date of the deposit of its instrument of ratification or accession.

3. The Secretary-General of the United Nations shall inform all Members of the United Nations, and other States which have signed or acceded, of the deposit of each instrument of ratification or accession.

Article 27

The provisions of the Covenant shall extend to all parts of federal States without any limitations or exceptions.

Article 28

The provisions of the present Covenant shall extend to or be applicable equally to a signatory metropolitan State and to all the territories, be they Non-Self-Governing, Trust, or Colonial Territories, which are being administered or governed by such metropolitan State.

Article 29

1. Any State Party to the Covenant may propose an amendment and file it with the Secretary-General of the United Nations. The Secretary-General shall thereupon communicate the proposed amendments to the States Parties to the Covenant with a request that they notify him whether they favour a conference of States Parties for the purpose of considering and voting upon the proposal. In the event that at least one-third of the States favours such a conference the Secretary-General shall convene the conference under the auspices of the United Nations. Any amendment adopted by a majority of States present and voting at the conference shall be submitted to the General Assembly of the United Nations for approval.

2. Such amendments shall come into force when they have been approved by the General Assembly and accepted by a two-thirds majority of the States Parties to the Covenant in accordance with their respective constitutional processes.

3. When such amendments come into force they shall be binding on those Parties which have accepted them, other Parties being still bound by the provisions of the Covenant and any earlier amendment which they have accepted.

Date Due

DEC 20 '70			
	PRINTED	IN U. S. A.	